Sweetness and Light

Sweetness and Light

The 'Queen Anne' Movement 1860–1900

MARK GIROUARD

OXFORD · AT THE CLARENDON PRESS
1977

Oxford University Press, Walton Street, Oxford OX2 6DP

OXFORD LONDON GLASGOW
NEW YORK TORONTO MELBOURNE WELLINGTON
IBADAN NAIROBI DAR ES SALAAM LUSAKA CAPE TOWN
KUALA LUMPUR SINGAPORE JAKARTA HONG KONG TOKYO
DELHI BOMBAY CALCUTTA MADRAS KARACHI

© *Oxford University Press 1977*

British Library Cataloguing in Publication Data

Girouard, Mark
    Sweetness and light.
    1. Architecture, Queen Anne
    I. Title
    720′.942   NA967   77-30113

    ISBN 0-19-817330-X

Printed in Great Britain at the University Press, Oxford by Vivian Ridler, Printer to the University

Contents

List of Illustrations

Colour Plates

Monochrome Illustrations

Acknowledgements

Among the many people who have provided me with help or information during the preparation of this book, I would especially like to acknowledge Gordon Barnes, Susan Beatty, John Brandon-Jones, David Cheshire, Tom Greeves, Martin Harrison, Anne Hawker, Nicolas Hellawell, Gervase Jackson-Stops, Professor Bill Jordy, John O'Callaghan, Valerie Pakenham, Bernard Richards, Andrew Saint, Gavin Stamp, Anthony Symondson, Robert Thorne, and David Watkin.

The former worshippers of bright, original, intelligent vivacious Gothica, turned their backs on her, to grovel in the dust before Queen Anne . . . One loved her for her homeliness, another for her dignity and picturesque grace; this admired her because she was so domestic and unpretending, that other because she was so rich and so queenly. She was pure English, pure Flemish, pure Italian . . . She spoke now in soft bastard Latin, now in French, now in Dutch, and now in pure Anglo-Saxon. Her age was as varied as her other characteristics, for her dress and style showed that she must be the contemporary of Julius Caesar, of Francis I, William the Silent, the Grand Monarque, Napoleon Buonaparte, the Brothers Adam, Norman Shaw, and John J. Stevenson. Pretty little lodges, dignified mansions, tall, gawky street fronts, and clumsy or picturesque temples called Board schools were erected in her honour, and she seemed to be installed as the architectural divinity, vice Gothica dethroned. The moral of this allegorical prelude is that the name of Queen Anne has been tacked on to things of very opposite styles, periods, and countries, with which the style of the real Queen Anne had no connection.

J. Moyr Smith, *Ornamental Interiors Ancient and Modern* (London, 1887), p. 68.

I   Sweetness and Light

'Queen Anne' has comparatively little to do with Queen Anne. It was the nickname applied to a style which became enormously popular in the 1870s and survived into the early years of this century. 'Queen Anne' came with red brick and white-painted sash windows, with curly pedimented gables and delicate brick panels of sunflowers, swags, or cherubs, with small window panes, steep roofs, and curving bay windows, with wooden balconies and little fancy oriels jutting out where one would least expect them. It was a kind of architectural cocktail, with a little genuine Queen Anne in it, a little Dutch, a little Flemish, a squeeze of Robert Adam, a generous dash of Wren, and a touch of François Ier. It combined all these elements and a number of others into a mixture that had a strong character of its own—particularly when they were mixed with skill and gaiety, as they very often were.

The mixture can easily be savoured today, for the style survives in large quantities. 'Queen Anne' covers large stretches of Chelsea, from Pont Street and Cadogan Square down to the Embankment. It breaks out in islands of red brick amid the stucco seas of Kensington and Bayswater; in houses built for artists or the artistic in Hampstead and Bedford Park; in riverside residences or seaside hotels, lively with balconies, turrets, gables, and green copper domes; in the pink and white daintiness of Newnham College, Cambridge, and the immediately recognizable silhouettes of the early London Board Schools. It can be followed overseas to America, where it was received with enthusiasm and developed rapidly and amazingly into what is known as the Shingle Style; or down the social scale to the undulating glass fronts, mirror-lined walls, and towering centre-pieces of the pubs of the nineties. It can be observed in its by-products, in wallpapers by Morris or Walter Crane, in pictures of Regency beaux and belles by Marcus Stone or picture books of quaintly pretty children by Kate Greenaway, in spindly black chairs with rush seats or many-shelved overmantels designed to show off the peacock feathers, and blue and white china collected by the aesthetic ladies whom George du Maurier caricatured in *Punch*.   1

It was a style which set out to please, and yet it was greeted on its appearance with howls of anger or derision. 'A bastard style', 'a contortion of every feature of architecture', 'abject copyism', 'effete feebleness and prettiness', 'excessively ugly', 'a regular tea-tray style', 'disgrace of the country', 'entirely contradicting the taste and feeling of the day', 'baneful influence over students', 'brilliant but dangerous', 'utterly commonplace' were among the expressions used about it. There were acrimonious and heated discussions wherever architects were gathered together. Aged Academicians wrote furious letters to the newspapers. The public were not deterred, and took to it with almost excessive enthusiasm.

Both the fury and the rapture seem surprising until one examines its background, out of which it appeared with something approaching inevitability. 'Queen Anne' flourished because it satisfied all the latest aspirations of the English middle classes. They had been growing in size, wealth, and sophistication, and the 1870s and 1880s found them at the height of their prosperity and power. England was then indisputably the greatest and richest nation in the world. No other nation as yet competed with its ironclads, no rivals seriously threatened its trade and industry. The upper and middle classes enjoyed this supremacy in something approaching equal partnership, into which the middle classes had fought their way through several decades of political and social agitation. When the working classes, or the greater part of them, had been given the vote in 1867 pessimists predicted revolution and social collapse, but apart from a little breaking of windows and tearing up of railings nothing happened; the balance of power was scarcely altered until the end of the century. The collapse of agriculture in the late 1870s under the impact of

REFINEMENTS OF MODERN SPEECH.

SCENE—*A Drawing-room in "Passionate Brompton."*

Fair Æsthetic (suddenly, and in deepest tones, to Smith, who has just been introduced to take her in to Dinner). "ARE YOU INTENSE?"

1. George du Maurier and the Aesthetes. Cartoon from *Punch*, 14 June 1879.

cheap American corn gave the upper classes a shock from which they never fully recovered, but the middle classes, whose wealth was mainly derived from the towns, were little affected by it.

But although the middle classes were formidable, they were not united. The children or grandchildren of the men who had made the money were reacting against the values which they had been brought up to accept. The earlier Victorian middle classes had been keyed up for a struggle; they were always girding up their loins to smite someone, in one cause or another. They fought to get money or power or social status, or to preserve religion from science or science from religion. Underneath they were often deeply insecure, but they papered over their insecurity with belligerence. Success was vital to them and to succeed they had to be tough and single-minded; their religion tended to be simple and dogmatic and to underwrite all the qualities that led to success; they were correspondingly scornful of failure and thought that if the poor remained poor it was their own fault. At their worst they were pushing, vulgar, greedy, and on the make; even at their best they tended to be intolerant and fanatical.

A Class in Search of an Image

From the 1860s there was a steady lessening of tension. Literally and metaphorically the next generation could afford to relax. Their views grew less dogmatic, their manners smoother, their prose lighter, and their morals easier. They looked with distaste at much that their parents had taken for granted. They needed a new life style.

Thackeray and others suggested to them how important it was to be a gentleman. Thackeray took the business of gentlemanliness very seriously, and his attitude cannot be dismissed as mere snobbery. As a young man he had satirized both the middle and upper classes without mercy; his attacks on the latter gained him the reputation of a dangerous radical. In later life money and success mellowed him; he concentrated less on attacking vices than extolling virtues, above all the gentlemanly virtues. But his standards had not changed all that greatly. A gentleman, as he used the term, lacked the arrogance and stupidity for which he had attacked the upper classes as well as the vulgarity and bigotry which he had satirized in the middle classes; a gentleman was relaxed, courteous, and considerate; he was never pushing, boastful, or fanatical; he was well-behaved but not prudish; he wore the right clothes and talked with the right accent; in fact he was like Thackeray.

This gentlemanly ideal was increasingly accepted both by the upper and middle classes. It was taught in the public schools, to which both classes sent their children, and practised in the clubs, which recruited their members from the public schools. It provided a common meeting-ground for the new and the old rich, and enabled one group to merge into the other. But although Colonel Newcome, or a slightly less innocent version of Colonel Newcome, was an adequate model for many Victorian clubmen, large numbers of the middle classes needed something a little more dynamic. They felt that it was important to be a gentleman, but not enough. However much in reaction against their parents, they were also conditioned by them. The earnestness of the earlier Victorian middle classes was not going to vanish in a generation, nor was their energy. Fathers who had spent their lives reading the Bible and making money with equally dedicated intensity very probably had agnostic children who were suspicious of the effects of money, and of the commercial society which produced it; but the tendency to dedication remained. Critical of their parents and in reaction against their way of life, they quivered with suppressed energy, ready to burst into activity as soon as they were given an outlet of which they could approve.

Matthew Arnold was not the first or the only person to suggest what were to prove two most fruitful outlets, but his *Culture and Anarchy* (1869) presented them in beautifully persuasive and readable form. As a famous son in reaction against an even more famous father, and a writer who concealed his seriousness under a coating of relaxed irony, he was nicely equipped to appeal to the younger generation. In *Culture and Anarchy* he pitched into both the upper and middle classes with enjoyable aplomb. He nicknamed the upper classes Barbarians because of their good looks, high spirits, passion for sport, and inaccessibility to ideas; he classed the middle classes as Philistines, and attacked them for being narrow-minded, fanatical, opinionated, and self-satisfied, for living in and creating ugliness, and for blindly pursuing money and personal freedom without knowing what to do with them.

In all this he was not so very different from Thackeray, but he was more constructive. He urged the middle classes not to remain satisfied with the Puritan or, as he called them, Hebraic virtues of energy, determination, concentration, and self-control, which he admitted that they possessed, but to cultivate the Hellenic virtues, which he contended that they had completely neglected. He summed up what he saw as the essence of Hellenism in a phrase that became famous: 'sweetness and light.' 'Sweetness' meant the creation and enjoyment of beauty in all its forms; 'light' was the result of intellectual curiosity, the desire 'to see and learn the truth and make it prevail'.

Here was a way out for all those who were no longer able to believe in conventional Christianity but who wanted to believe in something. They jumped on the band wagon of sweetness and light; they became devotees of the religion of beauty or the religion of enlightenment.[1] Even those who remained Christians found that liberal injections of sweetness and light would supply everything which they had felt lacking in their parents' beliefs and way of life. Sweetness would dissolve the ugliness of their houses and cities, light would smooth away their intolerance and narrow-mindedness. Moreover, those who felt increasingly unhappy because their pleasant and comfortable lives floated on top of a massive substratum of poverty and ignorance could ease their guilt by bringing sweetness and light to others less fortunate than themselves.

In the cause of light they agitated for education (and sometimes votes) for women and the working classes; they founded schools, museums, colleges, university extension courses, hospitals, and swimming-baths; they preached the need for health, temperance, welfare, Sunday opening, free libraries, pubs without beer, Churches without dogma, and clothes without corsets. In the pursuit of beauty they toured art galleries, frequented concerts, and even allowed their children to become artists; they brought beauty to the poor by founding free art galleries, organizing exhibitions of art in the East End, or lecturing on art at working men's colleges. At home they threw out their parents' furniture and ripped out their decorations; with interior decorators to advise them and antique shops and art-conscious craftsmen to make them new objects or sell them old ones, they redid their houses from ground floor to attic and worshipped at the shrine of their Morris paper, blue and white china, Italian primitives, Greek pots, Persian carpets, or eighteenth-century furniture.

Aesthetes and Progressives

Pursuers of beauty were known at the time as aesthetes; spreaders of enlightenment liked to think of themselves as progressives. The cult of aestheticism was brought to England from France in the 1860s by Swinburne and Walter Pater. In its pure form under the banner of 'Art for Art's sake', it completely disassociated art from morals; art had its own rules and it was impossible for a work of art to be immoral, whatever its subject-matter. This was too much for most people in England; they were prepared to detach art from religion, but Ruskin had conditioned them into tying it up closely with morals. The hard-line aesthetes remained a small and suspect group; most English aesthetes contented themselves more vaguely with cultivating their artistic sensibilities and trying to live beautifully in beautiful surroundings.

Their ideas of beauty were conditioned by what they disliked about their parents. Anything which the previous generation had admired, or which those they considered Philistines continued to admire, was suspect. Delicacy and refinement were preferred to toughness and vigour, the small scale to the large. Chunky heavy-weight furniture went out of fashion and spindly light-weight furniture came in; bright primary colours were rejected in favour of soft greys and greens; the coal-tar purples and magentas which had seemed such a triumph of mid-nineteenth-century science were utterly despised by the aesthetes. Generally speaking, they looked at modern technology with suspicion; artistically, it became progressive to be old-fashioned. Dislike of the present led them to the past, dislike of the town to the country. As an antidote to the present they recreated the past as an ideal world of pre-industrial simplicity, at once homely and Arcadian. Adjectives such as 'quaint' and 'old-fashioned' epitomized this world to them and were applied with an enthusiastic approbation which is hard to understand today. Children, because they seemed not yet to have left this innocent world, and because their ways were indeed so quaint and old-fashioned, became cult objects; so did any rural community which seemed untouched by industrial corruption or commercial vulgarity.

They utterly rejected their parents' tendency to argue either that one particular style was the best and right style, or that the Victorian age should create a new style. They were equally distrustful of all theories of beauty or proportion. 'Dogma' became a dirty word; in art as well as religion they believed in discriminating eclecticism guided by artistic sensibility. They agreed with Walter Pater when he wrote that the aesthete 'will remember always that beauty exists in many forms. To him all periods, types, schools of taste, are in themselves equal.'[2] All styles were allowable but, inevitably, some were more allowable than others. Japan, classical Greece, the Italian Renaissance, and the English eighteenth century became the vogue; the Middle Ages were still respectable, but suffered from their over-exposure in the previous thirty years. Originality came from combining elements derived from different styles rather than attempting to produce something completely new. As Mrs. Haweis put it in her book *Beautiful Houses*, 'Originality is like a house built of bricks taken from many places—it is the new disposal of the old bricks which makes the house an original one.'[3]

The nature of the light pursued, like the nature of the sweetness, was influenced by fashion. Progressives preferred their light diffused rather than concentrated; they were interested in everything and had a rather touching belief that almost everything could be reconciled with almost everything else. The older generation found this hard to understand. 'Is this the time for a maudlin universal sympathy?', Mrs. Humphry Ward makes a Tractarian clergyman ask in *Robert Elsmere*.[4] Progressive young couples in Chelsea, Hampstead, and Bedford Park thought that it was. Progressive young couples were also more likely to be interested in schools and education than health and hospitals—unlike their parents, whose generation had still been staggering from the effects of the cholera epidemics of the 1840s. Education, it was now felt, was going to solve all problems; education of every conceivable kind, but in particular education to prepare women for the vote which they ought to have, and the working classes for the vote which they had recently acquired. Hand in hand with education came Temperance. The subject of a terracotta panel depicting 'Knowledge strangling Ignorance', which was designed for the early London Board Schools in the 1870s, was repeated in a similar panel inserted into a coffee tavern in Streatham. Coffee taverns were intended to wean the local working classes away from alcohol; drunkenness was as much of an obstacle to enlightenment as lack of education. Enthusiasm for temperance and education, combined with a new sympathy for smallness of scale, tended to take progressives of the 1870s and 1880s into local government. Finally, like the aesthetes, they looked at the Victorian city with distrust. The same people who sat on School Boards and local Councils,

2. *My Lady's Chamber*, by Walter Crane. Reproduced as the frontispiece of *The House Beautiful*, by Clarence Cook, New York, 1878.

founded coffee taverns or campaigned for free libraries were likely to endeavour to bring the country into the city, by creating parks or planting trees, and to keep the city out of the country, by preserving commons and open spaces.

Both aesthetes and progressives tended either to do without religion, or to take to it stripped of dogma and even stripped of God. Some were attracted by Positivism, the religion of science to humanity with God left out, others attended Moncure Conway's chapel in South Place, where God was allowed in, but only in the most nebulous form. A few dabbled in Spiritualism. Alternatively they took to the extreme High Church. This may seem surprising, but the later Victorian High Church had radically changed its image from that of the earlier Tractarians. The change was conditioned by both sweetness and light. Ritualism provided all the beauty in both service and setting that aesthetes could wish for; many followed Walter Pater and attended High Church services for aesthetic reasons unsullied by belief.[5] Progressives were attracted because Tractarian emphasis on serving God through prayer and self-discipline was being replaced by the idea of serving God through service to others; the High Church was becoming socially conscious and politically radical, a movement that culminated in 1889 with the foundation of the Christian Social Union, which was both Left Wing and High Church.

From Pater to Green

'While all melts under our feet', wrote Pater, 'we may well catch at any exquisite passion, or any contribution to knowledge that seems, by a lifted horizon, to set the spirit free for a moment, of any stirring of the senses, strange dyes, strange flowers, and curious odours, or work of the artist's hands, or the face of one's friend.'[6] The aesthete burning with a hard gemlike flame, alone or with a friend in the seclusion of his exquisitely furnished rooms, might seem a long way removed from the do-gooder working himself to the bone for others in the dingy streets of the East End. But they were only different ends of the same Victorian loaf. In the 1870s and 1880s one constantly finds aestheticism and enlightenment next door to each other or mixed up together. It would be hard to think of a less socially aware aesthete than Walter Pater or a writer more earnestly dedicated to enlightenment than Matthew Arnold's niece Mrs. Humphry Ward. But they were friends, and Mrs. Humphry Ward's husband was for many years a fellow don of Walter Pater's at Brasenose.[7] The hero of her best-selling novel *Robert Elsmere* was a young clergyman who lost his faith, resigned his living, and found fulfilment and a heroic death spreading light and preaching an undogmatic religion of service in the East End slums. So much for light; sweetness was brought in in the shape of Robert Elsmere's sister-in-law Rose, an aesthetic beauty who with his encouragement sets out to become a professional violinist, thus striking two blows, one for art and one for the cause of women's independence.

Another character in the novel, Robert Elsmere's hero and mentor Professor Grey, is based on the Balliol don, Thomas Hill Green. Green was a formidable and somewhat austere character; more than anyone else he was responsible for indoctrinating young Oxford undergraduates in the 1870s with the ideal of service which sent them off to work in the East End or in local government. But he was also a friend of Walter Pater[8] and brother-in-law of John Addington Symonds, the historian of the Renaissance, who constructed his own personal religion out of poetry and art. Of the two gifted Nettleship brothers who were Balliol undergraduates of a slightly younger generation, one followed Green as a philosopher with an interest in local government, the other followed Rossetti and Swinburne (who had been friends with Green at Balliol) and became a painter of the extreme aesthetic school.

Octavia Hill, who had studied art under Ruskin, spent most of her life trying to improve the housing conditions of the working classes. But she always maintained her artistic interests;

among her side activities was the Kyrle Society, founded by her sister Miranda in 1877 to bring art and beauty to the poor. William Morris and Walter Crane both started life as pioneers of the aesthetic movement with radical sympathies, and developed in the 1880s into socialists. Frederic Harrison, the chief English advocate of Positivism and a man identified with every progressive cause, had aesthetic sympathies and an aesthetic wife who was painted by Walter Crane, posed in her drawing-room, surrounded by all the aesthetic trimmings.[9] Of the three formidable Garrett sisters, daughters of a Suffolk brewer, Elizabeth became the first qualified woman doctor in England and one of the two female members of the original London School Board; Mildred married Henry Fawcett, the blind radical politician, and became a pioneer suffragette; and Agnes, together with her cousin Rhoda, was among the first women who set up as interior decorators. They were also prominent suffragettes; their combination of interior decoration with votes for women was to be repeated a generation later by the Pankhurst sisters.

The Voice of the Philistine

The tendency of art and enlightenment to go together was satirized at the time, sometimes with a considerable degree of asperity. In *Monks of Thelema* (1876) by Walter Besant and James Rice, the hero (or anti-hero) Alan Dunlop is a young reforming landlord with aesthetic tastes who reads Swinburne, Morris, and Matthew Arnold and feeds his wife on Ruskin. He runs a co-operative farm on his estate, opens a bath house, public laundry, shop, and a bar selling only unadulterated beer in the village, regales the villagers with monthly festivals and theatrical performances, and turns a Dissenting chapel into a free library and reading room. His objectives are to bring 'books, joy and education, where there is nothing but squalor, dirt and beer'. He is portrayed as a prig and a fool, the villagers do not appreciate his efforts to improve them, and all his schemes end in fiasco.

By no means all the middle classes were converted to art or progress, and even those who were tended to disassociate themselves from the extremist element in either group, or the sillinesses which occurred on its fringes. The willowy aesthete ('he screams with a pretty feminine horror at the mention of mauve or magenta'[10]) or the gushing artistic lady is constantly made fun of in memoirs and journalism of the period. But however irritating, such people provided society with endless gossip and entertainment. Gilbert and Sullivan had a lot of fun with them in *Patience*, first produced in 1881; George du Maurier made his name with his cartoons of the aesthetic Cimabue Browns, Jellaby Postlethwaite, and Mrs. de Montmorency Tomkyns.

Gilbert and Sullivan's satire was of the most genial nature. Du Maurier knew how to satirize aesthetes because he moved in aesthetic circles; he later confessed that he had got extremely attached to Mrs. de Montmorency Tomkyns and her friends. Unlike the decadents of the 1890s even the sillier aesthetes aroused feelings of irritation and amusement rather than hatred and disgust. In the 1870s and 1880s it was hard for the middle classes to feel really angry or worried about anything. An atmosphere of good humour, tolerance, and extreme optimism pervaded their peaceful and prosperous world. Everything was surely going to be all right; superstition and ugliness would melt away, science would be reconciled with religion, art and education would civilize the working classes. High Church vicars sat amicably at the same tea-tables as agnostics; Conservatives invited Liberals to dinner; progressive ladies campaigned for the vote but felt as yet no urge to slash pictures or chain themselves to railings.

For increasing numbers of the middle classes serious-mindedness was cocooned and sweetened by inherited money; their life style was far more sophisticated and agreeable than that of their parents or grandparents. Young men could relax and enjoy themselves at public school and university knowing that there was a comfortable job waiting for them in the family business, or enough money to subsidize them in whatever career they chose, or even to support them in no career at all. A network of friends and relations provided them with useful and agreeable holidays. Steamships and railways were at hand to take them wherever they wanted in the world, and they had the money to travel in comfort. It was not surprising that they developed into agreeable people, or that they tended to gravitate into the agreeable society of the upper classes, even if they lacked the desire or the resources to rise into the upper classes themselves. With their newly developed sensibilities how could they fail to appreciate the way of life produced by what Mrs. Humphry Ward described as 'generations of rich, happy, important people, with ample leisure to cultivate all the more delicate niceties of social feeling and relation'?[11]

A distinctive feature of the later nineteenth century is the great band of thoroughly gentlemanly and 'nice' people, shading imperceptibly from the middle to the upper classes and living pleasantly on pleasantly adequate incomes in a pleasant world of tennis parties and dances and summers at the seaside. Within this world was an equally distinctive inner world of people who were artistic and progressive as well as nice, who felt a little superior to the Philistines, who travelled in Italy, went to the Grosvenor Gallery, and varied their agreeable tennis parties and dances with equally agreeable sessions with their decorator or committee meetings to improve this or to preserve that. This inner world also shaded from the upper to the middle classes; even if the middle classes provided most of its impetus, a small group of beautiful and noble ladies, suffused with sweetness and brimming over with light, reigned over it as constitutional queens, and held court at evening concerts and artistic soirées in their rich and tasteful houses.

It was these progressive, artistic, and gentlemanly people who seized with such enthusiasm on 'Queen Anne'. While their world was maturing in the 1860s, 'Queen Anne' was also quietly being brought to birth in inconspicuous corners by a few architects and artists. In the early 1870s the two met and, in spite of bitter opposition from some of the elder generation, married. To understand the reasons for the bitterness, and why, in spite of it, the two partners were so perfectly suited to each other, it is necessary to turn from the general scene to the particular background of 'Queen Anne'.

3. 'Queen Anne' daintiness. An illustration by Hugh Thomson for *The Ballad of Beau Brocade*, by Austin Dobson, 1892.

II The Origins of 'Queen Anne'

'Queen Anne' was the product of a small tightly knit group. Before its arrival and while it was germinating, there was a modest and quite separate revival of interest in the late seventeenth and eighteenth centuries. It did not amount to very much; it had little if any direct connection with, or even influence on, the artists and architects who produced 'Queen Anne'. But it is worth a brief preliminary discussion, because it helped to produce a public receptive to the style when it finally emerged.

In the 1850s, when Stuart and Georgian architecture were still generally despised, even by classicists, as being either corrupt or boring, odd little islands of what might be called neo-Georgianism stick out unexpectedly from the sea of Gothic and Italianate. They are both literary and architectural. In 1855, for instance, Charlotte M. Yonge in her novel *Heartsease* portrays a Whig peer, Lord Martindale, forced by the ambitions of a rich and imperious aunt, whose heir he is, to pull down his house with its 'old red pediment with the white facings' and rebuild it as a palatial modern classical mansion. In the course of the novel this is burnt down and replaced by a copy of the old red brick house, to everyone's satisfaction.[1]

In the same year as *Heartsease* was published, Wellington College started to rise from the barren heaths of south Berkshire. Although its buildings have a strong Victorian flavour, and include elements derived from French seventeenth-century architecture, they are predominantly a tribute to the red brick style of Wren and his associates. The architect of Wellington was John Shaw the younger. The commission had come to him on the recommendation of William Burn, who had turned it down because he was too busy. Burn at that time was the most successful country-house architect in Britain. He was prepared to work in almost any style, but his repertory included something approaching both Queen Anne and Georgian. His stone-faced stables at Kinmel in Denbighshire (1855) are an elaborate and convincing exercise in neo-Palladianism. The quieter (and no doubt cheaper) stable block at Dartrey in Co. Monaghan is equally eighteenth-century in style, but built of red brick with stone dressings. It can be grouped with the County Infirmary at Aylesbury, designed by another prolific country-house architect, David Brandon, at the instigation of Florence Nightingale's brother-in-law, Sir Harry Verney of Claydon. The Infirmary consists of a central block and wings, all of red brick with stone parapets and dressings, and is an unmistakable, if rather clumsy, version of a country house of the early eighteenth century.[2]

This group of buildings can perhaps be identified very tentatively as a down-to-earth country gentleman's alternative to the *palazzo* style of the Whig grandees on the one hand and the Gothic of the romantic or religious on the other. It was certainly what he saw as the down-to-earth qualities of the late Stuarts and the Georgians which appealed to Thackeray, who was more responsible than anyone else for reviving interest in the period. He had been fascinated by the eighteenth century since boyhood, and many of his later books deal with the Stuarts or Georgians. The period attracted him because, in contrast to contemporary bigotry and vulgarity, it seemed to him an age of good manners and common sense. Its aspects which he portrayed with sympathy were all in the middle ranges: the Cheshire Cheese rather than the Court of St. James, and writers, doctors, or honest country gentlemen rather than kings and grandees.

Architecturally, this meant Wren and red brick, rather than porticoes and Palladio. In 1860–2, at the end of his life and height of his fortunes, he built himself a red brick house in early eighteenth-century style on Palace Green, Kensington, opposite the genuine eighteenth-century red brick of Kensington Palace. His immediate inspiration was Wren's Marlborough

4

4. 2 Palace Green, Kensington. Built for himself by W. M. Thackeray, 1860–2.

House; he seems to have supplied sketches showing what he wanted to Frederick Hering, his rather dim architect. The result, with its plate glass sashes and clumsy detailing, was Queen Anne with a strong mid-Victorian accent. It gave great pleasure to Thackeray who was delighted with 'the reddest house in all the town'. But he lived in it for only a year and nine months before his death in 1863; the house aroused comparatively little interest and was certainly far less important in bringing the eighteenth century back into fashion than his writings.[3]

Thackeray may have prepared the ground for 'Queen Anne', but he did not sow the seed. To discover its origins and early growth one has to move to a different world: to a small group of architects and artists, in which the second generation of the Gothic Revivalists met the second wave of Pre-Raphaelitism.

In the 1850s and 1860s the Gothic Revival appeared to be at the height of its vigour and success. Although it was far from monopolizing contemporary architecture, it had enlarged its original mainly ecclesiastical base, and was capturing commissions for town halls, hospitals, hotels, and warehouses. Gothic Revival architects were able to recruit the cream of the new generation as pupils. They arrived full of enthusiasm for the movement, but gradually fell out of step with it. The process often took many years, but ended in what appeared to be a total abandonment of its doctrines.

They developed and changed in a similar way to that of other young men of their generation. To begin with, they tended to drop the religion out of Gothic. Pugin's statement that 'Gothic is Christian architecture' had been one of the main battle-cries of the Revival in its early days. Its protagonists had all been fervent Christians; the hard core of Gothic Revival buildings had consisted of churches, buildings with religious connections such as rectories and schools, or houses built for pious laymen. But the Christianity of Gothic no longer seemed so important to young architects, many (though by no means all) of whom were no longer committed Christians, or even Christians at all. Moreover, they gradually realized that the market was changing; religious shares were going down as domestic shares went up. Gothic, if it was to be justified, had to be justified by the standards of sweetness and light. They were increasingly attracted to it either for social reasons, as the product of a pre-machine age of craftsmen working freely in settings unstained by industry or smoke, or for aesthetic reasons, because their imagination was captured by Pre-Raphaelite visions of passionate kings and queens moving in richly mysterious chambers. They ceased to think of themselves as missionaries preaching dogma and began to think of themselves as artists, working by the light of their aesthetic sensibility.

Once this happened they inevitably began to mix with other artists, especially the circle of Rossetti, whose amoral and richly romantic view of the Middle Ages was exactly calculated to appeal to them. But from an aesthetic standpoint in particular, and the standpoint of the changing middle classes in general, undiluted medievalism, even when its religious element was played down, increasingly failed to satisfy them.

The first generation of Gothicists had been men with a mission. Their objective was to revive Gothic not just as one of a number of styles, but as the only style. They preached it with missionary fervour and also with missionary intolerance. Not only were all styles other than Gothic anathema; so was any period of Gothic other than the one they favoured. In the 1840s the approved period was English Middle Pointed, in the 1850s and 1860s it was Early French. The change was the result of a growing taste for the primitive and the powerful, in line with a general mid-Victorian taste for toughness. At the time, the nickname for it among architects was 'muscular'; muscularity went with the 'fire and energy' which Matthew Arnold complained that the middle classes preferred to sweetness and light.[4] Muscular French Gothic was an exciting style to use, and produced some impressive buildings, but it was notably lacking in sweetness.

In the 1860s the younger Gothicists began to react both against muscular Gothic in particular, and the idea that everything should be Gothic in general. Delicacy and grace became more sought after qualities than heaviness and strength; they reacted in the furthest possible direction against early French Gothic and even began to look with favour at English Perpendicular and Tudor Gothic, styles which had been despised by the Gothic Revival for at least twenty years. But why stick to Gothic? Why not listen to Walter Pater when he proclaimed that to the aesthetic 'all periods, types, schools of taste, are in themselves equal'?[5] If Gothic was to be admired because it was pre-industrial rather than because it was Christian, there seemed no reason why it should be preferred to other pre-industrial styles. They began to take an interest in the art and architecture of pagan Greece, of Muslim North Africa, and above all of Japan, which had just been opened up to the West and had become a fashionable subject of speculation in both France and England.

Nearer to home, and with more obvious results in their buildings, they began to look at English vernacular architecture as it had survived almost up to their own day in country cottages, farmhouses, country towns, and in the more old-fashioned areas of London. They began by reviving tile-hanging, weather-boarding, and half-timbering; they moved on almost immediately to revive elements from the homelier brick architecture of the seventeenth and eighteenth centuries. Suddenly, after years of vacations spent religiously scouring the Continent with their sketch-books, they realized there was a whole forgotten world at their doorsteps waiting to be rediscovered. Its buildings, as they knew from first-hand experience, were remarkably pleasant to live in; and as models, they were even more easily adaptable to contemporary needs than Tudor manors or half-timbered farmhouses.

There was another, and perhaps less creditable, reason why these architects began to chafe against modern Gothic; they felt that it was being vulgarized. Gothic had been taken up by commercial architects and adapted for a clientele wider and less discriminating than the clergymen and aristocrats who had originally patronized it. At every corner they saw Gothic shops, Gothic warehouses, and even Gothic public houses. This evidence that Gothic was being developed into a modern vernacular might have been expected to please hard-core revivalists, but it did not, because commercial Gothic seemed to have absorbed everything they disliked about contemporary society. As the 'Queen Anne' architect J. J. Stevenson later put it, Gothic had 'lent itself with fatal facility to the expression of loudness, vulgarity, obtrusiveness and sensationalism more objectionable by far than the dreariest classic of Gower or Wimpole Street'.[6] He and his friends disliked its plate glass windows and strident combination of hard washable materials of different colours; even more, they disliked the way in which it adapted and misused elements from their own much more discriminating 'muscularity'. Like other select coteries whose personal slang had been adopted and misused by the vulgar, they began to evolve a different idiom.

To move away from Gothic was almost impossible for architects of the older generation who had a complete emotional commitment to the style. It was a little easier for architects of the half-generation after that of Pugin and Scott, but even they tended to move only to a limited degree. Amongst the most gifted architects of this half-generation were William Burges (1827–81) and John P. Seddon (1827–96). Both of them were pioneers in the move from religious to aesthetic Gothic but neither was able to contemplate deserting Gothic altogether. From the 1850s both of them moved in artistic circles, had close personal friendships with artists, and employed Rossetti and others to decorate their buildings and furniture. Burges, in particular, seems to have had little religious commitment and was a pioneer in appreciating Greek, Moorish, and Japanese art; he incorporated elements derived from all three cultures into his own designs. But the work of both men remained unmistakably Gothic, of the most ponderous and muscular variety. When their friends among the artists and younger architects began to abandon medievalism they were unable to follow them, and indeed attacked them with considerable bitterness.

'Queen Anne' was developed by a circle which knew Burges and Seddon, but was a little apart from them. Its remote origins can be traced back to 1855–6, to the friendship which started in those years between Rossetti, who was an almost exact contemporary of Burges and Seddon, and William Morris, Edward Burne-Jones, and Philip Webb, who were several years younger. Morris and Webb had met in the office of George Edmund Street, one of the leaders of the muscular Gothic school. Morris soon gave up architecture, but Webb remained an architect, served as Street's chief assistant, and set up on his own in 1859. In 1861 the friends joined in founding the firm of Morris, Marshall, Faulkner and Co. The function of Marshall and Faulkner was to join with Morris, who had private means, in putting up capital. The designers for the firm were Morris, Webb, Rossetti, Burne-Jones, and Ford Madox Brown.

The firm started as a group of aesthetic Goths, artists all, fighting against contemporary commercialism and planning to produce every kind of furnishing for houses as well as churches. As art, in their view, rode above specialization, they were all ready to turn their hand to everything. Rossetti and Ford Madox Brown, the painters, designed furniture as well as decorated it; Webb, the architect, designed furniture and glass. To begin with what they produced was massive and medieval; apart from their own work, one of their earliest commissions was to decorate a ponderous Gothic chest which had been designed by J. P. Seddon for use in his own office. But almost from the beginning they began to move away from total commitment to medievalism. The way they were going was symbolized in 1862 by Rossetti's own physical move into a handsome red brick Georgian house in Cheyne Walk, Chelsea. In 1865 Morris, and Morris and Company with him, left the Gothic house which Webb had designed for him at Bexley Heath and went to another eighteenth-century house in Queen Square, Holborn. In the same year Burne-Jones moved into a similar house in Kensington Square.

The move from medievalism and massiveness was initiated by Rossetti and Ford Madox Brown, perhaps because, although they were older than Webb and Morris, they had escaped the Muscular-Gothic conditioning of Street's office. It soon involved a sizeable group of architects and artists, either members of the firm or connected with them. Among them were Algernon Charles Swinburne, the poet, and Simeon Solomon, the painter; the architects Norman Shaw, W. E. Nesfield, G. F. Bodley, George Gilbert Scott, junior, and E. R. Robson; and Warrington Taylor, penniless, consumptive, and of no steady occupation.

The movement in its early days is vividly brought to life by the surviving letters from Warrington Taylor to E. R. Robson, now in the Fitzwilliam Museum. The letters start in about the summer of 1862 and continue almost until Taylor's death. Taylor (*c.* 1837–70) was a strange, brilliant, sad figure.[7] He came from a well-to-do family and was educated at Eton, where he was a contemporary of Swinburne's. As a young man he went to Germany, became a Catholic, and was promptly disinherited by his father. In the 1860s he was back in London. As he was unable to find an adequate job, he was working as a book-keeper in Her Majesty's Theatre in the Haymarket, living in near poverty in Fulham with his wife and family, and spending much of his spare time with Rossetti, Morris, Philip Webb, and their circle, into which he may have been introduced by Swinburne.

E. R. Robson (1836–1917) was the son of a prosperous Durham builder, who served three times as mayor of Durham.[8] From 1853 to 1856 he was articled to John Dobson in Newcastle upon Tyne and from 1857 to 1860 was in London as an assistant in Gilbert Scott's office. He then set up his own practice, was appointed architect to Durham Cathedral, opened an office in the Adelphi in London, in partnership with J. W. Walton-Wilson, and for a time was also connected with a furniture-manufacturing firm started up in Durham by his father. When in Newcastle he had got to know the painter William Bell Scott, who put him in touch with Rossetti and his friends in London. Shortly after the firm of Morris, Marshall, Faulkner and Co. was founded in 1861, Robson obtained for it a commission to provide a stained-glass window for St. Oswald's Church in Durham. Taylor heard of him through his friends, came to his office, and introduced himself. A close friendship grew up between the two men, which lasted until Taylor's death.

In 1864 Robson was appointed City Architect of Liverpool. He closed his London office, and briefly lost touch with Taylor until he accidentally met him in Piccadilly when on a visit to London in 1865. Taylor had lost his job and was down and out. Robson invited him to come up to Liverpool as his secretary. He told Morris what he was doing, and Morris said 'We cannot let Taylor go out of London'.[9] The result was that Taylor was appointed manager of Morris, Marshall, Faulkner and Co. The appointment was a success. The survival of the firm was largely due to his reorganization of its finances and business methods, even though galloping consumption forced him to spend more and more time on the south coast, from which he directed the firm's affairs by letter. He died in 1870.

Although his official connection with Morris and Company* did not start until 1865, Taylor had been in the confidence of what he called 'the gang' since about 1860. Reading his letters is like listening to snatches of conversation, the rest of which has been lost—long enthusiastic conversations between young men in their twenties and early thirties, full of idealism and laughter, discussing and arguing into the small hours. One such evening, on 16 October 1867,

---

* Strictly speaking the firm remained Morris, Marshall, Faulkner and Co. until reconstituted as Morris and Company in 1875, but for convenience it is hereafter referred to as Morris and Company.

is briefly but vividly brought to life in the diary of the poet William Allingham. 'Cab to Euston Road, to Taylor's lodgings. T., Morris, Webb, D.G.R. lounges. I say the rhyme about "There's a louse on my back Twenty years old!" (which I heard Tennyson give). Morris repeats it with furious emphasis and gestures, making us all shout with laughter. Poor Taylor—tall, with eager hatchet face—is ghastly thin but full of mental energy—vociferates, then must stop to cough. "Won't go away this winter".'[10]

Taylor's letters were as impetuous and energetic as his conversation. They show how constructive a part he must have played in these discussions, both by stimulating the others to work out their ideas, and by throwing in ideas of his own. They are fascinating to read because as early as 1862 everything that was to develop into 'Queen Anne' is present in them in embryo—not just enthusiasm for products of the Queen Anne period, but also hatred of narrowness and commercial vulgarity, reaction against mid-Victorian heaviness and toughness, distrust of theorizing and the grand manner, concern for the under-dog, belief in art for art's sake, and a combination of interest in everything (including Japan) with an especial enthusiasm for the Englishness of England.

The earliest letters are particularly concerned with Robson's activities as a furniture designer. In 1862 Taylor writes: 'now concerning furniture the continual massive in style requires some change—and this I think is best gained by the constructive though light motifs of the Queen Anne style.' He elaborates on this in a letter which was probably written a few weeks later. 'Is not Queen Anne furniture better suited to our wants . . . constructional but light . . . The Japanese spirit of early Worcester china is good—The painted cabinets in Japanese style of Queen Anne time are good—the inlaid furniture of Queen Anne time is good it has something düreresque, and altogether does not Queen Anne furniture offer us the best motifs whereon to work now, compare these Queen Anne works with French rococo—how superior we English, Dutch are, Queen Anne staircases, clocks, old hall clocks, houses—have a try at their light but constructional work in furniture . . . cannot we learn from all ages?'[11]

Two more letters attack massiveness as being foreign to the English genius. 'Burges, Seddon et hoc genus omne being industrious but not men of genius seek to make impression by "stately" (qy pretentious?) Buildings—sensation!—all that is huge coarse in French Gothic they seize—but they have no feeling for the poetry of that very insular characteristic "littleness of English nature", everything English, except stockjobbing London or cotton Manchester, is essentially small, and of a homely farmhouse kind of poetry. . . . Above all things nationality is the greatest social trait, English Gothic is small as our landscape is small, it is sweet picturesque homely farmyardish, Japanese, social, domestic—French is aspiring, grand straining after the extraordinary all very well in France but is wrong here.'[12]

Discussion of art for art's sake is introduced by way of Swinburne and Viollet-le-Duc. Swinburne was one of the first to introduce the concept to England, in his review of Baudelaire's *Les Fleurs du mal*, published in the *Spectator* of 6 September 1862: 'Perfect workmanship makes every subject admirable and respectable.' In 1863 Taylor asks Robson: 'Have you seen Viollet-le-Duc's last volume—the article "maison" is very interesting . . . I think the theory well nigh right—that the architect painter must have no religion but poetry: he must not care for dogmas, he must have no bias.'[13] In an 1862 letter he asks 'Did you ever read any poetry by Swinburne, in my division at Eton, friend of Rossetti's', and on 27 October 1866, in one of the few dated letters in the correspondence, he defends Swinburne on the grounds that he must be judged by his poetry, not his morals: 'Read Swinburne in this the artistic sense.'[14] In and around 1862 he writes 'Theorizing generalizing on art is all twaddle' and 'I do not see that religion has one iota to do with art'. Art is enobling in itself: 'It is hellish wickedness to spend more than 15/- on a chair when the poor are starving in the street, because you do no good by it, but if you spend £5 on art in decoration you do somewhat to elevate your fellow creatures.'[15]

5. Great Woolstone Parsonage, Buckinghamshire. By William Butterfield, 1851.

By reading Taylor's letters one can savour the different shades of opinion existing within the group. The impulse towards lightness came from the artists rather than the architects; in 1862 'the painters like the light, the architects perhaps the massive'; 'What about moveable furniture —light sir—something you can pull about with the hand . . . Are not the Red Lion people in the right direction in this matter, they get gradually lighter, and Rossetti keeps them up to the point.'[16] The painters must have included Ford Madox Brown, who was designing extremely interesting furniture at this period. But Rossetti is the only one named, and for him Taylor has unstinted admiration: 'Next to Rome, Rossetti is infallible, this is the subject to savage Burges and all you architects with.' Among architects his heroes are Webb and Butterfield: 'Butterfield and Webb are English—as you ought to be, having such superb examples before your very eyes'; 'Webb is *delicate tender* in architecture—remember Ruskin on tenderness, the mark of a great man.'[17]

'Delicate' and 'tender' are hardly the words one would apply to the heavy-weight furniture which Webb designed for the firm in its earliest days. But he was ready enough to be edged away from the Gothic Revival, from heaviness, and from Street. His point of departure was his admiration for the architecture of William Butterfield. Butterfield was ten years older than Street and one of the few leading Gothic architects who had resisted the blandishments of France and Italy. His detail remained resolutely English in inspiration and his buildings were never as massive or ponderous as those of Street and Burges at the height of their 'muscular' period. Moreover, although remaining committed to the Gothic Revival, from the mid 1850s he boldly introduced small-paned sash or casement windows of early eighteenth-century type into his domestic buildings. His cottages and simpler rectories of red brick, sometimes tile-hung, with prominent hipped roofs, wooden sashes or casements, and the minimum of ornament were distinctive and delightful. Webb visited and sketched his work, and his first independent commission, William Morris's Red House (1859–61) was more strongly influenced by Butterfield than by Street.[18]

6. Milton Mill, Milton Ernest, Bedfordshire. By William Butterfield, 1856–7.

In the mid 1860s argument and discussion bore three-dimensional fruit. The results can be seen both in furniture designed by Morris and Company, and in buildings designed by Philip Webb and other architects in the circle. Morris and Company's furniture of this period is in need of research; a good many of the light-weight pieces described or hinted at by Warrington Taylor are probably still in existence and waiting to be identified. But one model, or rather group of models, has not only been identified but was to remain for many years the most successful line of furniture produced by the firm. This was the 'Sussex' chair, in all its numerous variations.[19]

The Sussex chair answered all Warrington Taylor's requirements. It was an elegant, simple, cheap, light-weight chair, rush-seated, made of wood usually stained either black or green. A number of variations on it were manufactured by the firm, some with arms and some without. It was first produced in about 1865. The credit for discovering the original model has been given to both Rossetti and Ford Madox Brown; one of the variants is described as the 'Rossetti' chair in later Morris catalogues. According to Mackail's biography of Morris, it was 'copied with trifling improvements from an old chair of village manufacture picked up in Sussex'. The original has long ago disappeared, but must have been a provincial version of a late eighteenth- or early nineteenth-century London model. Since accurate dating of eighteenth-century furniture was rare in the 1860s it was probably of this kind of chair that Warrington Taylor was thinking when he recommended 'constructional but light' Queen Anne furniture as a starting-point for contemporary design.

7. A table designed by Philip Webb, *c.* 1860, now at Kelmscott Manor, Oxfordshire.

In addition to Sussex chairs and, possibly, other Morris furniture still to be identified, from the mid-1860s a series of buildings were being designed in which the seventeenth- and eighteenth-century elements grew stronger, until by 1873 a new style had developed which was sufficiently coherent and widespread to be publicly recognized as 'Queen Anne'. All the relevant buildings of this decade were designed by architects in the Rossetti–Webb–Morris circle; or perhaps it would be more accurate to say by architects in a series of interlocking circles, in which everyone did not necessarily know everyone else, but at least knew somebody who knew them.

At this stage probably no one envisaged where the movement was going to end. Certainly Webb and others were thinking in perhaps illusory terms of non-style rather than new style. As Taylor put it to Robson 'You don't want any style, you want something English in character'; and in another letter, 'Style means copyism, the test of good work would be an absence of style.'[20] In practice architects used elements derived mainly from seventeenth- and eighteenth-century domestic architecture in a way that showed their Gothic Revival training. They abandoned symmetry whenever it seemed convenient to do so, and concentrated on features in which, as Morris later put it, 'some of the Gothic feeling was left',[21] such as prominent roofs and chimney-stacks and bay or oriel windows. They not only ignored the grammar of the orders but actively despised it, as pedantic and constricting; they avoided anything approaching the grand manner, and when they used classical features, tended to use them in their least correct form. They liked stumpy or bulging pilasters and pediments that were broken or used to finish off gables; they liked buildings such as the grammar school at Rye, with its pedimented dormers and row of homely brick pilasters, which Taylor was calling to Webb's attention with admiring affection in 1867–8.[22] Red brick, especially when combined with green foliage, had a symbolic value, for them, as the quintessence of Englishness.

8. A Sussex chair, of a type first produced by Morris and Company, *c.* 1865.

In Webb's own buildings one can watch a resolute attempt to obtain 'absence of style' combined with an increasing awareness of seventeenth- and eighteenth-century domestic architecture. There is a consistent development to be observed in five buildings designed by him in the years 1864 to 1868: a studio house for Val Prinsep, in what was to become Holland Park Road, Kensington, probably designed at the end of 1864, and built in 1865; a new entrance front and other additions to Washington Hall, Durham, designed and built for Lowthian Bell in 1865–7; a house for the Hon. George Howard on Kensington Palace Green (next door to Thackeray's house), designed in the summer of 1867 and built in 1868–70; an office block in Lincoln's Inn Fields, designed at the beginning of 1868 and built in 1869; and a house for George Pryce Boyce in Glebe Place, Chelsea, which was being designed in October 1868 and was built in 1869.

The patrons for these commissions are an example of the social mix of upper and middle classes, watered by money and manured by Art, which was to welcome and sustain the 'Queen Anne' style. Val Prinsep, artist and friend of Rossetti, came from a prosperous upper-middle-class background; his mother's parties in Little Holland were famous for their enjoyable potpourri of artists, intellectuals, and smart society. Lowthian Bell was a cultivated chemical manufacturer who was later to start a steel works at Middlesborough and make a great fortune. George Howard was an amateur artist, an aristocrat, and heir to the Earldom of Carlisle and to Castle Howard; he and his equally aristocratic wife were both in conscious reaction against their background and preferred the society of artists and writers to conventional upper-class society; in 1873 George

Howard's brother-in-law was to marry Lowthian Bell's daughter. G. P. Boyce was a professional painter with an architectural training, and an inner member of the Rossetti circle; his sensitive water-colours tended to depict the same kind of vernacular farm buildings or modest eighteenth-century town houses that were inspiring the architect members of the group.

For Prinsep, Bell and Howard Webb designed tall, asymmetric red brick buildings with prominent roofs, gables, and chimney-stacks and small-paned sash windows irregularly disposed. The Prinsep house, now 14 Holland Park Road, was the earliest and cheapest of the three, and the one closest to a Butterfield vicarage; its main features were two large studio windows under the gables, crowned with Gothic pointed arches but filled with small-paned sashes.[23] The new front at Washington Hall was a forceful and original asymmetric design, with a great Gothic-arched porch nicely balanced by a combined gable and chimney-stack, corbelled out at first-floor level; there were the usual sash windows and the multiple brick chimney-stacks were of seventeenth-century inspiration.[24]

9. Studio house for Val Prinsep, now 14 Holland Park Road, Kensington. Designed by Philip Webb, *c.* 1864–5.

10. Washington Hall (now Dame Margaret Training Centre), Durham. By Philip Webb, 1865–7.

George Howard's house, now 1 Palace Green, was an ambitious, splendid, and controversial   11, 12
building. In addition to its Gothic (or Gothic Revival) elements, its asymmetry, Gothic arches,
gables, oriel, and prominent steep-pitched roof, it had sash windows, brick cornices, brick
chimney-stacks, mouldings of cut and rubbed brick, brick aprons underneath the windows, and
wrought-iron railings, all of seventeenth- or eighteenth-century inspiration. But Webb gave every
element an individual character so that the total result was completely original.

It was not an originality that appealed to the elderly James Pennethorne, who as architect
to the Commissioners of Woods and Forests had to approve the design of houses built on Crown
land. The fact that Pennethorne could readily accept Thackeray's house in 1860 and violently
object to Howard's house in 1867 underlines the different approach behind the neo-Queen Anne

12. The dining-room
at 1 Palace Green,
before the interior
was remodelled.

◁   **11.** 1 Palace Green, Kensington. By Philip Webb, 1867–70.

of the one and the proto-'Queen Anne' of the other. Pennethorne found Webb's original designs 'commonplace' and 'perfectly hideous', objected to the lack of stone dressings to relieve the 'masses of red brickwork', disliked the gable and steep-pitched roof, and found the sash windows 'unattractive'. He brought in Salvin and T. H. Wyatt as referees, and they supported him. Webb's answer to their criticisms nicely summed up his own approach and the difference between two generations: 'That Messrs Salvin and Wyatt are "unable to discover what actual style or period of architecture" I have used, I take to be a sincere compliment.'[25] But even though George Howard was a client who could pull powerful strings, he was able to get the design through only by increasing the proportion of Portland stone dressings and adding a certain amount of extra ornament.

13   Webb's Lincoln's Inn office block was another original and effective mixture of Gothic and eighteenth-century elements, and showed an enjoyment of symmetry that was new for Webb. The same sense of enjoyment comes strongly across in his house for G. P. Boyce, now 35 Glebe Place, Chelsea, but here both the proportions and the flavour of the mixture have changed, with results that for the first time in Webb's work can be described as 'Queen Anne', rather than on

14   the way to it. It is not only that the entrance front of the house, with its hipped roof, symmetry, sash windows, and fan-lighted front door, is more strongly eighteenth-century in flavour than

13. 19 Lincoln's Inn Fields, London. By Philip Webb, 1868–9.

14. 35 Glebe Place, Chelsea. By Philip Webb, 1868–9.

anything Webb had designed previously. Webb's earlier buildings had had a big-boned no-nonsense element inherited from muscular Gothic, but the Boyce house has a delicacy in its symmetry, a daintiness in its scale, an elegance in details such as the attenuated first-floor windows, that recall Taylor's phrase 'delicate tender in architecture'.[26]

At the same time as Webb was working his way towards the seventeenth- and eighteenth-centuries, Richard Norman Shaw (1831–1912) and William Eden Nesfield (1835–88) were pursuing a parallel course. At this period Shaw and Nesfield were inside the Rossetti–Morris circle, even if they were not in the centre of it, like Philip Webb. Shaw had been in Street's office from 1858 to 1862; he overlapped with Webb there, and took over Webb's position as Street's chief assistant before he set up an office with Nesfield at 30 Argyll Street in 1863. He was friendly (though never friends) with Webb and admired his work; he also knew and admired the work of Butterfield. There is no certain evidence as to when he got to know Morris and Rossetti but his close personal friend in the 1860s was J. Aldam Heaton, an artist and decorator based at Bradford, who was also a friend of Rossetti's.[27] Heaton was concerned in Shaw's first important church commission, All Saints', Bingley (1864), for which Morris and Company provided the glass. Shaw continued to go to the firm for glass until the early 1870s, after which he drifted away from them.

Nesfield's closest friend, and frequent collaborator, was Albert Moore, the artist. The friend-ship was unlikely to endear him to Rossetti, who considered Moore 'a dull dog', but from about 1865 it brought him into contact with Whistler, who became friends with Moore in that year; at about this period Whistler is reported as going to Argyll Street to 'box with our friend Nesfield the architect'.[28] In the 1860s Whistler was seeing a good deal of Swinburne and Rossetti, and shared with Rossetti a passion for blue china and an interest in Japanese art. Nesfield had been interested in Japan since 1862, when the Japanese exhibits in the International Exhibition aroused great interest in advanced artistic circles in London (as is reflected in Warrington Taylor's letters). In Nesfield's notebooks there are sketches of 'drawings in a Japanese novel' made in 1862.[29] Another member of 'the gang' whom Nesfield got to know in the 1860s was Simeon Solomon, the painter. In about September 1869, Solomon described Nesfield to Swinburne as 'a fat, jolly hearty fellow, genuinely good natured, very fond of smoking and, I deeply grieve to say, of women. . . . His rooms are in Argyll Street near mine, and he has a very jolly collection of Persian, Indian, Greek and Japanese things that I should really like you to see.'[30] Many years later J. M. Brydon, who came to the Argyll Street rooms as an assistant in 1867, was to describe Nesfield's collection of blue and white Nankin china, Persian plates, and Japanese curios, and comment that his room resembled 'the studio of an artist rather than the business room of a professional man'.[31]

Shaw's and Nesfield's architectural development was in tune with the circles in which they moved and the ideas which circulated in them. From rooms decorated with Japanese and oriental china they set out to rediscover the English countryside, and sketch tile-hung cottages and half-timbered farmhouses in Kent and Sussex. From cottages and farmhouses they moved almost with inevitability to the plaster and half-timbered or red brick and sash-windowed houses of country towns, and the craftsmanship of rubbed and cut brick, elaborately turned joinery, or richly modelled pargetting that embellished them. They came back to London to design buildings in which Gothic merged into farmhouse vernacular, and farmhouse vernacular into builder's classical; and on plaster coves inspired by their country tours they incised delicate ornament derived from Japan.

15, 16

By mixing Streetian Gothic with farmhouse vernacular (with a little Elizabethan and Japanese thrown in) Shaw and Nesfield rapidly developed what came to be called their 'Old English' manner. From their interest in builder's classical of the seventeenth and eighteenth centuries there developed, rather more slowly, what came to be called 'Queen Anne'. For many years their clients tended to be given one or the other, according to taste; Shaw, unlike Nesfield or other

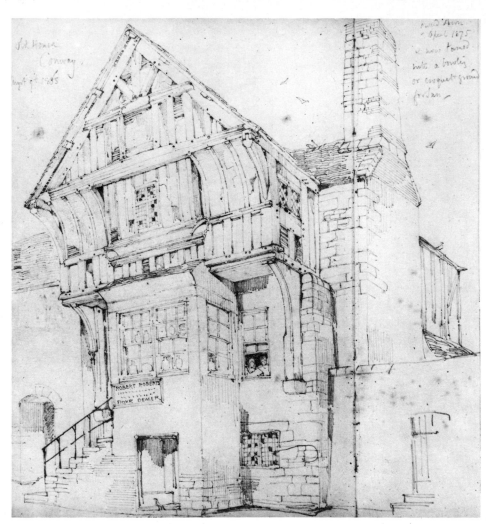

15. A house in
Conway, Caernarvon-
shire, drawn by
William Eden Nesfield,
9 August 1865.

16. Nesfield's sketch
of Fenton House,
Hampstead, drawn
1870.

17. Design by Norman Shaw for cottages at Bromley, Kent, *c.* 1864.

members of the group, tended to keep 'Queen Anne' for the town and 'Old English' for the country. This book is not concerned with the long and wildly successful career of 'Old English' but it is impossible to separate the two styles completely, because one merged into the other.

Perhaps there is a modest foretaste of 'Queen Anne' in the many-paned windows with wooden glazing bars of one of Shaw's earliest and most delightful buildings, a warehouse (long since demolished) in Narrow Street, Shadwell. It was designed late in 1862 or early in 1863, probably for the Shaw Savill shipping line, of which Shaw's brother was the founder. Seventeenth- and eighteenth-century elements are much more in evidence in a row of brick cottages designed for Coles Child, perhaps as early as 1864, at Bromley in Kent. These have massive ribbed chimney stacks of seventeenth-century type, windows with small panes paired in the Butterfield manner, and doors with fan-lights and bracketed-out canopies.[32]

17

At Fowler's Park, in Kent, where Shaw designed an extension and new entrance front to a plain late eighteenth-century country house belonging to James Gow-Steuart, one can watch 'Queen Anne' emerging from the chrysalis. Shaw's first design, dated 3 December 1864, was remarkably eclectic, and also remarkably clumsy. It looked like a late eighteenth-century house mutilated by Elizabethan mullioned windows and the addition of a clumsy porch on the ground floor, and oversized dormers and a mansard roof on top. In the second and executed design, dated February 1865, the dormers have been reduced in size, and the mullioned windows replaced by paired sashes framed by brick pilasters and pediments. The result is still eclectic, the rhythm of the windows is still different from (and more complex than) what it would have been in the seventeenth and eighteenth centuries, but the eye of the artist has been at work and the design has suddenly come alive.[33]

18, 19

18. Shaw's first design for additions to Fowler's Park, Kent, 1864.

19. The final design for Fowler's Park, 1865.

20   At the end of 1866 Nesfield designed his first known building in a post-Gothic manner. This is the well-known lodge in Kew Gardens, designed, presumably, to tone in with the so-called Kew Palace, a homely red brick house of the mid-seventeenth century with Flemish gables, of the type that Shaw and Nesfield had learned to appreciate. It used to be thought amazingly advanced for its date, but now turns out not to have been quite so much of a pioneer. It remains, however, perhaps the first building of the 1860s in which one of the essential elements of 'Queen Anne' is to be found—not just eclecticism, but also that delicate exaggeration of period which was to delight the public in the 1870s. All its elements can be related to buildings of the seventeenth century, but almost all the proportions have been changed: the roof is taller, the walls lower, the chimney-stacks slenderer, and the pilasters squatter than they would have been, and the result is entirely distinctive and delightful. Similar exaggeration is to be found in the lodge which

21   Nesfield designed at Kinmel Park, Denbighshire, in 1868. This is a more elaborate and Frenchified version in stone of the Kew lodge, and has the extra diversion of a rich incrustation of sunflowers —in stone or wrought iron, on their own or sprouting out of two-handled pots.[34]

Sunflowers, like so many of the elements that were to coalesce into 'Queen Anne', had been set in circulation by Morris, Rossetti, and Burne-Jones. Perhaps Blake's 'sunflower weary of time' and Tennyson's 'heavily hangs the broad sunflower' had something to do with their vogue, for both poets were admired in Pre-Raphaelite circles. In Morris's *Story of an Unknown Church* (1856) he tells of 'many sunflowers that were all in blossom on that autumn day', and in 1857

20. Lodge at Kew Gardens, Surrey, by W. E. Nesfield, 1866.

sunflowers filled the foreground of his contribution to the Oxford Union frescoes, which depicted the unrequited love of Sir Palomydes for La Belle Iseult. From 1857 until the early 1860s both Rossetti and Burne-Jones were bringing sunflowers into their work; Burne-Jones at this period had an especial fondness for them.[35] He and his friends may have used them as symbols of physical love and the world of the senses; in Rossetti's *Mary Magdalene at the house of Simon the Pharisee* (1858) a sunflower and a lily, each in a pot to either side of the door of Simon's house, seem to suggest the physical and spiritual worlds between which Mary Magdalene is poised.[36]

In the mid-1860s sunflowers spilled over into decoration. Nesfield's spread of stone and metal sunflowers on the lodge at Kinmel was matched by the equally lavish array of sunflower tiles with which E. J. Poynter (Burne-Jones's brother-in-law) surrounded the stove in the grill-room in the South Kensington Museum at approximately the same time.[37] In 1868 Philip Webb introduced brick sunflowers more discreetly into the exterior of George Howard's house in Palace Green, Kensington. Nesfield at Kinmel was perhaps the first architect to follow Rossetti's example and pot them; but his pots, which were to be endlessly imitated, were not handleless tubs, as in

24

21. (*Far left*) Sunflowers on the lodge at Kinmel Park, Denbighshire, by W. E. Nesfield, 1868.

22, 23. (*Top and bottom left*) Sunflower details from 72 Cadogan Square, Chelsea, and Carlyle Mansions, Chelsea Embankment.

24. (*Top right*) Sunflowers rampant. 'Childe Roland to the dark tower came' by Burne-Jones, 1861.

Rossetti's *Mary Magdalene*, but had twin handles, a form possibly derived from the flowerpots on the pargeted façade of Sparrowe's House in Ipswich.[38] From 1868 Nesfield, Shaw, and other architects, artists, and decorators used sunflowers in increasing numbers, potted, unpotted, and sometimes paired off with lilies, as in Rossetti's drawing. By the 1880s the aesthetic world was swamped with sunflowers, and their original sponsors were sick of the sight of them.

The last of the pioneering 'Queen Anne' buildings to be produced by Shaw and Nesfield in the 1860s was Shaw's enlarging and remodelling of West Wickham House in Kent for W. M. Steuart.[39] This was drawn out in October 1869 and built in 1870–1, an elegantly simple design of red brick and white woodwork, with rows of sash windows elongated as in Webb's house for Boyce and grouped in pairs under a hipped roof with pedimented dormers. Its mixture of symmetry and irregularity was to become typical of the 'Queen Anne' movement; the entrance block forms a symmetrical pavilion but at right angles to it is attached an asymmetrical one-storey stable wing with cupola, so that the whole is an irregular and picturesque composition.

To Nesfield and Shaw on the one hand, and Webb following Butterfield on the other must be added the third group which pioneered 'Queen Anne', the architects who had been trained in the office of Sir George Gilbert Scott. Of these the first in the field in the 1860s were G. F. Bodley and G. G. Scott, junior, but they were to be joined early in the 1870s by E. R. Robson, J. J. Stevenson, Thomas Graham Jackson, and R. J. Johnson. These were the cream of Gilbert Scott's assistants. Their wholesale conversion to 'Queen Anne' was impressive evidence of the collapse of the Gothic Revival, at least in the form in which it had been so assiduously preached by their old master.

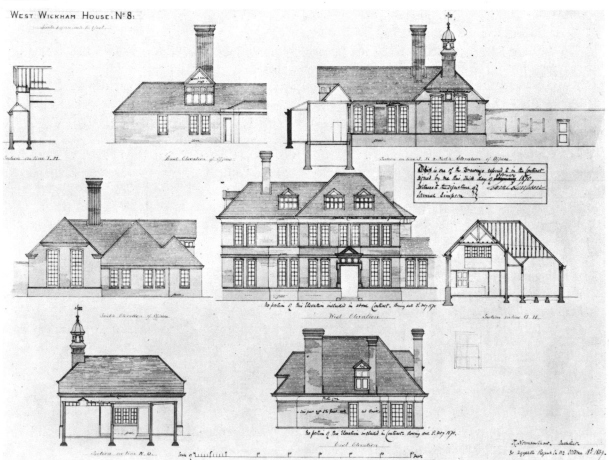

25. Designs by Norman Shaw for West Wickham House, Kent, 1869.

The pioneer of 'Queen Anne' among them was almost certainly the oldest member of the group, Scott's own brother-in-law, George Frederick Bodley (1827–1907). Bodley had left Scott to set up on his own by at least 1857, but he kept closely in touch with the younger men in Scott's office. In about 1870 Thomas Garner left Scott to become his partner (a project by Bodley to go into partnership with Robson having fallen through), and shortly afterwards Bodley, Garner, and G. G. Scott, junior, joined in starting up Watts and Company, a decorating firm of a similar nature to Morris and Company.[40] Bodley had known Rossetti since at least 1856, when Rossetti enrolled him in the abortive Hogarth Club, an association of artists out of sympathy with the Academy. When Morris and Company was formed Bodley was one of their earliest and best patrons, at St. Michael's, Brighton (*c.* 1861–2), St. Martin's, Scarborough (*c.* 1862–3), All Saints', Selsley (1862), and All Saints', Cambridge (1864–6).

As a young man his work was almost inevitably 'muscular' and French, notably in St. Michael's, Brighton, which he later referred to as a 'boyish antagonistic effort'. Unlike Burges and Seddon, who were his exact contemporaries and whom he resembled in his early career, Bodley developed away both from muscularity and total commitment to Gothic. By the mid-1860s his Gothic was turning English and delicate. With English Gothic churches came houses that were not Gothic at all—even though they were built for clergymen.[41] The earliest of them is probably the vicarage of St. Martin's, Scarborough, dated 1867 on the fabric and perhaps designed in 1866. This inexpensive but pleasing house could be described as Butterfield with the Gothic left out. It has sash windows paired in the Butterfield manner, but instead of Gothic arches there are brick pediments over the windows and doorway. The main windows are grouped into three slightly projecting bays, which rise above the roof into gables and supply a gently regular rhythm in a building otherwise asymmetrical. 　26

The other non-Gothic houses known to have been designed by Bodley in the 1860s include the vicarage of St. Augustine's, Pendlebury, near Manchester (which has been demolished), and a group of houses at Malvern Link built for the Revd. George Herbert or his family and finished in 1869. Father Herbert was the founder and first vicar of J. L. Pearson's Holy Trinity, Vauxhall (1863). His father was a builder, and it was possibly for him that Bodley designed the four houses at Malvern Link. One was the Herbert family house, one (dated 1869 over the door) was lived in by Canon Spooner, vicar of St. Leonard's, Newland. The other two were built as private houses, but in 1879 were taken over by the Community of the Holy Name, an order of Anglican nuns founded by Father Herbert in Vauxhall; the convent later expanded to take in the other two houses, and all four appear to have been added to in the same style as the original work. This makes their exact original design a little hard to work out, but their general character is still clear. They have hipped roofs with dormers, sash windows with wooden external shutters, projecting weather-boarded bays, a sprinkling of Venetian windows, and the by now familiar mixture of symmetry and asymmetry. The eclecticism, ranging from farmhouse vernacular to 　27 Palladian, represents a different mix to that of the Scarborough vicarage, but the character is much the same—relaxed, unassuming, and agreeable.[42]

George Gilbert Scott, junior (1839–97), was in his father's office as a young man. Among his fellow assistants he formed an especially close friendship with E. R. Robson, who taught him how to trace.[43] In 1863–7 he was at Jesus College, Cambridge, where he became a Fellow in 1870. These were the years in which Bodley was restoring the college chapel and employing Morris and Company to decorate the new roofs; Scott must have seen a good deal of them in Cambridge, and became a regular visitor to 'the shop' in London.[44] In about 1869–74 he brought in Morris and Company to provide stained glass and other decorations for Peterhouse, which he had been commissioned to restore and embellish.

Scott's work at Peterhouse was Gothic; but in about 1868 or 1869 he was asked to design a large country house at Garboldisham in Norfolk, for Cecil M. Montgomerie, and followed the

27. House at Malvern Link, Worcestershire. By G. F. Bodley, *c.* 1869.

rest of the group in experimenting with a non-Gothic design.[45] Three of the façades were predominantly Tudor or Jacobean in style, but on the entrance front Scott designed something closer
to the mid-seventeenth-century façades of Raynham Hall in the same county. The main entrance
had rusticated columns and a pediment; similar combinations of pediments and columns appeared
as centre-pieces of the shaped 'Flemish' gables of the flanking wings. George Devey had used
Flemish gables at Betteshanger (*c.* 1860) and in other houses of the 1860s, but there is no certain
evidence that these were known to Scott or his friends. Within the group he was probably the
pioneer of a feature that was later to be run to death in the service of 'Queen Anne'.

To judge from photographs (it has been demolished), Garboldisham was a somewhat clumsy
and heavy design, conspicuously lacking in, for instance, the delicate prettiness of Bodley's houses
of the same date. Scott may have been circumscribed by the need to provide something sufficiently
dignified and important to live up to Victorian conceptions of a country house. He was far more
successful with the stable block, which fortunately survives. Here a wooden cupola surmounts
the Flemish gable of the centre-piece, there are less elaborately shaped gables on the wings, and
the design is unified by alternate stripes of red and white brick (did Scott know the banded
seventeenth-century façades of Moulton Hall in Yorkshire?). When originally built it must have
looked pretty and very gay; in the last hundred years wood and brick have weathered together
into a gentle mellowed decay.

28, 29

◁ **26.** St. Martin's Vicarage, Scarborough, Yorkshire.
By G. F. Bodley, *c.* 1866–7.

28. Cupola of the stable block, Garboldisham Hall, Norfolk. By George Gilbert Scott, jun., *c.* 1868–9.

29. The stable block, Garboldisham Hall, photographed shortly after completion.

Two architecturally minded laymen spoke up in these years for the buildings of the late seventeenth and early eighteenth centuries. In May 1865, Alexander Beresford Hope, in a lecture to the Architectural Association at Conduit Street, was reported as remarking that 'he wished to plead for a class of buildings to which adequate justice had not been done. He referred to the houses in our towns and a smaller class of country houses built between 1660 and 1710. At that time there seemed to be a great feeling for quiet proportions, quiet comfort, and adaptation of the structure for the position in which it stood, which characterized a great amount of studied refinement. These houses were generally admirably placed in the garden, and had a good architectural effect.'[46]

In the autumn of 1867, Hope's plea was repeated by the Revd. J. L. Petit, speaking to the St. Albans Architectural and Archaeological Society. 'The domestic style of architecture which prevailed in Queen Anne's time, at least such specimens as do not exhibit the Classical orders too prominently, has always appeared to me to harmonize exceedingly well with Gothic buildings, and it is a style which might be used in the present day without giving the idea that we are adopting the manner of an age different from our own.' The architecture of this period satisfied modern requirements 'whether we want size or number of rooms, fine proportions, good ventilation and lighting, convenience of passages and staircases, or a stately and dignified aspect.'[47]

Hope and Petit had many connections with the architectural world. It is hard to believe that they were unaware of the interest which some of the younger Gothic Revival architects were already showing in buildings of the late seventeenth and early eighteenth centuries. The way in which the tide was turning was further demonstrated in 1870, when R. Almond gave a paper at the Architectural Association on 'Domestic Architecture during the reign of Queen Anne'.[48] 'Queen Anne' was in the air; and although the term does not seem to have been applied in print to new buildings until 1872, it seems likely that from the late 1860s it was already in use in architectural circles as a convenient, if not very accurate, way of referring to what Webb, Shaw, Nesfield, Bodley, and Scott were doing.

III 'Queen Anne' Goes Public

The Buildings

Looking back over the 1860s one can see that by the end of the decade the mixture that was to be branded 'Queen Anne' was almost ready for launching. Webb, Shaw, Nesfield, Bodley, and Scott had evolved a basic vocabulary. The early and mid-seventeenth century had supplied them with gables, whether straight or Flemish, brick pilasters, brick pediments, ribbed chimney-stacks, and prominent plaster coves; from the late seventeenth and eighteenth centuries came sash windows, hipped roofs, wooden cupolas, external shutters, fan-lights, brick aprons under the windows, and wrought-iron railings; the architects had mixed them all together, made roofs and chimney-stacks especially prominent, been asymmetric when they felt like it, paired or elongated their sash windows, and thrown in the occasional sunflower to add an aesthetic flavouring.

The results were enjoyable, but still largely unknown. None of the buildings described in the last chapter was illustrated, or even mentioned in the building periodicals, let alone anywhere else. Between 1870 and 1873 the situation was transformed. The small group previously working in the style were strengthened by new recruits, such as J. J. Stevenson, E. R. Robson, and Basil Champneys. Many more buildings, including schools and offices as well as houses, were built in the new manner; some were of considerable size, some in prominent positions, and a good many of them were described and illustrated in the press. The *annus mirabilis* for the style was 1873, when 'Queen Anne' can reasonably be described as going public. In that year a group of new 'Queen Anne' buildings received maximum publicity and the style became the subject of furious discussion, first by architects and then by everyone else. The term 'Queen Anne' was taken up by the public and, in spite of protests from some architects that 'Free Classic' or even 'Re-Renaissance' would be a more accurate description, was irrevocably fastened to the style.

Two buildings, both designed in 1871, were to be especially influential. Norman Shaw's New Zealand Chambers in the City showed that 'Queen Anne' could be used just as well for offices as for houses, and supplied his fellow-architects with a whole new range of motifs. J. J. Stevenson's Red House in Bayswater provided the 'Queen Anne' answer to the problem of designing a London terrace house.

The Red House was Stevenson's first building in the new manner; but he would almost certainly have been involved in the movement several years earlier, if he had not been practising out of London. The Stevensons[1] were a textbook example of the way in which a middle-class family could blossom out in the second or third generation of wealth. They had been farmers in Ayrshire, then merchants in a small way in Glasgow, until J. J. Stevenson's father founded a chemical works on the banks of the Tyne at Jarrow, and made a considerable fortune. His eight children included his eldest son, J. C. Stevenson, who ran the family business and became a Liberal M.P. and the chairman of the Tyne Improvement Commission; Alexander, who moved in artistic circles and collected pictures and furniture; Flora, who became one of the original members and ultimately Chairman of the Edinburgh School Board; and Louisa, a founder of the Edinburgh School of Domestic Economy, promoter of medical and university education for women, and a suffragette. Among the family's cousins and connections were the Andersons, shipowners originally established at Peterhead near Aberdeen, who came down to London in the nineteenth century and founded the Orient Line in the 1870s; in 1871 one of them married Elizabeth Garrett, England's first qualified woman doctor.

John James Stevenson (1831–1908) was educated to become a minister of the Scottish Free Church, to which his family belonged. While studying theology in Germany he picked up liberal notions and decided that the ministry was not his vocation. He became an architect instead. From 1856 to 1858 he was in the office of David Bryce in Edinburgh, from 1858 to 1860 in the office of George Gilbert Scott in London. His contemporaries in Scott's office included G. G. Scott, junior, E. R. Robson, T. G. Jackson, Thomas Garner, and R. J. Johnson; in these years he almost certainly got to know Bodley. In 1860 he became partner of his friend Campbell Douglas in Glasgow. In 1866 his father died and left him a share in the Jarrow Chemical Works. It was probably this legacy which encouraged him to set up in London and enabled him to take the move in an unhurried spirit. In 1867 he started discussions about entering into partnership with E. R. Robson, who was unhappy in his job as City Architect of Liverpool. In 1868 he wound up his partnership with Campbell Douglas and spent two leisurely years writing and holidaying, in Paris and Broadstairs. In 1870 he rented a furnished house in London; early in 1871 he began to build the Red House; in September 1871 his partnership with Robson formally began. Robson had meanwhile, in July, become Architect to the London School Board, a part-time job which did not preclude him from private practice.

Once he moved south Stevenson can have had no difficulty in picking up the latest architectural trends in London. Apart from his friendship with Bodley, Scott the younger, Robson, and others from the Scott kindergarten, his former assistant in Glasgow, John McKean Brydon, had moved down to London in 1867 to work for Nesfield and Shaw;[2] through him he had first-hand access to what was going on at 30 Argyll Street. It seems likely that through Robson he met Rossetti and William Morris. In his two years of comparative leisure he had plenty of time in which to work out an architectural philosophy; in this period, according to his own account, he had begun to write what was ultimately to develop into his two-volume book *House Architecture*, which was not published until 1880. Moreover, unlike the other architects in the group, he had the money to build his own house on a sufficiently lavish scale to demonstrate his ideas and advertise his abilities. In calling it the Red House he may have been alluding to more than just its colour. In the Red House at Bexleyheath William Morris had used his private means to demonstrate the possibilities of aesthetic Gothic, in furniture and decoration as well as architecture. In his own Red House Stevenson dug into his capital to give an equally comprehensive demonstration of the potentialities of 'Queen Anne'—or as he preferred to call it, 'Free Classic'.

The Red House[3] was to be very widely imitated, inside and out, but this was not because it was strikingly original, but because it could be imitated easily. The exterior was worked out according to a straightforward formula: strip the stucco off the standard terrace house of the 1860s and replace Italianate detailing by 'Queen Anne'. London builders of the 1860s had tried to bring a little variety to the type of flat-fronted stucco house with columned porch which they had inherited from the 1850s. One way in which they achieved this was by building a bay window on one or both sides of the porch; another was by putting prominent dormer windows flush with the main façade above the cornice, and giving them elaborate architectural treatment. Both these devices were used at the Red House. But instead of being faced with stucco it was built of exposed brown stock bricks with red brick dressings; Stevenson almost certainly derived this combination from the eighteenth-century buildings at Kensington Palace, which were in sight of his house. All the detail was 'Queen Anne': the dormers had Flemish gables and brick pilasters, the usual plate-glass sashes were replaced by sashes with small panes and louvred external shutters, the standard builder's ironwork was replaced by a mixture of sunflowers and eighteenth-century scrollwork, the standard pillared porch was replaced by a brick one with an oval window, surrounded by seventeenth-century-style brick mouldings, above an arch. Even the brick pedimented gateway leading to a covered way from street to front door was a 'Queen Anne' version of the innumerable iron and glass canopies which were tacked on to the nearby

30

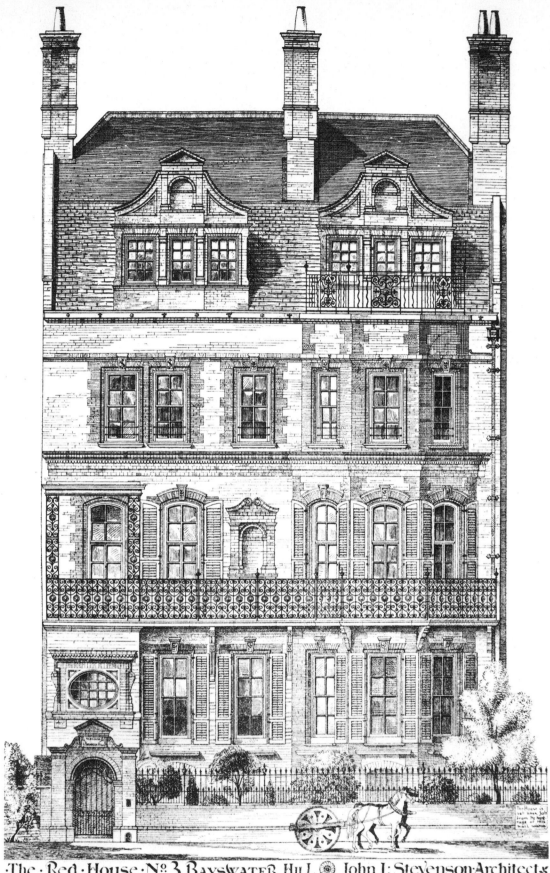

·The·Red·House·Nº 3 Bayswater Hill ⊙ John J: Stevenson·Architect·

30. The Red House, Bayswater Hill, London. By J. J. Stevenson, 1871–3. (Demolished.)

31. The staircase at
the Red House, from
a drawing probably
by J. J. Stevenson
or A. J. Adams.

stucco houses of Holland Park and Notting Hill. A brick alcove on the first floor held a blue and white 'Nankin' vase. There was a little variation in the spacing of the windows on each floor, but the fenestration was not as complicated as in some of the buildings of Webb and Shaw. The house was familiar enough not to alarm, yet novel enough to attract attention.

The interiors survive, in Stevenson's own drawing of the staircase, in contemporary descriptions, and in photographs taken shortly before the house was demolished after the last war, when it was empty and derelict. They suggest the same kind of eclecticism apparent in the exterior, enriched by ideas picked up from visits to the houses of Rossetti and other artists. There were water-colours by Rossetti and by Stevenson's Scottish friends, Orchardson, MacWhirter, and Hunter, wallpaper and stained glass by Morris and Company, and library fittings designed by Bodley.[4] But there was also much that dated from before the nineteenth century, for the house was an aesthetic mixture of periods and places: Dutch and Persian tiles, Chinese and Italian

31

32. 8 Palace Gate, Kensington. By J. J. Stevenson, 1873–5.

pottery, Dutch furniture, Chippendale and French eighteenth-century chairs, an Italian cabinet, and a Venetian mirror. On the staircase the balusters were a synthesis of early eighteenth-century and Jacobean types; the fireplace was designed to incorporate old tiles and carving; the swags in the deep plasterwork frieze were of late eighteenth-century inspiration, as was the plasterwork in the drawing-room.

32   Similar swags (and another Nankin vase) appeared on the exterior of 8 Palace Gate, which was designed by Stevenson in 1873 for Henry Francis Makins.[5] Its façade was a version of that of the Red House, also built of stock bricks with red brick dressings, but with slightly more elaborate detailing. It is an agreeable enough design, but not an especially distinguished or distinctive one; the quality of the Red House was probably very similar. Its best feature is its
1   ornamental detail; its wrought ironwork and decorative brickwork are a pleasure to study. Detail of this quality (which Webb had anticipated, in simpler form, at 1 Palace Green) was to remain typical of Stevenson, and his example was to be followed by other 'Queen Anne' architects; the largely defunct craft of rubbed and moulded brickwork was brought to life again by the style, with agreeable results for London.

33   Like the Red House, New Zealand Chambers[6] was a demonstration of how the gains of trade and industry could be applied in an artistic manner. Stevenson's family firm, the Jarrow Chemical Works, provided the money to pay for the Red House; New Zealand Chambers was built as the headquarters of the Shaw Savill shipping line, which ran a service to and from New Zealand. The two buildings were designed within a few months of each other; the contract drawings for the Red House are dated March 1871, the drawings for New Zealand Chambers followed in July.

33. New Zealand Chambers, Leadenhall Street, London. By Norman Shaw, 1871–3. (Demolished.)

But the two are (or were, for both have been demolished) very different designs. New Zealand Chambers was a piece of prestige advertising by a much more brilliant architect than Stevenson. Although the Red House was to exert great influence in the long run, it was neither central nor striking enough to cause an immediate stir. New Zealand House was in the news from the start. It was in Leadenhall Street, in the heart of the City. It was in brilliant and blatant contrast to everything around it. It provoked immediate fury or enthusiasm and was followed by innumerable imitations. More than any other building it put 'Queen Anne' on the map.

The City had been increasingly dominated by the stone-faced offices and warehouses disguised as great Italianate palaces which Edward l'Anson and other architects had designed in the 1850s and 1860s. Shaw's objective was to outshine such buildings in brilliance and outdo them in convenience. He made New Zealand Chambers into a lantern of glass, notably better lit than any of its rivals. His starting-point was far removed from the grand manner of the *palazzi*. In general, it was the type of timber-framed town house, rewindowed and partly remodelled in the seventeenth and eighteenth centuries, which Nesfield, Shaw, and their associates were sketching in the later 1860s and early 1870s. In particular, it was Sparrowe's House at Ipswich, a timber-framed house of the early seventeenth century remodelled in 1656, which as a synthesis of Jacobean structure and Carolean ornament was exactly calculated to appeal to 'Queen Anne' tastes. Its main features were its row of first-floor oriel windows with arched central lights (a

34. Sparrowe's House, Ipswich, Suffolk, the main prototype for New Zealand Chambers.

common type in the mid-seventeenth century) and its lavish use of pargeting. Both reappeared in expanded form at New Zealand Chambers. The windows were based on those at Sparrowe's House but were given little pediments and expanded both horizontally and vertically in a manner probably suggested by the virtually all-glass Jacobean façade of Sir Peter Pindar's house in Bishopsgate (now in the Victoria and Albert Museum). Pargeting of splendidly lush quality was applied both below the windows, as at Sparrowe's House, and on the immense coved cornice which crowned the façade. Above this were dormer windows, joined together by narrow strips of glazing so that there was continuous glazing almost the whole length of the roof. On the ground floor, bay windows of seventeenth-century type glazed with leaded lights were replaced by shallow oriel windows based on those in eighteenth-century shop-fronts, with a grid of wooden glazing bars; above them was a brick frieze of 'pies', circular motifs of Japanese derivation much favoured by Shaw and Nesfield. In the centre the combination of pedimented doorway and oval window (similar to the oval window at the Red House) was the only asymmetric element of the façade; it was a gesture of independence and a demonstration that Shaw, unlike conventional classical architects, was not a slave to symmetry. Similar gestures were to become more or less obligatory in any otherwise symmetrical 'Queen Anne' building.

All the windows were recessed between piers of red brick. This device enabled Shaw to get round the building laws, which laid down that wooden window frames had to be set back into the face of the building. By arguing that the brick piers, even though they made up only a small proportion of the whole façade, were technically the building face, Shaw got round the District Surveyor.[7] Once the windows were recessed the great cove was a natural means of joining the wall face to the eaves; Shaw had the ability to make aesthetic capital out of his difficulties. The end effect suggested a rippling glass wall between buttresses; it was as though the façade of Henry VII's Chapel, Westminster, had been translated into seventeenth- and eighteenth-century language. No doubt Shaw appreciated and enjoyed this.

The country houses designed in the same years as the Red House and New Zealand Chambers form an impressive group, but it was not through them that the style came to public notice. This was partly because country houses are by their nature withdrawn from the public eye, partly because Nesfield and Webb, the architects involved, disliked publicity and on principle neither exhibited their designs at the Academy nor allowed them to be illustrated. The first and biggest house in the group was Nesfield's Kinmel Park in Denbighshire,[8] designed for H. R. Hughes, whose great fortune derived from a copper mine in Anglesey. Nesfield's sunflower-bespangled lodge at Kinmel, designed in 1868, has already been referred to. In the same year, inspired by a visit to Hampton Court with the Hughes family, he designed a new house too palatial even for a client as anxious and able to spend money as Hughes was. The existing house (a remodelling and enlargement of the previous one) was designed in about 1870 and built in 1871–4. It was less 35, 36

35. Kinmel Park, Denbighshire. By W. E. Nesfield, *c.* 1870–4.

36. The central pavilion at Kinmel Park. The house was gutted by fire in 1976.

grand than the original design, but still grand enough, with the influence of Hampton Court still much in evidence. Its size, its lavishness, and its abundant use of stone dressings and carving to set off the red brick placed it a little apart from other 'Queen Anne' buildings, but it was based on the same brand of eclecticism and the same method of design.

The main façades are reminiscent of Hampton Court, but the high roofs and some of the detailing give the house more of the feeling of a seventeenth-century château. The decoration includes sunflowers in pots and even the occasional Japanese detail. The immensely extended range of main building, chapel, service wing, and outbuildings is abundantly picturesque and irregular; the main entrance and garden fronts are largely symmetrical. But even within this symmetry there are variations. On the entrance front the balance of the central pavilion is abruptly broken by the off-centre chimney-stack. A similarly placed chimney-stack is the only interruption of the symmetry of the new front which Nesfield added to Bodrhyddan, a few miles from Kinmel, in 1872–4.[9] This front is typically eclectic; the main block, with its hipped roof and dormers, is in the English late seventeenth-century manner, but the centre-piece is a mixture of Nesfield's own devising and culminates in a boldly shaped gable of, if anything, Elizabethan origin.

I. Porch of 8 Palace Gate, Kensington. Designed by J. J. Stevenson, 1873–5.

II. One of E. W. Godwin's designs for Kensington Vestry Hall, 1877.

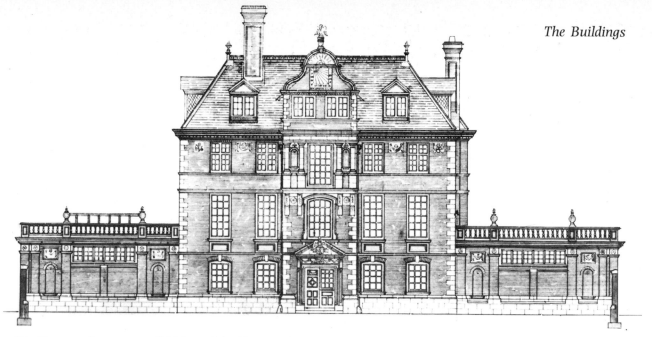

37. Elevation by W. E. Nesfield for Bodrhyddan, Denbighshire, 1872.

38. Joldwynds, Surrey. By Philip Webb, 1872. (Demolished.)

In 1872 Webb designed two country houses both of which have been demolished. Rounton Grange in Yorkshire was his second commission for Lowthian Bell, whose interests had now shifted from chemicals to steel, and from Durham to Middlesborough. Joldwynds, near Dorking was for William Bowman, an eminent ophthalmic surgeon who looked after Rossetti's eyes. It must have been a delightful house; as Lethaby put it 'it looked as if human people might live in it'. It was built of red brick, but the first floor was tile hung and surmounted on each front by three weather-boarded gables. There were tall chimney-stacks of ribbed or arcaded brick; the windows were all sashes with small panes, and those on the first floor had little wooden pediments. All this was very much in the 'Queen Anne' mood, but there were other elements that were less so. The mouldings and detailing of the ground floor and the cornices inside were all in Webb's highly personal manner, a kind of simplified Gothic. This idiosyncratic detailing was even more

39. Elevation by Philip Webb for the garden front of Rounton Grange, Yorkshire, 1872. (Demolished.)

39   in evidence at Rounton Grange, a stone house in which one can watch Webb detaching himself from the 'Queen Anne' stream which he had helped to set moving. And yet in its high bold silhouette with prominent roofs reminiscent of the seventeenth century, its combination of symmetry and asymmetry, its sash windows and occasional pediment, Rownton was still recognizably related to other buildings being designed by the circle at this date.[10]

Three capacious houses designed within a few months of each other, at the end of 1872 or beginning of 1873, were in fact built in towns though they would not have looked out of place in the country. They were Oak Tree House, Hampstead, designed by Basil Champneys for Henry Holiday, the artist; Lowther Lodge, Kensington, designed by Norman Shaw for the Hon. William Lowther, M.P.; and Leamington House, Leamington Spa, designed by G. G. Scott, junior, for the Revd. Septimus Carus Wilson, as the vicarage for the proposed church of St. Mark's.

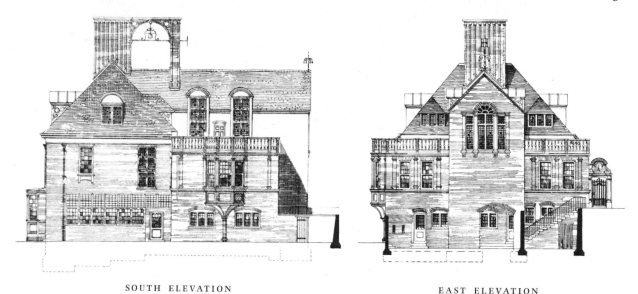

SOUTH ELEVATION   EAST ELEVATION

40. Oak Tree House, Hampstead. By Basil Champneys, 1872 3. (Demolished.)

Basil Champneys (1842–1935) was the grandson of Paul Storr, the silversmith, and the son of a Low Church clergyman who was a popular writer on religious subjects and later became Dean of Lichfield. He was educated at Trinity College, Cambridge, and for a few years was in the office of J. P. Seddon's partner, John Prichard of Llandaff. He set up in independent practice in about 1868, possibly on the strength of the commission to design St. Luke's, Kentish Town (1868–70), which came to him by way of his father. It was a big, handsome, muscular Gothic church; but by the end of the 1860s Champneys had moved into the Rossetti–Morris orbit, and his buildings soon showed their influence. He may have first got to know Rossetti as a result of Rossetti's work for Prichard and Seddon at Llandaff Cathedral; he certainly met him at the house of Sidney Colvin, art critic and historian, who had been his close friend since Cambridge days and had become friends with Rossetti and Burne-Jones in 1868. In that year or 1869 Champneys set up his office in 32 Queen Square, a few doors away from No. 36, where Morris lived and Morris and Company had its offices. He moved in about 1872 to 39 Great Marlborough Street, round the corner from Shaw and Nesfield. Here, until about 1875, he shared an office with Shaw and Nesfield's former assistant J. M. Brydon.[11]

Champneys brought in Morris and Company to design stained glass for two windows in St. Luke's, Kentish Town, but the majority of the glass was by another member of the circle, Henry Holiday.[12] Holiday was an artist as well as a stained glass designer; he had been friendly with Rossetti and Burne-Jones since the early 1860s, and was a close friend of Simeon Solomon's. At the end of 1872 he decided to build himself a house in Hampstead, on the edge of the heath, and employed Champneys to design it. Building started early in 1873. It was not in fact Champneys's first 'Queen Anne' building; it had been pre-dated by a few months by his design for Eel Brook Common Board School, Fulham, which is described in the next chapter.

Champneys was not an original architect, but he could develop on the work of others with the greatest facility and charm. He seized on the potentialities of prettiness and delicacy in 'Queen Anne' and exploited them to their utmost. Oak Tree House (which has been demolished) was an extremely clever design.[13] It gives the feeling of having been thought out from the roofs downward. The roofs, with attendant dormers and chimney-stacks, were T-shaped and completely symmetrical. The long stroke of the T contained the nave, so to speak, of the studio, which expanded at lower level into aisles with flat roofs which could serve as look-out terraces for the

40

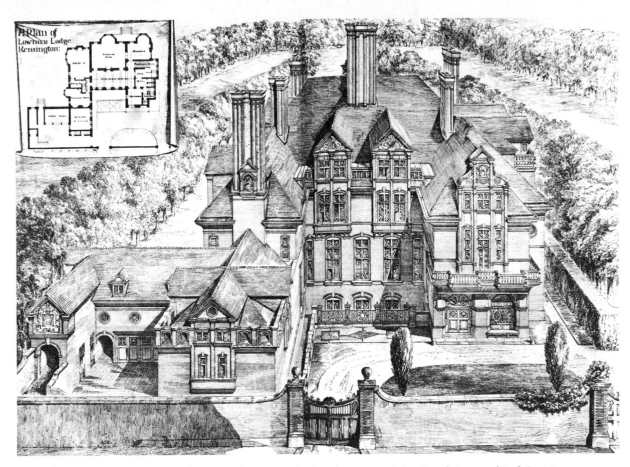

41. Lowther Lodge, Kensington Gore, London, now the headquarters of the Royal Geographical Society. By Norman Shaw, 1872–5.

view over London. The kitchens were below the studio; the cross stroke of the T contained bed-rooms and living-rooms. All the flues were carried up into two immense chimney-stacks, set at right angles to each other and joined by an arch. Beneath the roofs the fenestration was very irregular. The basic symmetry of the scheme was only in evidence from the east; from other directions the house assumed a variety of highly picturesque groupings. Charming details abounded; a bell was hung from wrought-iron supports in the arch of the chimney-stacks, the windows shifted prettily from sashes to leaded lights, the studio aisles were articulated by delicate brick pilasters (derived from Nesfield's lodge at Kew) and flowered out to the south in a little oriel window supported on brick vaulting (derived from Webb's No. 1 Palace Green). For a rising artist of the 1870s nothing could have been more suitable.

41, 42, 43   Lowther Lodge[14] was designed by Shaw, probably a few months after Oak Tree House, almost as if to show Champneys that, pretty and quaint though his house might be, Shaw could design even more prettily and even more quaintly. Lowther Lodge was more complex and highly wrought than any of his previous 'Queen Anne' houses. Its charms were displayed with brilliant virtuosity in a bird's-eye view exhibited at the Royal Academy in 1874. It demonstrates to perfection the differences between Queen Anne and 'Queen Anne'; it is a *divertimento* on a Queen Anne theme. The theme is clearly visible and gives the design its basic shape: a red-brick house of half-H plan, with coved cornice, hipped roof and two wings, of a type found by the dozen in cathedral closes or set in green parkland all over England. But there are innumerable diversions which overlap, burst out of, sink into, or push in front of this basic shape. Chimney-stacks break

42. A detail of the garden front of Lowther Lodge.

43. The inner hall, Lowther Lodge.

unexpectedly through the roofs and soar to dizzy heights; dormer windows slide down in front of the main façade, the main façade vanishes behind a stable block; there are minute circular windows, little aerial arcades of brick, little railed in platforms up in the roof, little windows poked into the bases of the chimney-stacks; the main entrance, instead of being sensibly in the centre, is to one side of a side wing; and high up on the skyline brick scrolls curl and sunflowers sprout in the Flemish gables.

44   After all this, Scott's Leamington House, agreeable though it is, seems a little pedestrian. The commission came to him in 1872, but the final design was not evolved until 1873; the house was furnished and decorated by the newly founded firm of Watts and Company, which Bodley, Garner, and Scott had started up in about 1874. The client was paying for both house and church; he seems to have had sybaritic tastes, for the rectory was built before the church (the exact opposite of the normal mid-Victorian practice) and included a marble-lined bathroom.[15] The design relates closely to Scott's work at Garboldisham: it employs chimney-stacks and Flemish gables of the same pattern, and shows the same fondness for horizontal stripes of contrasting colours, obtained at Leamington by introducing courses of stone into the red brick. In comparison to the subtle variation of Lowther Lodge, the main block is stiff and box-like, with rather heavy square bay windows on the south front; the east front and asymmetric entrance front to the west are simpler and more agreeable.[16]

44. Leamington House, Warwickshire. By G. G. Scott, jun., 1872–4.

These three houses, although designed for towns, were free standing and set in large gardens. In 1873 the first expansion of the Red House formula was built, in the form of a row of terrace houses in Upper Berkeley Street, on the Portman estate. In Stevenson's own words 'the lessee of a plot (Sir Baldwin Leighton) who took an interest in architecture, was allowed to build a red brick house in the freest form of Classic with a fantastic gable in front. But it was insisted that the other houses in the block should have precisely the same details, and the same fantastic gable. This is altogether contrary to the spirit of the style attempted, the essence of which is variety.'

45

Later attempts, by Stevenson and others, to give variety to London terraces were sometimes to be more confused than successful. The Upper Berkeley Street houses (Nos. 1 to 5) were not a very distinguished group, but this was less because of their repetitive design than because of the quality of their detailing. The architect was T. H. Wyatt, who only a few years before had been supporting James Pennethorne in his condemnation of Webb's 1 Palace Gate. In the interval he had been one of the very few older architects to be converted to 'Queen Anne'. But he was not, at the best of times, a distinguished designer, and his 'Queen Anne' houses retained many vestiges of mid-Victorian heaviness; in particular, although the upper windows had small-paned sashes, the windows of the principal floors were filled with sheets of undivided plate glass.[17]

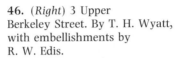

45. (*Below*) 1–5 Upper
Berkeley Street, London.
By T. H. Wyatt, 1873.
(Demolished.)

46. (*Right*) 3 Upper
Berkeley Street. By T. H. Wyatt,
with embellishments by
R. W. Edis.

The first tenants of No. 4 Upper Berkeley Street were Elizabeth Garrett Anderson and her husband; they brought in her sister and cousin Rhoda and Agnes Garrett (fresh from eighteen months' training under J. M. Brydon) to decorate it for them in the 'Queen Anne' manner.[18]

46 No. 3 was the central house in the row, and a few minor variations in the exterior were allowed by the Portman estate. The architect employed to provide them was another recruit to 'Queen Anne', R. W. Edis. Edis had probably got to know Morris and other members of his circle as a result of joining the Artists' Volunteer Rifle Corps, which was formed during the anti-French scare of 1859. Its gifted and, in some cases, unlikely recruits included Millais, Holman Hunt, Leighton, Swinburne, Rossetti (who would only obey orders if the reasons for giving them were explained to him), and Morris (who when ordered to turn right invariably turned left). Edis remained an active member of the corps for many years, and ultimately became its colonel in succession to Leighton.[19]

Edis had also become friends with Norman Shaw as early as 1859, when Shaw proposed him for membership of the Architectural Association.[20] His variations in the design of 3 Upper Berkeley Street show that he had absorbed rather more of the spirit of 'Queen Anne' than Wyatt. They included a different gable, swags of moulded brick between the windows, and different glazing. The upper windows had rather smaller panes than in those of the other houses; the

47. The Ingham Infirmary, South Shields, Durham. By R. J. Johnson, 1871–3.

lower windows had small panes in the top half of the sash and plate glass in the lower half. This compromise between 'Queen Anne' and technology was ignored by other 'Queen Anne' architects at the time but was to be widely imitated when 'Queen Anne' became part of the commercial builders stock-in-trade in the 1880s and 1890s.

Work of these years other than houses included a hospital in County Durham, which caused no stir at all, and the buildings put up by the London School Board, which aroused at least as much interest as New Zealand Chambers. The hospital was the Ingham Infirmary at South Shields, designed by R. J. Johnson, and built between March 1871 and May 1873. Although not a building of the first class it is worth a brief discussion, both as an early example of 'Queen Anne' and because its architect has been undeservedly forgotten.

Robert James Johnson (1832–92)[21] was the only member of the Scott kindergarten to settle permanently out of London. He was one of the assistants in Scott's office in the late 1850s, and at the time when they were all muscular Goths together travelled in France with E. R. Robson, making drawings which were published as *Specimens of Early French Architecture* in 1861. In 1862 he became a partner of Thomas Austin of Newcastle. He remained in Newcastle for the rest of his life. His clerk of the works at the Ingham Infirmary was T. A. Page; J. J. Stevenson had brought him down from Scotland in 1864 as clerk of the works for the new Gothic house which he designed in that year for his brother J. C. Stevenson at Westoe, the best residential quarter of South Shields.[22]

The design of the Ingham Infirmary shows that Johnson had kept in touch with his old associates. Its style was described by the local paper in 1873 as 'a modification of what was common in the reign of Queen Anne'.[23] It was in fact much closer to an actual building of the late seventeenth or early eighteenth century than most of those put up by the group. In this it forecast his subsequent development, for though at least one of his subsequent buildings showed the influence of Norman Shaw, others were handsome classical buildings nearer to what we would call neo-Georgian than to 'Queen Anne'.[24]

48. Offices of the
School Board of London,
Thames Embankment.
By G. F. Bodley, 1872.
(Demolished.)

The numerous schools designed for the School Board of London by Basil Champneys, E. R. Robson, and J. J. Stevenson from 1872 onwards were such influential and widely publicized examples of 'Queen Anne' that they have been reserved for the next chapter. The School Board **48** Offices on the new Victoria Embankment can be discussed in this one. The building was designed by G. F. Bodley, as his entry for a limited competition held at the end of 1872, and was awarded the first prize in January 1873. Bodley wrote in the report accompanying the design that 'the style adopted is a free form of Classic or Renaissance. The style allows of the freedom and pliability characteristic of Gothic, and has the advantage of giving ample window space and square headed windows instead of pointed ones.' The *Architect* at the time described the style as 'Antwerp classical',[25] but the building owed as much to François Ier as to Antwerp. Bodley, perhaps on the grounds that English brick vernacular was not monumental enough for a prestige building on the Thames, had gone for inspiration to early French Renaissance châteaux and the sixteenth-century town halls and great merchant houses of the Low Countries. 'Freedom and pliability' enabled him to place the two great gables which dominated the design slightly off-centre, and to push the main entrance to one side. 'Ample window space' was obtained by filling all the intervals between his three rows of pilasters with glass, so that the building (which has been demolished) was almost as well windowed as New Zealand Chambers.

Bodley's previous lapses from Gothic had been in obscure locations and received no publicity. The School Board Offices gave public and prominent witness that one of the leading architects of the Gothic Revival had deserted the cause. According to one source, Street was so infuriated that he 'kept George Bodley out of the Academy as long as he could because Bodley had . . . dallied with the Renaissance'.[26] But for the members of Bodley's own circle the building suggested a way of enriching their vocabulary. So far (apart from some French influence at Kinmel) they had kept to English sources: 'Flemish' gables had been domesticated in England since the sixteenth century. From now on a French, Dutch, or Flemish strain became increasingly apparent in buildings designed by members of the movement and made the name 'Queen Anne' even more inapposite.

Criticism: the Professionals

In 1872 'Queen Anne' began to be mentioned for the first time in the architectural press. On 31 May, for instance, the *Building News* described a cabinet in the International Exhibition as exhibited by Morant, Boyd, and Blanford 'but evidently from the designs of some architect . . . mediaeval, but freely treated, with a good deal of impure classic details, introduced after the fashion of the Queen Anne period, now so much and so foolishly imitated by some of those young men who strive to appear original by following some queer out-of-the-way type.' On 9 July J. P. Seddon, who was probably responsible for the comment just quoted, initialled an article on 'Spurious eclecticism' in the same paper, in which 'Queen Anne' is summarily dealt with: 'Of réchauffés, of even Elizabethan architecture, and certainly of the Queen Anne style, lately come into fashion, we have had more than enough . . . their hybrid jumbles of detail are not sufficiently eclectic in any good sense to deserve imitation at our hands.'[27]

Seddon's angry scorn was to be typical of the reactions of all the older Gothicists as they watched the younger generation desert the Gothic Revival. But there were younger contributors to the building periodicals whose reactions were more favourable. On 8 June Edward W. Godwin wrote a short description of Stevenson's Red House. Although he still felt bound to describe as 'peculiar' the 'fancy we have more than once lately had to note for the elaborate brickwork of the last century', he added, 'we cannot but remark the excellence both of the materials and workmanship'.[28] E. W. Godwin (1833–86) was one of the most brilliant and original designers of his generation. His close friendship with William Burges had probably helped to keep him away from 'Queen Anne' in the 1860s, but from the early 1870s his buildings began to show its influence and his criticisms, in the *Building News* and other periodicals, to help popularize it. In 1872 he was joined on the *Building News* by Maurice B. Adams (1849–1933). Adams, unlike Godwin, was a permanent member of the staff rather than a contributor. He soon became an enthusiast for 'Queen Anne'. Passmore Edwards, the proprietor of the magazine, radical, pacifist, and supporter of every progressive cause, was unlikely to have discouraged him. Within a year or two the *Building News* was actively supporting the style, and Adams was illustrating all the most important 'Queen Anne' buildings in engravings to which he managed to impart an agreeably aesthetic flavour.[29]

This was in the future, however. In 1873 'Queen Anne' received far more publicity than in 1872 but in the *Building News* as well as in the other building periodicals the publicity was of a mixed nature. It was sparked off by the style's first prominent showing in the Architecture Room of the Royal Academy. As the *Building News* put it in its issue of 9 May, 'the curious and growing passion for Late Elizabethan work which has developed itself among a certain set of "advanced" architects has come to the front in a way which has not been hitherto customary'.[30] The article goes on to make clear that by 'Late Elizabethan' is meant what was already widely nicknamed

'Queen Anne', especially Shaw's designs for New Zealand Chambers, Bodley's for the School Board Offices, and Robson and Stevenson's for the Board Schools. The designs were distinctive enough in themselves, and in addition the actual buildings were readily accessible or about to be: New Zealand Chambers already up, and the School Board Offices rising, in prominent positions in central London; the Board Schools less central but sprouting, it must have seemed at the time, like mushrooms at every suburban or slum-land corner.

All three sets of designs were given full coverage, and a very mixed reception. They were clever, no doubt, but also startling and even shocking. The *Building News* found New Zealand Chambers 'the most remarkable of a series of semi-Elizabethan contributions . . . thoroughly truthful, very clever, but contriving to form an anachronism of the most startling quality'. In the School Board Offices it saw 'somewhat of the same taste for debased Renaissance'. The *Architect* wrote them off as 'utterly common place', thought New Zealand Chambers 'brilliant but dangerous', and in general attacked at length the 'effete feebleness and prettinesses' of 'a bastard style'. As for the Board School designs 'these three drawings set forth the danger we have hinted at in a "Queen Anne" revival; here we have three buildings of the usual dull character of building, peculiar to London houses in the beginning of the eighteenth century, treated certainly with some little originality, and with, of course, something of quaint picturesqueness about them, but withal excessively ugly, with great windows divided into little panes and curiously shaped and pedimented gables'.[31]

The *Builder* was torn between admiration and dismay. It had nothing good to say for the School Board Offices and found the Board Schools 'one of the most singular whims of architectural archaeology'. New Zealand Chambers was a brilliant design but 'why sacrifice everything to the picturesque? . . . Why affect so unnecessarily the manner of a bygone age. Mr. Shaw is an architect of genius; he is one of the few who appear to know wherein lies the "poetry" of building; yet we feel sure that, with his talents, he could give us this poetical and picturesque element without so entirely contradicting the tone and feeling of his own day.'[32]

On 23 May the *Building News* published an Irish attack on 'Queen Anne' made by W. M. Mitchell in an address to the Irish Architectural Association in Dublin: 'The present attempt to introduce the long, square headed windows and broken pedimented gables of Queen Anne's reign, the lumpy furniture of the Cromwellian era, and the ingenious but semi-barbaric ornament of China and Japan, indicate the extravagant lengths to which a certain school is inclined to go in its search after novelty.' On 24 May the *Architect* produced a cautious leader on the new style. It was more informative than critical, and included a useful list of the leaders of the school; these were said to be 'besides Mr. Norman Shaw and Mr. Bodley, Mr. Nesfield, Mr. Webb, Mr. Stevenson, Mr. Gilbert Scott Junior and—let not the reader be too much astonished—Mr. Butterfield, with one more moving spirit, artistic rather than architectural, in the person of Mr. Rossetti.'[33]

Meanwhile New Zealand Chambers had been brought to the attention of the seventy-eight-year-old Professor T. L. Donaldson, the Nestor of English architecture, ancient but still powerful. He simmered for several months and finally exploded in a letter headed 'The New Old Style' published in the *Builder* on 9 August. 'I cannot conceive', he wrote of the design, 'what motive could have induced its author, a man of acknowledged talent, to rake up a type of the very lowest state of corrupt erection in the City of London, of a period that marks the senility of decaying taste . . . a contortion of every feature of architecture . . . the last somersault or gambol of the agile gymnast, who seeks at the end of his performance to extort a laugh from the spectators at whatever cost of contortion and personal effort. But such a work of the Gold Medallist of the Royal Academy and Silver Medallist of the Institute is a sad spectacle of the abuse of high powers.'[34]

In January 1874, William H. White, the secretary of the R.I.B.A., mounted an attack on 'Queen Anne' at the Architectural Association, and parodied 'Queen Anne' buildings in a drawing that grotesquely failed to catch their quality. In the discussion that followed R. W. Edis came to the defence of the London Board Schools and provoked White into calling them 'the disgrace of the country'.[35] But in the same month Robert Kerr wrote an article in the *Architect* that was by no means hostile, and in June J. J. Stevenson defended the new style in a paper on 'The recent re-action of taste in English architecture' given to the third General Conference of Architects (held in Somerset House under the auspices of the R.I.B.A.).[36] This was widely reported and was the first full-length defence of the style to be published in the architectural magazines. The *Building News* followed up its report with an engraving by Maurice B. Adams of the Red House, published on 18 September 1874. Stevenson had previously boosted 'Queen Anne' in an article on 'Our Dwelling Houses' published in *Good Words* in October 1873. He delivered another defence of it at the Architectural Association in February 1875, and provoked Richard Phené Spiers to protest at the style's 'baneful influence over students' and T. Blashill at its 'abject copyism, not of beauty but of ugliness'.[37] In spite of his late arrival on the scene Stevenson was now accepted as one of the leaders of the new school, or, as the architect Lacy W. Ridge put it in March 'one of the great apostles or ministers of Queen Anne'.[38]

Criticism: the Amateurs

In the non-architectural press 'Queen Anne' was greeted much more calmly. The *Globe*, in an article on 'The style of Queen Anne' published on 13 January 1874, thought that 'in itself this return to the style of Queen Anne cannot be reckoned a very important thing'. It saw it as a natural reaction to the 'high claims and furious aggressiveness' of the Gothic Revival and as expressing 'desire for lighter grace of composition'. It praised it without much enthusiasm for being unpretentious and 'sufficiently modest', but the author clearly looked back with some nostalgia to the days when giants clashed with giants over 'some of the profoundest questions known to aesthetics'. As he put it 'There was something great about the Gothic Revival'.

The *Saturday Review* on 31 July 1875 greeted 'The Queen Anne Craze' with 'perfect good humour and equal scepticism . . . the history of the Queen Anne propaganda as the serious and scientific development of a successful national style out of an existing English type will have been written on water'. This was because it was based on an entirely artificial eclecticism, instead of an eclecticism that had developed naturally. But the article admitted that the style 'will have played a not inconspicuous part in the rapid transformation of the grim stale London of our youth'.[39]

The difference in reaction was not especially surprising. The critics of the *Saturday Review* and *Globe* (did they belong to the elder generation?) might find it difficult to take 'Queen Anne' altogether seriously, but to laymen there was nothing shocking about the style. Many architects found it very shocking indeed. The dedicated Gothicists were, for obvious reasons, infuriated. As Burges later put it, 'Queen Anne' architects were 'simply deserters from the Gothic school'.[40] Classicists were almost equally infuriated because 'Queen Anne' seemed to them a travesty of classicism. It broke all the rules, ignored the grammar of the orders, and derived inspiration from a type and period of classicism which they had been brought up to despise.

Their angry onslaughts inevitably provoked the 'Queen Anne' architects to retaliate. They were, however, less inclined to rush into print in support of 'Queen Anne' than the Gothicists had been in support of the Gothic Revival. The movement produced no equivalent to Pugin or Gilbert Scott as an apologist. Webb, Shaw, Nesfield, and the younger Scott kept quiet; so did Bodley, except in so far as his brief explanation of his School Board Offices, submitted for the competition, was subsequently published. The main defence came from J. J. Stevenson, Basil Champneys, and Thomas Graham Jackson.

Theory: a Development not a Betrayal

Stevenson's papers and articles have already been referred to. They were the only ones to be given full coverage in the architectural press, but Champneys and Jackson had in fact preceded him. From 1871 Champneys was writing on architecture for the *Portfolio*, an ambitious new art periodical started up in 1870 by the publishing firm of Seeley and Company. Champneys's connection with the *Portfolio* probably originated in the fact that Seeley's had originally specialized in religious books, and had published a number of Dean Champneys's Low Church tracts. By the 1870s the firm had been taken over by the son of the founder. He and Champneys were in parallel reaction, Champneys against the Gothic Revival, and the younger Seeley against the firm's evangelical reputation, as established by his father. In 1871 Champneys wrote about Wren churches and eighteenth-century furniture; in 1873 he defended 'Queen Anne' in an article on 'Gothic and Renaissance Architects'; and in 1874 there was much that was relevant in his articles on 'Winchelsea, Rye, and the Romney Marshes'.

Meanwhile in 1873 T. G. Jackson (1835–1924) had published *Modern Gothic Architecture*. Jackson had been in Scott's office at the same time as Stevenson, Robson, Scott, junior, and Garner. He seems to have been friendly but not intimate with them (his close friend in the office was John Oldrid Scott), and was never more than on the fringes of the 'Queen Anne' movement. But the arguments in his book were exactly applicable to 'Queen Anne' and brought him the admiration and support of Norman Shaw. In his autobiography he wrote that *Modern Gothic Architecture* was finished in 1870, but failed to find a publisher for three years.[41] This seems very likely, for the arguments and points of view put forward by Jackson, Champneys, and Stevenson were only developments or expansions of those expressed by Warrington Taylor in 1862–4, or in Webb's letters to the Department of Woods and Forests in 1867. Such arguments must have been common property in the group during the ten years before public interest resulted in their publication.

The arguments against 'Queen Anne' could be roughly grouped into aesthetic (shading into moral) and practical. There were the arguments that it was 'hybrid', 'bastard', or 'corrupt', favoured by classicists, and the Gothic Revival argument that it was a betrayal. There was the argument that it was artificial, in that it was based on a self-conscious rather than organic eclecticism. There was the argument that it was 'effete' or small-minded—to quote Burges again, 'a regular tea-tray style'. Finally, there was the argument that it was inefficient, not to say anti-efficient, in that it rejected modern methods and comforts and affected 'so unnecessarily the manners of a bygone age'. Ostensibly this was a practical argument, but it engendered a great deal of emotional heat among those who felt committed to 'progress'.

As all the leading 'Queen Anne' architects were children of the Gothic Revival, a large part of the efforts of their apologists naturally went to contesting the charge that they were traitors. Their argument was simple; they were not betraying the Gothic Revival, they were developing it. The main thesis of Jackson's *Modern Gothic Architecture* was that Gothic could only become relevant to nineteenth-century conditions if it abandoned the letter of Gothic and concentrated on its spirit. 'The moment we begin to use the forms of Gothic architecture simply because they are called Gothic . . . that moment does the work in our hands cease to be Gothic at all.' 'Gothic is to be developed into a living art' by 'the gradual removal of archaisms' and 'the incorporation into it of modern ideas and the utilization of modern discoveries.' 'Gothic may lose *all* those features by which we know it, and yet for our purposes be Gothic in the truest sense after all.' The main difference between the Middle Ages and the nineteenth century was five or six hundred years of experience, and it would be absurd not to take advantage of it: 'this consideration should suggest to us the advisability, nay more, the necessity of a judicious eclecticism.'[42]

Apart from putting in a word for the 'wonderful naturalism' of the best early Renaissance ornament,[43] Jackson was vague as to what form this 'judicious eclecticism' should take. Stevenson, in his various papers, was more explicit. Unlike Jackson, he isolated the area in which Gothic was unsatisfactory. Essentially, it had evolved as a style for building in stone, and for building churches; it was therefore by its nature hard to adapt when building in brick and building houses, quite apart from the fact that standards of comfort had improved since the Middle Ages. A Gothic-arched window was naturally adapted to light a vaulted building, but was an inefficient way of lighting a room with a flat ceiling. In contrast 'the brick architecture of the restoration, of Queen Anne and the Georges', was a style in which 'Englishmen working in brick, and using sliding sash windows according to the custom of the land . . . found the natural expression of their feelings'. By adapting it for nineteenth-century houses, 'with some new life from Gothic added . . . the true spirit of Gothic was better expressed than by copying . . . Gothic forms'.[44]

Stevenson elaborated on 'the true spirit of Gothic' and its effect on the architects of the Gothic Revival. It had led to 'the impulse to cast aside laws which trammelled freedom of planning and design' and 'the insisting on naturalness of construction and truth of materials'. All this could be expressed just as well with later details as with Gothic ones. Naturalness of construction and truth of materials were already to be found in the brick architecture of the seventeenth and eighteenth centuries. But 'freedom of planning and design', the freedom to have irregular plans and asymmetric façades whenever it was convenient to do so, was not a characteristic of the period. This was (the metaphors are mine not Stevenson's) the pinch of salt which brought 'new life from Gothic' to the brick vernacular, the solvent which turned Queen Anne into 'Queen Anne'.

Theory: the Idea of the Vernacular

In doing so it took it even further away from the architecture of the Renaissance which was its immediate source, let alone from the architecture of Greece and Rome. It was this, from their point of view, corruption of what they considered an already corrupt development of the classical tradition which infuriated Victorian classicists, and led to the outbursts of Donaldson and others. The 'Queen Anne' architects retaliated with spirit. Pure classicism was as unsuitable for modern houses as pure Gothic. As Jackson put it, neither 'the peculiar monotony' of Greek architecture nor 'the costly and monumental character' of Roman could satisfy the complex requirements of Victorian society.[45] For Champneys and Stevenson the domestic architecture of the seventeenth and eighteenth centuries was neither 'corrupt' nor 'debased', it was 'vernacular'. It had adapted the classical vocabulary so that ordinary people could use it naturally and unselfconsciously. Champneys described how the Renaissance had started as a scholarly style 'derived from special study', but the 'necessity that it should become adapted to varied acquirements' had led to the development of an English domestic style 'which became almost as universal and vernacular as the style of the Middle Ages', but which 'from its proximity to our own time fulfils far more thoroughly the practical requirements of contemporary life'.[46] Stevenson briefly and neatly summed up the qualities of the style which appealed to him. It was wrong for domestic architecture to aim either for 'the purity of Greek or of thirteenth century Gothic . . . it should rather be homely, like colloquial talk'.[47]

Similar arguments could deal with the accusations that 'Queen Anne' was an 'effete' style, in terms reminiscent of those in which Warrington Taylor had contended that 'everything English . . . is essentially small, and of a homely farmyard kind of poetry'. 'Queen Anne' was not only unaggressive and anti-heroic, it gloried in it. In his articles on Winchester, Rye, and Romney Marsh Champneys drew an interesting parallel between mid-nineteenth-century taste in architecture and in landscape. 'Scenery-hunting' in Switzerland had led to people losing their eye for the delicacy of homely scenes and worshipping nature in 'her most sensational and most violent types'. In architecture a similar 'craving for grandeur' and 'familiarity with the imposing productions of continental art has blunted our sense of the more quiet but often more genuine charm of the unpretentious monuments of native architecture'.[48]

The widely voiced complaint that 'Queen Anne' was a 'Backward Ho' style had enough truth in it to be best met by head-on tactics: there were occasions on which it was progressive to look backward. As Stevenson put it 'it may be a characteristic of an age, and the truest sign of its advancement, to look back with admiration on some former time'.[49] This could be expanded into a defence of 'Queen Anne' as a compromise between aesthetics and practical needs. A style was needed which was suitable for unselfconscious, everyday use—in other words, a vernacular. In so far as a vernacular existed in the 1870s it was too hopelessly vulgarized and commercial to satisfy anyone with aesthetic tastes. The only hope was to look for a vernacular style that was at once aesthetically acceptable and not too remote from current practice, and to develop from that. The London brick architecture of the seventeenth and eighteenth centuries provided the answer. It was the style in which contemporary building practice had its roots; Stevenson went as far as to claim that it was 'fundamentally the same as the common vernacular style, which every workman has been apprenticed to'.[50] So it was sufficiently practical as well as artistic. Stevenson could even claim that the use of small panes instead of sheets of plate-glass, the example of 'Backward Ho' which most shook contemporaries, had practical advantages as well as aesthetic ones. Apart from carrying the wall surface over the openings in a basically Gothic manner, it provided psychological security; unlike the gaping voids of plate glass, small panes produced 'a feeling of enclosure and comfort within'.[51]

Theory: 'Let us have Artists'

But however much Stevenson might play with practical arguments, the driving force behind 'Queen Anne' architects was their conviction that they were artists. It was as artists that they revolted against the ugliness and crudity of their environment, it was as artists that they proposed to fuse their wide range of sources together, it was as artists that they cheerfully condemned or ignored scholarship, rules, systems of proportion, the language of the orders, anything that would inhibit their creative freedom. 'Henceforth, then,' wrote Jackson 'instead of architects, painters and sculptors, let us have *artists*.'[52]

As artists, they reflected the mood of their fellow artists. The right path for development was not by trying to be completely original; Stevenson dismissed 'the common cry for a new style' as 'foolish'.[53] The way lay in eclecticism; and the *Saturday Review*'s contention that 'Queen Anne' would be written on water because it was artificial was invalid because the style was the product of creative eclecticism, based not on theory but on sensibility. Champneys, whose friendship with Sidney Colvin and Walter Pater[54] put him closely in touch with contemporary views on art, elaborated on this. He attacked both the intrusion of morality into art, and 'the intrusion into valuable works of imagination of a reflective and *doctrinaire* element . . . After all, observation is the only practical education in art. Sensitiveness to the most subtle and infinitesimal relations of form and colour is the quality of perception on which art-appreciation relies . . . And this sensitiveness is to be gained neither by analysing nor by taking thought, but by looking at things. The true function of the critic is to make people look at one thing rather than another, and to lead them to derive from observation neither abstract theories nor universal principles, but merely an education of those perceptions to which alone the unanalysable and infinitesimal conditions of art are manifest.'[55]

III. Design by G. G. Scott, jun., for a house for A. H. Whipham of Middlesbrough, 1874–5.

IV. Design by J. J. Stevenson for T. H. Green's house, 27 Banbury Road, Oxford, 1881.

This reaction against dogma and theory, of which the mid-Victorians had had all too much, was the main reason why 'Queen Anne' produced comparatively little literature. The movement had no Pugin because it did not want one. Even Jackson, Champneys, and Stevenson often give one the feeling that they are thinking up reasons after the event, to justify choices taken by instinct. Some of their lines of defence were more convincing than others. That there was something in the argument that 'Queen Anne' was a potential vernacular was shown by the enthusiasm with which London builders took it up—and very dreary results they all too often produced. But it is hard to accept that its originators believed all that seriously in 'Queen Anne' as a plain man's style, considering the heights of sophistication and artificiality to which they quickly developed it. Nor were their arguments that Gothic could not be adapted to nineteenth-century conditions very convincing. Commercial Gothic had proved adaptable enough, indeed its popularity with the vulgar was one reason why 'Queen Anne' architects so disliked it; and if they wanted something more aesthetically satisfying, Tudor Gothic was a genuine Gothic vernacular which could have been (and indeed was) brought as picturesquely up to date as Queen Anne.

But 'Queen Anne' succeeded not because it was sensible but because it was pretty, and because by the 1870s it exactly suited the mood of the public. Older laymen could refuse to take it seriously, or like Herbert Spencer, when his friend Moncure Conway settled in the 'Queen Anne' suburb of Bedford Park, express amazement 'that a "progressive" should go far back in matters of architecture'.[56] Older architects could mutter that it was 'corrupt' or a 'betrayal'. Those under forty, especially those who considered themselves advanced or artistic, found that it gave them everything they had been looking for. Those who were bored by or sceptical about religion, took to 'Queen Anne' because it was emphatically secular. To those in reaction against contemporary values 'Queen Anne' seemed deliciously old-fashioned. It was gentlemanly but not aristocratic, middle-class but not bourgeois, eclectic but not uncouth, pretty but not frivolous, unassertive but chic, reminiscent of the country but adaptable for the town. They took to it for its sweetness, and used it for the spreading of light. Their new enthusiasm for living beautifully poured into 'Queen Anne' houses filled with delicate and pretty objects, from all countries and of all dates. In the service of enlightenment they built 'Queen Anne' schools, colleges, hospitals, libraries, and swimming-baths. All over London outbursts of red brick began to interrupt the smooth expanses of stucco. Soon the style was erupting all over the country. 'Queen Anne' had become the fashion.

IV   The Architecture of Light

The Board Schools

Sherlock Holmes's reaction to the London Board Schools probably summed up the feelings of many of his contemporaries. While in a train crossing the viaduct near Clapham Junction, on his way back from investigating the case of the stolen Naval Treaty, he looked out of the window and addressed the inevitable Watson.

> 'Look at those big isolated clumps of buildings rising up above the slates, like brick islands in a lead coloured sea.'
> 'The Board Schools.'
> 'Lighthouses, my boy! Beacons of the future! Capsules, with hundreds of bright little seeds in each, out of which will spring the wiser, better England of the future.'[1]

The same sentiments were expressed rather less vividly by Charles Booth in his *Life and Labour of the People of London*. 'In every quarter the eye is arrested by their distinctive architecture, as they stand, closest where the need is greatest, each one "like a tall sentinel at his post", keeping watch and ward over the interests of the generation that is to replace our own . . . Taken as a whole, they may be said fairly to represent the high-water mark of the public conscience in this country in its relation to the education of the children of the people.'[2]

Towering above terraces of little houses all over London, the Board Schools captured the imagination of the public as impressive and immediately recognizable symbols of enlightenment. They also helped to convert it to 'Queen Anne', as the style of the moment and the style of progress. Foster's Elementary Education Act of 1870 had been a disappointment to the progressives of the National Education League, who had agitated for a complete national system of primary education that would be both free and compulsory. The Foster Act produced a system of non-compulsory state schools as a supplement to, rather than replacement of, the existing voluntary schools, most of which were run by one or other of the religious denominations. School Boards financed by a local school rate were to be set up in the towns only, and (except in London) at the discretion of the Department of Education, to build and run what became known as Board Schools. To the chagrin of the reformers the Boards were given no control over the voluntary schools in their area. The latter continued to function side by side with the Board Schools, and were given state aid as long as they fulfilled certain conditions. Religious instruction in the Board Schools was limited by the Cowper-Temple clause, an amendment passed in the House of Commons by Rossetti's friend and patron and Nesfield's client, William Cowper-Temple,[3] to the effect that 'No religious catechism or religious formulary of any particular denomination shall be taught in the schools'. This satisfied the non-conformists and the progressives, who were prepared to accept religious teaching in the schools as long as it involved religion without dogma.

The Act may have been a compromise, but it resulted in the setting-up of hundreds of School Boards and in the building, within a few years, of thousands of new schools all over the country. The School Boards consisted of members each of whom represented a district, and were elected by the rate-payers. Women were eligible both to vote and to stand for membership. Along with Hospital Boards, School Boards were among the first public bodies open to both sexes, so that progressive women deprived of other outlets for their energies and ambitions were naturally attracted to them. As the Boards also tended to attract radicals, non-conformists, agnostics, and even socialists, many people regarded them with suspicion.

Inevitably, the London School Board (strictly speaking, the School Board of London) was the biggest and most powerful of the new boards. The first elections for members were held in 1871. The first chairman was Lord Lawrence, ex-Governor General of India, and the vice-chairman (chairman from 1873) was Charles Reed, a prosperous non-conformist printer. Among the first members were two distinguished women, Emily Davies, campaigner for education for women and in 1871 in the process of founding Girton College, and Elizabeth Garrett Anderson, England's first qualified woman doctor.

The building of new schools was put under a Works Committee, of which Charles Reed was the chairman. Its two other most active members were Edmund Hay Currie, who owned a distillery in Bromley and was active in philanthropic work, and Thomas Chatfield Clarke, an architect with an interest in working-class housing.[4] In May they recommended the appointment of a part-time architect at a salary of £500. His job was not intended to include the designing of schools. He was to report on existing buildings which might be taken over, and to deal with 'questions of sites, plans, drainage, ventilation, alterations and the like'. New school buildings were to be designed by outside architects, on the basis of limited competitions. In June the Works Committee selected a short list of six from the eighty-four applicants. E. R. Robson was among them, and was appointed by ballot of the whole Board on 5 July. This was two months before the beginning of his partnership with J. J. Stevenson.[5]

The job at this stage was well below Robson's capacities. One would like to know what lay behind the brief official notices of reports and meetings in the surviving minutes. Did Robson merely see it as a useful stop-gap until his partnership with Stevenson got under way? Or had he been told that it was likely to develop into something bigger—as a year later it did? Did he have encouragement or support in his application? Was the Rossetti network in operation? Did William Cowper-Temple put in a good word? Was it of any relevance that Charles Reed had once been a friend and partner of Thomas Plint, who was Rossetti's best client until his unexpected death in 1862?[6]

Whatever the background Reed, Currie, and Clarke loyally backed and promoted Robson from the start. In February 1872 the Works Committee asked him to produce a sketch plan for the Board's new offices on the Embankment. On 26 June Reed proposed to the Board that Robson be officially appointed architect for the offices, but an amendment that it be put out to competition was narrowly carried by sixteen votes to fifteen. On 31 July Reed proposed, this time with success, that Robson's salary should be increased to £1,000, and that he should 'give his time to the Board' and be put in charge of designing and building its schools. Twenty-seven schools by outside architects were already under way, but from then on virtually all the Board's innumerable new schools were designed by, or under, Robson.[7]

The pressures and conditions under which the outside architects were originally chosen can only be guessed at. On the whole they were an undistinguished collection, but Robson clearly tried to involve architects from his own set. G. G. Scott, junior, was invited to compete in February 1872, but declined. Basil Champneys competed for Johnson Street School, Stepney, in February–May but was only placed fourth; in June, however, he competed successfully for the Eel Brook Common School in Harwood Road, Fulham. Other successful competitors in the same month included R. W. Edis and Bodley and Garner.[8] On 29 July the Works Committee, having failed to get the job for Robson, suggested that Matthew Digby Wyatt, Waterhouse, J. Oldrid Scott, and Edward Barry should be invited to compete for the School Board Offices, with Bodley in reserve in case any of the others declined.[9] Wyatt, Waterhouse, Scott, and Barry were names likely to appeal to the Board as suitably well known for a prestigious job; Bodley was perhaps considered too much of a church architect. One wonders whether Robson or his committee knew in advance that at least one of the other four would decline. At any rate the final competitors proved to be Scott, Wyatt, Bodley, and Arthur Blomfield. In January, the Works Committee selected Bodley's

49. Board School, Eel Brook Common, Harwood Road, Fulham. By Basil Champneys, 1872.

design.[10] Meanwhile Robson, presumably with his committee's approval, had brought in his partner Stevenson to collaborate on the new schools.

On 20 June 1872 G. P. Boyce (Webb's client at Glebe Place, Chelsea) wrote in his diary: 'Called upon Mr. Robson and Mr. J. J. Stevenson about the proposed Board School next door to me. Mr. Stevenson produced my "Back of an Old House, Dorchester" drawing, which seemed to be in his office for the sake of making people, who would otherwise prefer purple slates on drab stocks and cement and thin window bars and plate glass, swallow red tiles and red brick and thick window bars.'[11] Were the 'people' aimed at just Stevenson's own private clients, or were he and Robson already trying to sell 'Queen Anne' to the School Board Committees? For Boyce's visit took place at a time when the first designs for a 'Queen Anne' school were about to be accepted.

The London School Board style became so well known and successful that there seems to have been a certain amount of jockeying for the prestige of having invented it. T. G. Jackson, who had been with Robson and Stevenson in Scott's office, gave the credit to Stevenson as 'the real originator, as is believed among architects, of the sensible and manly style of the School Board buildings in London'.[12] Robson's son, on the other hand, was unenthusiastic about Stevenson's contribution and wrote that his father was 'occupied often in the afternoon rubbing out what John had done in the mornings'.[13] In fact although it seems possible that at the time of Boyce's visit Robson or Stevenson was already sketching out suggestions for 'Queen Anne' schools, the first Board School in the style to be accepted was designed neither by Stevenson nor by Robson but by Champneys. His Harwood Road school was designed in June and July 1872, before Robson's responsibilities had been extended to cover design.[14] It had the high-gabled silhouette, big chimney-stacks, dormer windows, Flemish gables, and many-paned sash or casement windows that were to make the Board Schools of the future so familiar.

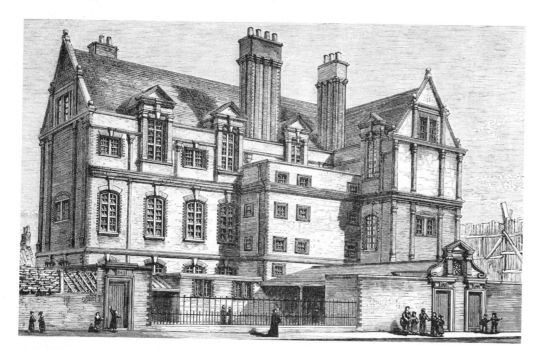

50. Board School, Orange Street, London (1873).

51. Board School, Angler's Gardens, London (1873).

The first four schools designed under Robson were worked out between the end of July and October: they were Broad Street, Ratcliff; Hammond Square, Hoxton; Creek Road, Deptford; and Winstanley Road, Clapham. 'Messrs. Stevenson and Robson' exhibited unnamed designs for three schools at the Academy in May 1873. From other sources these are known to have included Winstanley Road and, almost certainly, Creek Road; the third design was probably either for Hammond Square or for Broad Street. Eleven school designs followed at the end of the year, including Wornington Road, Notting Hill; another fifty-six were designed in 1873.[15] In 1874 Robson published his *School Architecture* in which he illustrated a number of London Board Schools designed by outside architects, including Champneys's Harwood Road, and ten by his own department, the most recent of which was New North Street, Shoreditch, designed in

50, 51

52. Board School, Caledonian Road, London (*c.* 1878).

February 1874. In his book Robson acknowledged that 'several of the designs selected for illustration are from the pencil of my partner, Mr. Stevenson'. Stevenson, when discussing the schools in his *House Architecture*, stated that 'for the architecture of a few of the earliest of these I am responsible, having found by the practical experience of a house I built for myself in this manner, that the style adapts itself to every modern necessity and convenience'.[16] These two statements make it clear that Robson and Stevenson designed schools separately, rather than collaborating on them, and that Stevenson's schools were 'Queen Anne'. The partnership broke up in 1876, but there seems no certain evidence that Stevenson designed any schools after the end of 1874. In 1875 A. J. Adams, who entered a brief partnership with Stevenson in 1876, was employed by the Board for a year as a 'temporary additional draughtsman' and may have designed some schools in that period.[17]

Of the first four schools produced under Robson the most ambitious, Winstanley Road, was Gothic rather than Queen Anne. A number of other Gothic schools followed in 1872 and 1873, including Mansfield Place, Kentish Town; Camden Street, Camden Town; Victory Place, Lambeth; and Globe Terrace, Hackney. Their Gothic displayed the influence of Butterfield and Webb; they had white-painted wooden casements or sashes and very little ornament. The idiosyncratic nature of Winstanley Road in particular suggests an attempt at Webb's 'absence of style'. It may be that Robson originally designed in Gothic and Stevenson in 'Queen Anne', but that 'Queen Anne' proved so successful that Robson increasingly adopted it. This is only a hypothesis and in any case the credit for pioneering the style for schools must remain with Champneys.

The 'Queen Anne' Board Schools succeeded because they were cheap, convenient, attractive, and easily recognizable. They were built on small budgets and usually on constricted sites. They were planned in accordance with the educational standards of the day, which required complete separation of boys from girls, as well as separate, co-educational infant schools. All three divisions had to have their own big schoolroom in which all members of the division could be seated, as well as large separate classrooms. The prevalent pupil–teacher system, which meant that many of the teachers had to be supervised as much as the children, made it desirable that it should be easy to see from one classroom into another, and from the schoolroom into the classrooms. Other requirements included lavatories, cloakrooms, teachers' rooms, a certain amount of covered but not enclosed space for playgrounds in wet weather, openings to either side of the classrooms to provide cross-ventilation, thirty square inches of glass to each square foot of floor, and (for reasons which remain obscure) a ceiling height of at least fourteen feet for both classrooms and schoolrooms.

The early Board Schools developed out of these constraints. They were usually at least three stories high, in order to fit the necessary accommodation on the site; division was stacked above division and the ground floor sometimes left open to act as a covered playground. Lavatories, cloakrooms, and teachers' rooms, which required lower ceiling heights, were placed behind or to the side of classrooms, with different floor and ceiling levels and separate access from the stair-cases. There were no corridors, to economize on space, and the top floors rose into prominent roofs and were lit by dormer windows, to economize on walling. Classrooms had windows either at both ends or both sides, for through-ventilation. The accepted ideal plan was H-shaped, with, on each floor, a central schoolroom between pairs of classrooms, for easy supervision. If space allowed, the infant school was built as a separate single-storey building, since the ideal room width for infants was different from that for children.

'Queen Anne' provided Flemish gables for the dormers and gable ends of the classrooms; small-paned sashes for the small rooms, and huge grids of timber and glass, with hinged lights, for the classrooms; decoration at minimum cost by means of pilaster strips, raised panels of brickwork, and colour contrasts between brown stock bricks, red brick dressings, and white woodwork; round arched arcades for the covered playgrounds; and prominent ribbed chimney-stacks for the schools which were heated by open fires (but open fires increasingly gave way to central heating). Small-paned windows could be defended on practical as well as aesthetic grounds; local hooligans threw stones at the new schools, and it was cheaper to mend a small pane than a sheet of plate glass. The only occasional extravagance was a panel of ornament in moulded brick or terracotta. Rossetti's friend Spencer Stanhope designed a panel showing 'Knowledge strangling Ignorance' which was used in some of the first schools to be built;[18] later ones had panels of sunflowers, or just the date and the initials of the London School Board.

Bold, sensible, picturesque, and adaptable, the Board Schools of the 1870s, if not quite as striking as they appear in the vigorous engravings by H. W. Brewer which illustrate Robson's book, were a remarkable achievement. Although similarity in planning, outline, and detail gave them a basic unity, each site was a different shape and each school had slightly different requirements. 'Queen Anne' proved capable of adapting to different sites and of ringing changes on the details, so that the schools, although all recognizably related to each other, exhibited a great deal of variety. In the schools of the 1880s and 1890s the planning was improved but the architecture comparatively little altered; the freshness and originality of the first schools of the 1870s were never quite recovered.

Newnham College

The down-to-earth and big-boned London Board Schools perhaps diffused more light than sweetness. Both sweetness and light gushed out of the buildings of Newnham College, Cambridge. Here Basil Champneys was the college architect for over thirty-five years. Between 1874 and 1910 he designed a series of 'Queen Anne' buildings of delicate and intimate prettiness, grouped with comfortable informality round an immense tree-studded lawn.

At Newnham 'Queen Anne' demonstrated its ability to provide a setting for what Tennyson had called 'sweet girl graduates with their golden hair'. It also reinforced its claim to be the style of progress. In 1847, when Tennyson had created Princess Ida and her women's university in the wilds, university education for women was a titillating fantasy. By the early 1870s it had become a practical, but controversial reality, supported by the enlightened but much mocked at by the conventional. The groundwork was carried out in the late 1840s and the 1850s, when various schools providing good secondary education for women were founded (Queen's College, Harley Street, 1848; Bedford College, 1849; North London Collegiate, 1850; Cheltenham Ladies' College, 1858). In 1867 Emily Davies, who for many years had dreamt of the possibility of a university college for women, wrote to her friend Barbara Bodichon that 'the scheme is about to be brought down from the clouds'. It took her, in fact, four years before she could raise the money with which to start building Girton College, Cambridge, in 1871. In 1869 the College had started in a small way in a rented house at Hitchin; it moved into the new Girton building in 1873.

Meanwhile, in 1869, the Association for Promoting the Higher Education of Women in Cambridge had been founded at a meeting in the house of Elizabeth Garrett Anderson's sister, Millicent, and her husband Henry Fawcett, the blind Radical politician and Professor of Political Economy at the University. The Association's secretary was Henry Sidgwick, then a thirty-one-year-old don at Trinity College. In 1871 Sidgwick persuaded Miss Anne Jemima Clough, sister of the poet, to settle with a group of five women students in Regent Street, Cambridge. From 1872 to 1874 they rented Merton Hall, behind St. John's College. In 1874 the Newnham Hall Company Ltd. was founded as a non-profit-making association of shareholders, with Sidgwick as its dominating force. Its aims were to build and run a residential hall for women students, and to organize their studies. Newnham Hall went up in 1874–5 and Miss Clough moved into it as the first Principal. In 1880 Newnham Hall developed into Newnham College.[19] A. J. Balfour, whose sister Eleanor married Sidgwick in 1876 and succeeded Miss Clough as Principal in 1892, was one of the first shareholders. Others included Thackeray's novelist daughter Anne, and Miss Mary Anne Ewart, the comfortably off daughter of a Liverpool merchant, who in 1884–5 was to employ Philip Webb to design her a house, called Coneyhurst, in Surrey.[20]

In 1871 Emily Davies told Sidgwick that he was 'the serpent that was eating out her vitals'.[21] Although both were fighting for university education for women they were at loggerheads about methods. The Girton line was all or nothing; women must do exactly what the men did. Girton was only open to women reading for an honours degree. Newnham in its early days was much more easy-going. It was sympathetic to anyone who wanted to improve her education; it tried to work out individual courses suited to each person's needs and capacity. To begin with only a few of its students were reading for honours. Accordingly Girton despised Newnham for being pusillanimous and Newnham disliked Girton for being doctrinaire.

The difference was largely one of generation. Sidgwick was eight years younger than Emily Davies and eleven years younger than her friend and benefactor Barbara Bodichon; the majority of the first shareholders in the Newnham Hall Association were in their twenties and thirties. Girton expressed high Victorian toughness, Newnham late Victorian sweet reasonableness. It was typical of Sidgwick to choose as Newnham's first Principal someone as unlike Emily Davies as could be. Emily Davies was both formidable and prudish; it was only with the greatest difficulty that she was persuaded that her college should be at Cambridge, and even then she insisted that it should be in a village two miles from the town to keep her girls out of reach of the under-graduates. At Newnham, a few minutes walk from the centre of Cambridge, Miss Clough was kindly, motherly, and fussy. She urged her students to 'take the little pleasures of life', and when she 'could find nothing to say to a passing girl, she kissed her instead'.[22]

The difference in life style between the two colleges was expressed by their architecture. Emily Davies chose Waterhouse as early as 1867, apparently on the strength of his work at Balliol. Girton was minimally Tudor Gothic and suggested, rather depressingly, the bracing of the moral fibre. Emily Davies wrote to Barbara Bodichon, 'As we cannot have tradition and associa-tion, we shall want to get dignity in every other way that is open to us.'[23] Neither Newnham nor the 'Queen Anne' style was after dignity, and they merged together with disarming appropriateness.

Champneys was probably chosen as architect because he had been friends with Sidgwick when he was an undergraduate at Trinity and Sidgwick was a young and approachable don there.[24] His claims may have been reinforced by his friend Sidney Colvin, who was a Fellow of Trinity from 1868 and the first Slade Professor of Fine Art at Cambridge from 1873. The building operations at Newnham were put under a building committee on which the dominating personality seems to have been Miss Ewart.[25] Champneys presented his plans for Newnham Hall on 25 Feb-ruary 1874. Revised estimates for £6,922 were accepted from William Bell and Sons of Saffron Walden in June, and the building was ready for occupation in the next year.[26] In 1879–80 North Hall (now Sidgwick Hall) was built, Newnham Hall was renamed South Hall (it is now called Old Hall), and the two Halls jointly became Newnham College. At this stage they were divided by a public road. This was closed in the 1880s, when Sidgwick Avenue was laid out to replace it. The College now gained uninterrupted possession of what was to become a great irregular rectangle of grass and trees, and gradually developed round three sides of it. South Hall was extended to the north in 1883–4. In 1886–7 Clough Hall was built to the west of North Hall; it included a very big dining-hall which could be used as an assembly hall for the whole college. A gatehouse, known as the Pfeiffer building, filled the gap between North and South Halls in 1892–3. In 1894 the archway was fitted with gates made by Thomas Elsley, to Champneys's designs, as a memorial to Miss Clough; and Sidgwick and his wife, who was now Principal, moved into the rooms above it. The library was added behind Clough Hall in 1896. The Kennedy building completed the north side of the rectangle in 1905, and the last Champneys building was Peile Hall, built along its west side in 1909–10.[27] Minor Champneys works are the old laboratory on an island site in the garden, and the delightful little gymnasium to the east of the Old Hall, both built in 1878. The college has never had a chapel, largely because Sidgwick 'abstained from identifying himself with every form of institutional Christianity'.[28]

Newnham was lucky in its architect. Champneys maintained his standards of design for thirty-five years; the fact that all the many buildings of these years are by the same architect gives the college an agreeable consistency but within the consistency there is considerable variety.

53. (*Right*) The original Newnham Hall,
now Old Hall, Newnham College, Cambridge.
By Basil Champneys, 1874–5.

54. (*Below*) Clough Hall, Newnham College.
By Basil Champneys, 1886–7.

55. The Pfeiffer Building, Newnham College. By Basil Champneys, 1892–3.

Each block has a different character. Old Hall is pretty but a little prim, Sidgwick confident and   53, 54, 55, 56
relaxed, Clough almost overpoweringly dainty, Pfeiffer sumptuous and concentrated; Kennedy and Peile are drier than the earlier buildings, but still very handsome. The elements throughout are the familiar 'Queen Anne' ones. Champneys had an especial fondness for broken pediments, not shared initially by his committee; on 16 March 1874, he was writing to Miss Ewart 'I rather regret the elimination of broken pediments' on Newnham Hall, and in the end they were retained.[29] Although he had a greater taste for symmetry than some of his 'Queen Anne' contemporaries the loosely rambling general layout prevents the college from having any feeling of formality. The Pfeiffer gatehouse is a nice example of the 'Queen Anne' method of putting Gothic Revival   55 principles into seventeenth-century dress; one of its turrets contains a staircase and the other provides bay windows for rooms, so the staircase turret is bigger than the other, and has windows on different levels, producing an approximate symmetry that is very agreeable.

57. A student's room in
Newnham College, from
a contemporary
water-colour.

But perhaps the architectural feature of Newnham that sticks especially in the memory is its multitude of bay and oriel windows. They range from the two great cylindrical bays of the Clough dining-hall, with their matching copper domes, to the pair of pocket oriels that sprout out of the side elevation of Sidgwick. Inside, in both large and small rooms they produce a pleasing combination of major spaces with minor spaces opening out of them; but, as tends to happen with the 'Queen Anne' style, the buildings are less interesting inside than out, though the galleried library is agreeable enough. All the halls have rooms letting on to corridors instead of the traditional Oxford and Cambridge staircases; at Newnham Hall Miss Clough insisted that the corridors should have windows at both ends because 'it was cheering to look out as one walked along the passages'.[30] The students' rooms (unlike those at Girton) had open fireplaces; they were furnished with Morris 'Sussex' chairs and writing desks of Georgian pattern; old photographs and drawings show Morris wallpapers, Japanese fans and parasols, and vases or pots of flowers in abundance. Mary Paley, who was one of the first students, describes in her memoirs how 'we papered our rooms with Morris, bought Burne-Jones photographs, and dressed accordingly' and how she and her friend Jane Harrison designed the embroidery for their tennis dresses: 'Hers was of pomegranates and mine of Virginia creeper, and we sat together in the evenings, and worked at them and talked.'[31]

57

◁ **56.** Looking along Clough Hall to Sidgwick Hall
(formerly North Hall), Newnham College.

Jane Harrison was described at the time as 'tall, willowy, in the tight fitting olive-green serge of the days of the aesthetic craze, her hair in a Greek coil' or 'like a beautiful green beetle'.[32] She later became a Greek scholar of great distinction. In her memoirs she tells of visits by Turgenev, Ruskin, and Gladstone to Newnham and how the Newnham girls 'used to wait outside Macmillan's shop to seize the new installments of *Daniel Deronda*'. On one occasion George Eliot actually appeared in her room, which had been newly decorated with Morris paper, and 'said in her shy and impressive way "Your paper makes a beautiful background for your face"'.[33] Her friend Mary Paley taught at Newnham after she had graduated (a pupil gushed 'She *is* a Princess Ida')[34] and married Alfred Marshall, the economist, for whom J. J. Stevenson designed Balliol Croft in Cambridge in 'Queen Anne' style in 1885. Another of the first students, Ellen Crofts, married Charles Darwin's son Francis in 1883; they built and settled in a 'Queen Anne' house on the Huntingdon Road. In the same year Maud Du Puy, a visiting American who was about to marry another Darwin brother, described 'quite a number of aesthetic costumes' at a Newnham garden party.[35] It seems to have been only later that Newnham caught something of the Girton spirit and it became possible to refer disparagingly to 'the drab Newnham girls'.[36]

Three Town Halls

In the later nineteenth century local politics became increasingly prestigious. Chamberlain's historic mayorship at Birmingham (1873–6) received the greatest publicity, and introduced new conceptions of local government based on popular support and the assumption of much greater responsibilities. In a smaller but extremely influential way T. H. Green's session on the Oxford City council (1876–82) made local politics fashionable among idealistic intellectuals. It was inevitable that the progressive 'Queen Anne' style should endeavour to produce new solutions for municipal architecture. But it achieved much less success in local politics than in education. There were two main reasons for this. One was that in the local politics of the 1870s and 1880s the progressives were fighting against deeply entrenched local power-structures, often dominated by local tradesmen and shopkeepers, who saw municipal building mainly in terms of providing a nice opportunity for their wife's nephew, who happened to be an architect. The other was that municipal buildings in general, and town halls in particular, were expected to express civic dignity, and 'Queen Anne' was not thought of as a dignified or important style.

Both forces can be seen at work in the cases of the Municipal Buildings at Leicester, the Town Hall at Wakefield, and the Vestry Hall at Kensington. At Leicester the town council personally voted in a good 'Queen Anne' design, somewhat against the advice of their assessor, but perhaps not for the most creditable reasons. At Wakefield an eminent assessor selected a 'Queen Anne' design, to the bewilderment of the council; however, they loyally accepted it, and grew to be proud of it. In Kensington the vestrymen ignored all their assessors' recommendations, actively sneered at some of the best 'Queen Anne' designs of the 1870s, and selected a second-rate classical entry, by an architect with local connections, of which Kensington has been rightly ashamed ever since.

Leicester had originally held a competition for their municipal buildings in 1871. Street was the assessor, and selected a fine Gothic design by Edward Godwin, which the town council turned down because they did not like London architects.[37] A new competition was held at the beginning of 1873, with T. H. Wyatt as the assessor. 'Queen Anne' still had no history of competition success except for Bodley's victory with his London School Board Offices in January, which probably came too late to influence entries. The competitors, with one notable exception, seem to have kept clear of the style; even G. G. Scott, junior, in collaboration with his brother John

Oldrid, sent in a Gothic design. The exception was an excellent 'Queen Anne' design by Francis John Hames.

In June, before the results were decided on, the entries were publicly exhibited, and discussed in the building periodicals. The quality of Hames's design was recognized both by the *Builder* and the *Building News*, though both were critical of it. The *Building News* thought it 'a clever design . . . after the fashion of Hampton Court Palace', but complained that 'the long square windows cut up into minute squares by wide sash bars, and other vagaries of the style, are carried to exaggeration'. The *Builder* described it as 'in the Queen Anne style which, corrupt and unsatisfactory as it is in many ways, has a character of its own which has been here thoroughly appreciated and consistently worked out'. However, 'we should scarcely wish to see so important a building erected in this style'.[38]

T. H. Wyatt, the assessor, was one of the few older architects sympathetic to the movement; as related in the previous chapter, in 1873 he was actually building a row of houses in Upper Berkeley Street which were undeniably, if rather dimly, 'Queen Anne'. He was required to select, but not grade, five designs on which the council would vote. Hames's design was among the five. Wyatt's report on it was sympathetic and, though critical of some features of the planning, he commended its style: 'the elevations have much originality and would, I think, make, with some slight additional study, a very picturesque and imposing group of municipal buildings, even though they may not be of a very pure period of art.' Nevertheless, his report, though not grading the designs, unmistakably gave preference to a more conventional classical one by Ordish and Traylen. But when the council voted on the designs in July, they gave the first prize to Hames.[39]

Hames was resident in London at the time of the competition but came from Leicester, where he had been articled to a Leicester architect, William Millican. The councillors' votes for his design probably expressed a preference for local talent rather than aesthetic discrimination. But although Hames came from Leicester, his architecture came from London, more exactly from 30 Argyll Street, where he had been (and probably still was) working as Nesfield's assistant. The sketchbook given to him by Nesfield in 1871 is in the R.I.B.A. Drawings Collection; it bears a friendly inscription 'with best wishes for lots of good things in the book'. The good things came, in the shape of delicate and sensitive sketches of old buildings, drawn very much in the style of Nesfield. The subjects are what one would have expected from a young man working in Nesfield's office: eighteenth-century ironwork, seventeenth-century joinery, Flemish gables at Broome Park, and a fanciful and beautiful late seventeenth-century house at Enfield are interspersed with Gothic churches and picturesque town houses of the type that Nesfield and Shaw loved.[40] *58*

The architecture of Leicester Town Hall is also what one would have expected from Argyll *59* Street: the hipped roofs crowned by wooden balusters, the elongated sash windows and chimney-stacks, the round windows, the combination of general symmetry in the main elevation with asymmetry in the placing of details, even the sunflowers on the chimney-stacks, derive from Kinmel; the central gable and balconies on stone brackets derive from Bodrhyddan. But however derivative the details, they are very competently put together and the result is an agreeable building, dignified and friendly, and not at all pompous. But after Leicester Town Hall, Hames is heard of no more; did he die young, did he emigrate, or did the town hall owe a good deal to the helping hand of Nesfield?

The Wakefield and Kensington competitions followed on in 1877. They took place at almost exactly the same time, but under very different conditions; the smooth progress and successful conclusion at Wakefield were bitterly commented on by the disgruntled entrants in Kensington. Wakefield corporation had been empowered by a private act of 1876 to build a Town Hall. A competition was advertised in February 1877; the building was to cost not more than £35,000 and it was stipulated that 'the style of architecture is to be of such a character as will harmonize with the public buildings adjoining'. As these were classical, and included the Grecian Mechanic's

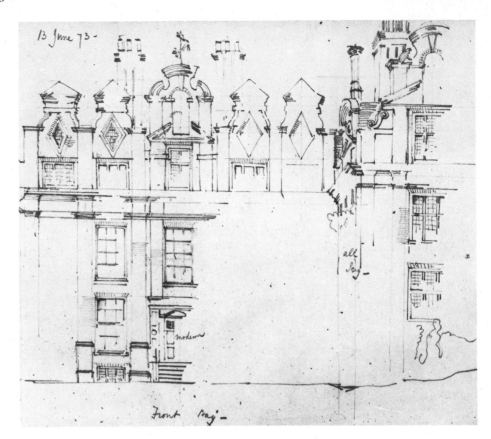

58. Broome Park, Kent, from a sketch by F. J. Hames made in 1873.

Institute and the Courthouse, which had a prominent Doric portico, it was widely believed that only a classical design had any chance of winning. In March the Borough Surveyor informed the entrants that this was not the case, but even so most of the entries were classical, to a greater or lesser degree.[41]

There were thirty-five entries, which were exhibited both to the council and the public in April. The Corporation's Building Committee, fortified by a tour of recent town halls, selected ten designs, from which a professional assessor was to select a first, second, and third. Waterhouse was invited, but declined, and at the end of April Street was invited and accepted. This perturbed the *Wakefield Express*, on the grounds that 'he is a gentleman holding a very high position if not the highest in his profession, but he is, we hear, more noted as a Gothic than a classical architect'. The Corporation were even more perturbed when Street came down from London, looked with horror at the selected ten, and asked to see the others. He then gave the first and third premiums to designs which the Corporation had rejected, although the second went to a design from the selected ten, by a Wakefield architect. The winner was a design by Thomas Edward Collcutt (1840–1924).[42]

The Corporation accepted Street's award, and grew to like it, in spite of a good deal of sniping from some councillors. The *Wakefield Express* later commented that 'In certain quarters there has doubtless been a desire to see a revival, though faint, of the glories of the Propylaea and Parthenon'. At a celebratory dinner held after the laying of the foundation stone in October, the councillor who toasted 'the Architect and Builder' revealed himself 'free to confess that he, along with many others, did not care very much for Mr. Collcutt's design at the first sight, but the more attention they gave to the details, the more satisfactory the design became'. Their satisfaction continued, even though there were the inevitable rows during the course of building, as the costs escalated far beyond the stipulated £35,000.[43]

59. The Municipal Buildings, Leicester. By F. J. Hames, 1873–5.

Street's adjudication suggests that he was a good politician. He cannot have thought much of the design to which he gave the second premium, for it was a commonplace example of Victorian classicism; but a second prize for a local architect was a useful sop to local pride. Collcutt had sent in two designs, the second of which was an extremely fine Gothic one, on a similar plan to his 'Queen Anne' winner;[44] it is hard to believe that Street did not prefer it, but if so he must have decided that there was little chance of the Corporation accepting Gothic and gone for the classical design with the most Gothic feeling in it. However, he left a loophole for Gothic in his report; he stated that, while it was impossible for him to premiate both of Collcutt's entries, 'it will be for your committee, I think, to take both of his designs into consideration in the execution of the work'.[45] The third premium went to an able and, for the time, unusual entry in full-blown mid-eighteenth-century style, by Austin, Johnson, and Hicks of Newcastle.[46] This was almost certainly designed by R. F. Johnson, whose Ingham Infirmary was described in Chapter III and whose 'Queen Anne' excursions tended to have a much stronger flavour of what we would call neo-Georgian than those of his friends.

A potentially embarrassing fact came to light soon after the competition results were announced. Collcutt had been Street's assistant. Street rode over the situation with aplomb. 'Many years ago he was in my office . . . Since that time I am not sure that I should know him if I met him in the street.' Admittedly he had told the mayor 'that I suspected I knew the author of the design' but he had been thinking of someone else. He was glad that it turned out to be Collcutt 'as I doubted whether the gentleman in question was quite equal to the work'.[47] Street was probably telling the truth, for he was both a man of high principles and a notoriously remote employer. But who could 'the gentleman in question' have been except Godwin, whose professional career was currently suffering both from his unconventional sex life and the embarrassing inability of his two Irish country houses to keep out the damp? And how, in the light of the whole competition and Street's award, can one believe Blomfield's story, that Street kept Bodley out of the Academy for as long as he could because he had betrayed the Gothic cause by designing the School Board Offices?[48]

Collcutt had overlapped with Shaw in Street's office, and since setting up on his own had designed furniture of high quality (and a shop to show it in) for Collinson & Lock, and a house in Bloomsbury Square. Wakefield Town Hall was his first big architectural commission. Its style was described by him as 'Renaissance, freely treated',[49] by a local historian as 'French Renaissance', by Murray's Guide as 'French Gothic', and by the *Buildings of England* as 'Free Tudor'. The *Building News*, more accurately, defined it as 'Queen Anne' without actually saying so: 'the author has more the feeling of a true Gothicist than a classicist; the masses and groupings are thoroughly Gothic in spirit . . . We almost fancy that the author had the New Zealand Chambers before his eyes when designing the Wood Street elevation'.[50] The narrow elevation to the main   60 street, the only part of the building which is at all prominent, is indeed a clever variation on New Zealand Chambers, executed in stone instead of brick and timber, and with the three oriels carried up through the eaves to pedimented gables, instead of being crowned by a cove. Set back to the right of the façade is a tall tower (increased in height from that shown in the competition entry, at the request of the Council) of decidedly Gothic Revival silhouette. The result, compressed and lofty on its narrow frontage, is entirely successful. The change-over to stone from the brick and timber more usual in 'Queen Anne' works without a flaw; the effect is handsome but not pompous; the three great lanterns of glass in enfilade, with the tower shooting up beyond them, form a memorable combination, and the tower on its hilltop provides a civic symbol visible from miles around.

Behind the main frontage the rest of the building is much more utilitarian, and is planned, not especially conveniently, round a narrow internal courtyard which has almost inevitably been filled in with later accretions. The handsome council chamber, on the first floor behind two

◁ **60.** The Town Hall, Wakefield, Yorkshire.
By T. E. Collcutt, 1877–80.

61. Competition design for Kensington Vestry Hall. By J. J. Stevenson and A. J. Adams, 1877.

of the oriels, has lost its Collcutt furnishings in recent years; the best surviving room is the former Mayor's parlour up in the roof, more Jacobean than eighteenth century in feeling, with a fireplace in a deep alcove, much stained glass, and a great barrel-vaulted ceiling enriched with a running design of hundreds of plaster birds (executed by Walter Smith of London). The 'magnificent Persian rug', originally before the fireplace in the Council Chamber must surely have been chosen by Collcutt, and dispatched as a little outpost of Chelsea fashion among the Yorkshire councillors.[51]

A competition for a new Kensington Vestry Hall was announced early in 1877, and entries had to be in by 26 March. It was to be one of a string of new London vestry halls, town halls of the future, the inevitable result of what had been country parishes round London finding themselves with the population of sizeable towns. But by the standards of Leicester and Wakefield it was a modest affair, with a ceiling of £18,000 instead of £35,000, as at Wakefield, and £30,000 as at Leicester. The stipulation that 'a classical form of architecture is to be employed' led the *Building News* to express fear that 'a commonplace Italian design' would be selected, and their fears were to be abundantly justified.[52]

A site a few minutes' walk from Kensington Palace and Kensington Square proved irresistible to 'Queen Anne' architects, and at least eight 'Queen Anne' designs were sent in, as well as one captioned 'Queen Anne is dead'. All the designs were exhibited to the public in April, and aroused much comment. The five main 'Queen Anne' entries were 'Old Kensington', 'Kensington', and 'Alpha', later to be revealed as by J. J. Stevenson and A. J. Adams, J. Oldrid Scott, and J. M. Brydon, and 'Xmas' and 'Utility', of which the former was certainly, and the latter probably, by E. W. Godwin.[53]

The site was an L-shaped one with only one good frontage, to Kensington High Street. The competitors fell into two main divisions, those who put the big hall in front, a position which had certain practical disadvantages, and those who put it at the rear, and as a result produced a less impressive entrance façade. Stevenson and Adams's entry had a hall at the rear and, although

62. Competition design for Kensington Vestry Hall. By J. M. Brydon, 1877.

ably planned, its appearance suffered as a result; moreover, the elevation suggested a failure to escape sufficiently from the Board School formula. In contrast Brydon's design, which was widely and rightly admired, had a festive richness exactly suited to a small but prestigious town hall. J. O. Scott's design was described by Scott himself as 'Classic, with a studious avoidance of so called Queen Anne barbarities'; in effect this meant symmetrical 'Queen Anne' with the oriels and sunflowers left out. Godwin's designs, unlike the other three, were never engraved, but two preliminary drawings survive. An especially enchanting one shows rows of paired sashes between pilasters, five *œils-de-bœuf* in little Flemish gables, and a big hipped roof with off-centre clock and tower. It can probably be identified as 'Utility', commended in the press as clever and 'of thorough Old Kensington type', but heavily criticized for its planning.[54]

In May it was announced that Thomas Whichcord had been chosen as assessor. Then nothing happened. By 22 June an angry letter to the *Building News*, signed 'A Competitor' was asking why there had been a delay of three months, when the Wakefield competition had been settled in three weeks: 'Rumour, with its hundred tongues, is by this time pretty busy with all sorts of stories.' The result was not announced until the end of July. Whichcord had placed Stevenson and Adams second and J. O. Scott third, but had given the first award to a classical design by Frederick Mew, architect of the Hampstead Vestry Hall. The Building Committee had ignored his awards, selected three of their own, and palmed off Mew with the fourth premium. The winner was a dreary classical design by Robert Walker. Mr. Freeman, a member of the Building Committee, announced that 'he objected to the Queen Anne style, which the professional advisor had a fancy for, on the ground that we had enough of it in the School Board'. Freeman, incidentally, was on the London School Board's Works Committee; he must have been a thorn in the side of poor Robson.[55]

The decision was not well received in the building press. Stevenson capitalized on his disappointment by adapting his design for the new City offices of the Orient Line, recently started by his cousins the Andersons.[56] Others made a great fuss. In September it was revealed that none of the designs chosen by the Building Committee could be built for less than £20,000. In October an angry 'FRIBA' wrote to the *Building News* complaining that of the three prizeholders 'one . . ., I am led to believe, was the son of a vestryman, and another associated in the work with the surveyor of the vestry board'.[57] The vestrymen of Kensington were unperturbed; Walker's building went ahead, and was completed in 1880.

A Miscellany of Enlightenment

There were to be no more 'Queen Anne' town halls of the quality of Leicester and Wakefield. In 1878 Collcutt was given the second premium for a 'Queen Anne' design for Barrow-in-Furness Town Hall, but the winning design was a Gothic one. Minor, but agreeable town halls in the style include one at Yarmouth, designed by J. B. Pearce, and one at Pontefract designed in 1881 by a Leeds firm, Perkins and Bulmer.[58] Brydon's first successful competition was for the Chelsea Vestry Hall, in 1885; but by then he had moved away from 'Queen Anne', and his winning design was a straightforward essay in the manner of Wren.

'Queen Anne' kept its corner in education. Within the field it consolidated its hold on Board Schools, and schools and colleges for women. Much remains to be discovered about 'Queen Anne' schools and college buildings of this period, but it seems unlikely that more than the occasional building of the quality of Newnham or the London Board Schools will come to light. The Board School style spread out gradually from London, rather as the Hertfordshire school style spread in the 1950s, but there were always areas to which it never penetrated. Newnham was followed at Oxford by Somerville College, founded in 1879, and Lady Margaret Hall, founded in 1878. Both acquired 'Queen Anne' buildings, those at Somerville designed by Thomas Jackson in 1882, those at Lady Margaret Hall by Champneys in 1881–3.[59] Another Oxford example of 'Queen Anne' by Jackson is the former High School for Girls (now the University Department of Metallurgy), a gently festive building of 1879–81 at the southern end of Banbury Road. The Girls' Public Day School Company, which was founded in the late 1870s, built a number of 'Queen Anne' schools in the London area; Robson designed the earliest, built at Blackheath in 1880. One of the pioneer schools for women, Miss Buss's North London Collegiate School, acquired a new building on a new site in 1877–8; almost inevitably, it was 'Queen Anne', an agreeable design by E. C. Robins, with a big hall in which Miss Ewart distributed the prizes in 1878.[60]

Other school work by Champneys includes a new building at Bedford Grammar School (1886) and the Museum at Harrow (1884–6).[61] The latter is Champneys's most impressive 'Queen Anne' building. Tall and festive, with a double-ridged roof ending in twin Flemish gables, it rides its dramatic hill-side site like a Board School on which, for a change, there was money to spend and on which money had been well spent. On the side away from the road is an unexpected delight; an open staircase, in the manner of southern France or Italy, which climbs all the way up one corner of its four lofty storeys.

Other enlightened causes which were provided with 'Queen Anne' buildings included hospitals, swimming-baths, low-income housing, and libraries. A humane and charming design of 1877 for a small children's hospital in Cardiff by J. D. Sedding (who had been in Street's office with Webb, Shaw, Morris, and Collcutt) seems never to have been built.[62] Among the best surviving 'Queen Anne' hospitals are Johnson's pioneer Ingham Infirmary, described in Chapter III, and St. Peter's Hospital in King Street, Covent Garden, designed by J. M. Brydon and built in 1881. A description of the latter in the *Building News* refers to Brydon's 'endeavour to secure the

63. The external staircase of the Museum, Harrow School, Middlesex. By Basil Champneys, 1884–6.

64. Cottage Hospital, St. Leonards-on-Sea, Sussex. By W. Hay Murray, 1881.

home-like character so desirable'.[63] 'Queen Anne' was in theory well adapted to redeem hospitals from the institutional Gothic or monumental classic which made many of the big new hospitals of the mid-century remarkably un-homelike. It did not always succeed, although it is often difficult to judge the original designs, which tend to have been obscured by later additions. Brydon's Hospital for Women in Euston Road, designed for Elizabeth Garrett Anderson in 1888–90, has been a good deal altered but can never have been as agreeable as St. Peter's Hospital.[64] Cottage Hospitals, a new phenomenon of the later nineteenth century, were more suited to the 'Queen Anne' approach than big metropolitan ones. Very pleasing examples were designed at Newmarket (with almshouses attached) by Frederick R. Roper in 1880 and at St. Leonards-on-

64   Sea by W. Hay Murray in 1881.[65]

There are a number of 'Queen Anne' public baths in existence, and a good deal of 'Queen Anne' working-class housing was erected by public or philanthropic bodies, but neither type always managed to escape a drab institutional character. By rights they should have, for the whole ethic of 'Queen Anne' was that it should produce friendly buildings, built to a human scale. One sympathetic case in which 'Queen Anne' succeeded was at Lime Tree Walk in Sevenoaks.[66] This was a piece of private philanthropy by T. G. Jackson and his father. They had noticed with distress that the centre of Sevenoaks (where they lived) was being redeveloped for middle-class housing and the working classes being pushed out. The Jacksons disapproved both of 'the mischievous sorting out of classes into distinct districts for rich and poor, which always has the effect of creating as it were two hostile camps' and of 'workmen . . . having to walk miles from home and back again twice a day'. In 1878 they bought a field close to the centre of the town, which had not yet been built on, and covered it with small houses and three-storey flats, designed by T. G. Jackson and let to working people at low rents.

65   The buildings were 'Queen Anne' at its simplest, somewhat under the influence of the low-cost houses being designed at the same period by Norman Shaw for Bedford Park. They had dormers, tile-hung gables, windows with small-paned sashes or casements, and the occasional shallow bow window, like an eighteenth-century shop-front. The flats had timber access galleries supported on brick Tuscan columns. In the centre of the estate was a coffee house of slightly more elaborate architectural character, adorned with Flemish gables and a cupola.

To provide the area with a coffee-house rather than a pub revealed an ambition to improve the working classes from which even philanthropic schemes as humane and unpatronizing as

65. Lime Tree Walk, Sevenoaks, Kent. By T. G. Jackson, 1878, from a drawing by him made in 1890.

this one were seldom free. Coffee public houses, designed to wean the working classes away from alcohol, were a favourite product of the enlightened in the 1870s and 1880s, and 'Queen Anne' was the favourite style in which to build them. Along with their spiritual half-brothers, the 'improved' public houses, and their illegitimate offspring, the brashly commercial 'Queen Anne' pub of the 1890s, they are discussed in Chapter VIII.

A coffee tavern was one of the many progressive features of the little mill town of Leek in Staffordshire.[67] Leek was an example of a provincial town which reacted with enthusiasm to sweetness and light in general, and William Morris and Norman Shaw in particular. It had its own especial link with William Morris. George Wardle, who was employed as a book-keeper and draughtsman by Morris and Company from about 1866, and became manager after Warrington Taylor's death in 1870, had a brother, Thomas Wardle, who owned a dye works in Leek. As early as 1868 Mrs. Thomas Wardle had founded the Leek Embroidery Society, under Morris's influence; it anticipated by several years the Royal School of Art Needlework, which was founded in 1872 by a group of artists' wives and artistic ladies, most of whom were connected in one way or another with the Morris circle.[68]

For three years, from 1875 to 1877, William Morris frequented Thomas Wardle's works in Leek, in order to learn the technique of dyeing. It was a connection that worked two ways, for besides learning from Wardle, Morris aroused his interest in reviving the use of vegetable, instead of aniline, dyes. From 1876 Wardle started dyeing Morris textiles with the soft 'natural' colours derived from vegetable dyes which the aesthetic movement was united in preferring to aniline mauves and magentas.[69]

It was probably during these years that Morris got to know William Larner Sugden (1850–1901) the son of a well-established Leek architect, who was working in his father's firm and went into partnership with him in 1881.[70] Larner Sugden became an enthusiastic disciple. He was one of the first members of the Society for the Protection of Ancient Buildings, which Morris and Webb founded in 1877;* when Morris became a Socialist he followed his example; in the 1890s he was involved in the Co-operative Movement, and designed a number of co-operative shops in Leek. Like Morris he was unable to accept conventional Christianity, and was one of the founders of the William Morris Labour Church at Leek, where religion was preached stripped of every possible shred of dogma—at his funeral 'Adonais' was read instead of the Bible. He passed on his particular brand of idealism to his friend Raymond Unwin, one of the pioneers of the garden city. Another friend, Keir Hardie, said of him that 'he looked out upon life with the eye of the artist and the heart of the lover. He saw the hideousness with which commercialism has clad this fair land of England and the mean and poverty-stricken life which it brings to the English people. He hated the ugliness and pitied the poor, and sacrificed himself freely to redeem the one and save the other.'

But although Morris dominated his beliefs, the dominant influence on his architecture, especially in the 1880s, was Norman Shaw. This may also have started through personal contact; Sugden probably met Shaw when the latter was designing Spout Hall in St. Edward's Street, Leek, in 1871–3.[71] The innumerable banks, shops, and houses designed by Sugden in Leek and its neighbourhood are permeated with the influence of Shaw's Old English and 'Queen Anne' manners —with, it must be admitted, a strong provincial accent.

66   Sugden, Morris, Shaw, art and enlightenment all coalesced in the Nicholson Institute at Leek. The intention to build this was first made public under suitably aesthetic circumstances by Sir Philip Cunliffe Owen, the director of the Victoria and Albert Museum. The occasion was the opening of an exhibition of work by the Leek Embroidery Society, the Royal School of Art Needlework, and Morris and Company, held at the Leek Mechanics' Institute in November 1881. Sir Philip announced that Thomas Wardle had put him in touch with 'another worthy townsman, Mr. Joshua Nicholson', who intended to build a combined library, art gallery, museum, and art school at Leek, and that the plans for this had already been drawn up.[72]

They were in fact by Sugden. Nicholson was a Liberal non-conformist manufacturer who owned a silk mill in Leek. He had first thought of founding the institute in 1874, as a memorial to Richard Cobden, and his ideas had been growing more ambitious ever since. The foundation stone was laid early in 1882, and the Institute was opened in 1884.[73] In obedience to the principles of Morris and the S.P.A.B., a seventeenth-century house on the street frontage of the site was lovingly preserved, even though it blocked the best view of the new building; according to the *Builder* its 'quaint garden of sunflowers and hollyhocks . . . imparts a charming old-world flavour to the whole scene'. The Institute towered up bravely behind it; rich with broken pediments, huge windows of many lights and busts of famous men, with a great red-brick Flemish gable at one end and a Wren-like tower capped by a green copper dome at the other, it still dominates the skyline at Leek—a secular church dedicated to the new religions of culture, art, and education.

---

* The S.P.A.B., being concerned with protecting old buildings rather than putting up new ones, is only marginal to the subject-matter of this book. But in its reaction from mid-Victorian methods, its appreciation of the mellowness and texture of old buildings, and its contention that they were valuable in so far as they displayed the work of different generations and lost most of their point if 'restored' back to conformity with some supposed best period in their history, the Society was closely linked to the 'Queen Anne' point of view. Most of the people, laymen included, discussed in this book were members; a number of architects, however, including Shaw, Champneys, and Bodley, never joined, apparently not because they disapproved of its principles but because a kind of architectural freemasonry made them dislike the idea of a lay pressure group designed to keep architects under control.

66. The Nicholson Institute, Leek, Staffordshire. By W. L. Sugden, 1881–4.

V Sweetness at Home

The House Beautiful

Even more than in the omnipresent Board Schools, it was in the architecture of private houses that 'Queen Anne' made its most typical, successful, and publicized contribution. For the cultivated businessmen and aesthetic housewives who took with enthusiasm to the religion of Beauty, the obvious place in which to put their principles into practice was in their own homes. They set to work with a will, and an increasing mass of literature, with interior decorators to back it up, helped them on their way.

So did an increasing mass of satire, aimed at those who so self-consciously set themselves apart, as aesthetes among the philistines. The aesthetes took it all in good part, conscious that they after all were the pace-setters. In 1882 an aesthetically conscious magazine, the *Burlington*, sketched the transformation of the house even of an imaginary Mr. Philistine Jones: 'He has a dado, and blue and white china may be espied in nooks and corners—he has eschewed gilt—he has ceased to care for stucco—he lives in a Queen Anne house and actually has begun to think about the shape of his jugs. This improvement is rapidly spreading through all classes of society —good taste is no longer an expensive luxury to indulge in . . . And to whom are we indebted for those advantages? Why, to the Aesthetes, the fools and idiots of Philistine phraseology.'[1]

The aesthetes had a good deal to be complacent about, on architectural as well as artistic grounds. By 1882 the norm of stucco and plate glass had been replaced by the norm of red-brick and small (or at least smaller) panes. In London in the 1850s and 1860s one-off houses were the prerogative of the very rich, of the Duke of Buccleuch at Montagu House in Whitehall or the millionaire R. S. Holford at Dorchester House in Park Lane. Most people, including not a few dukes and millionaires, bought or leased houses put up by speculative builders. A few spent time and money on interior decoration, but the majority handed their houses over to fashionable shops to furnish: many new houses were put on the market complete with wallpapers and decoration. By the 1880s the number of one-off houses had enormously increased, and they were being built for clients much further down the social scale. For those who lacked the money or the confidence to build their own house a wide range of housing was available, put up by enlightened speculators to standards that aesthetes could approve of. These ready-made houses still left plenty of scope for the aesthetic housewife to express her taste in furnishing and decoration; and the less adventurous were at least beginning to call in a decorator rather than a shopkeeper for advice.

An aerial view of London in the 1880s would have shown acres of new red brick coagulating round the skirts of London. The first impression would have been of an indiscriminate eruption, but closer inspection would have revealed a more complex pattern of growth. Typically, development started in the 1870s with a few artists or artistic people building one-off houses in neighbourhoods which for one reason or another they found attractive. These small and select nuclei then attracted more one-off houses and a certain amount of speculative building, usually of high quality and moderate scale. In the 1880s much bigger terraces of much more standard design made the original nuclei into sizeable neighbourhoods. The final great outburst of 'Queen Anne' came in the 1890s, filling gaps and erupting over the suburban fringes. By now 'Queen Anne' was thoroughly commercialized and often only a travesty (though sometimes an enjoyable one) of its origins. Inevitably, it ceased to be a style for the initiated, who moved on to other things.

The ideal terrain for a successful growth of 'Queen Anne' combined genuine early eighteenth-

67. House for
Kate Greenaway,
39 Frognal, Hampstead.
By Norman Shaw,
1884–5.

century houses with existing artistic or literary associations. The two were often found together because of the tendency of cheap and old-fashioned neighbourhoods to attract artists and writers. As already related, Thackeray, after many years of residence in old houses in the neighbourhood of Kensington Palace and Kensington Square, built his own Queen Anne house on Palace Green in 1860–2 and was followed by George Howard on the adjacent site in 1866. Meanwhile Burne-Jones had settled in an eighteenth-century house in Kensington Square in 1865. The north and south sides of Kensington Gardens received J. J. Stevenson's Red House on Bayswater Hill (1871), his house for H. F. Makins in Palace Gate (1873), and Shaw's house for the Lowthers on Kensington Gore (1873), all designed for clients undeterred by (though scornful of) the stucco Italianate housing already built around them. During the remainder of the 1870s a kind of ding-dong battle went on between red brick and stucco, the effects of which are especially noticeable in Queen's Gate. Inevitably, red brick won in the end and high-class commercial 'Queen Anne' arrived with Shaw's Albert Hall Mansions in 1879 and the flats and terraces of Kensington Court in the 1880s.

The old red-brick houses and innumerable artistic associations of Hampstead attracted architects, artists, and writers, including three of the original pioneers of 'Queen Anne', Shaw, Champneys, and G. G. Scott, junior. Scott settled in an early eighteenth-century house in Church Walk in 1872; on the slopes between Hampstead village and St. John's Wood Shaw and Champneys designed 'Queen Anne' houses for themselves, and others for Henry Holiday (Champneys, 1871), Edwin Long (Shaw, 1878 and 1888), Frank Holl (Shaw, 1881), and Kate Greenaway (Shaw, 67

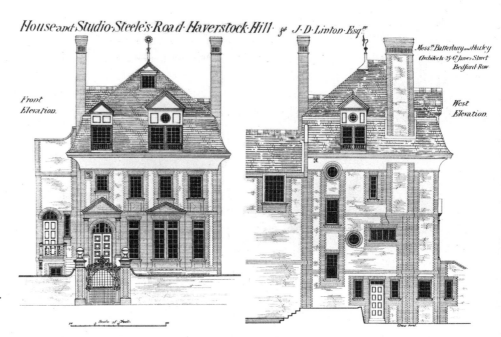

House and Studio Steele's Road Haverstock Hill for J. D. Linton Esq.

Front Elevation.

West Elevation.

Mess. Batterbury and Huxley Architects 25-6 Janes Street Bedford Row

68. Studio house, Steele's Road, Hampstead. By Batterbury and Huxley, 1877.

68

1885). Further houses were contributed by J. J. Stevenson and Philip Webb; and the firm of Batterbury and Huxley set up as a kind of poor man's Shaw and indefatigably plugged the gaps between the houses by the better-known men.[2]

A more compact, but exceedingly prestigious outburst of 'Queen Anne' was taking place at much the same time, as the result of Lord Ilchester's decision to bring a little money into the Holland Park estate (which he had taken over from his cousin, Lady Holland, to rescue her from bankruptcy) by demolishing Little Holland House and developing its site. In the 1860s Mrs. Prinsep, with Watts as her tame household genius in one wing and Tennyson, Gladstone, and Rossetti rubbing shoulders at garden parties on the lawn, had made Little Holland House famous for its enterprising mix of high life and Bohemianism. Her son Val Prinsep and her friend Frederick Leighton had already built houses next door, so that when Watts decided to stay on part of the redeveloped site (the lease had run out) and build himself a studio, the nucleus of an artistic colony was already in being. Melbury Road was laid out on the Little Holland House site in 1875, and the clumsy 'Queen Anne' studio-house designed on it for Watts by F. P. Cockerell was immediately joined by a more distinguished group of red-brick houses. Among these were houses designed for themselves by William Burges and Hamo Thorneycroft, one still resolutely Gothic, the other, if anything, Old English; but the houses designed by Norman Shaw for Luke Fildes and Marcus Stone, and by J. J. Stevenson for Colin Hunter, were notable examples of 'Queen Anne'. After that the supply of available and sufficiently prosperous artists seems to have run out, and the remaining sites were filled by houses put up by speculative builders in their own commercial variety of 'Queen Anne'.[3]

But it was in Chelsea that 'Queen Anne' in its earlier days made the biggest inroads, as a result of the simultaneous development of the Metropolitan Board of Works' property along Chelsea Embankment and Tite Street, and of the property belonging to Lord Cadogan and Smith's Charity to the west of Sloane Street. Old Chelsea, even more than Old Kensington, had the requisite combination of old buildings and an existing colony of artists and writers. Carlyle's move to Cheyne Row in 1834 had been followed by Rossetti's to Cheyne Walk in 1862, Whistler's to Lindsay Row in 1863, and Bell Scott's to Cheyne Walk in 1870. All these moved into eighteenth-century houses, but in 1868 George Boyce had employed Webb to design him his pioneer 'Queen Anne' house in Glebe Place.

Early in the 1870s the Metropolitan Board of Works developed its policy of embanking the Thames, and acquired the river frontage of Chelsea together with an access road along what was to become Tite Street. The embankment was completed by 1875 and the ground along it (and a year or two later, along Tite Street) was let for building. In view of the neighbourhood it was not surprising that the resulting houses were almost all 'Queen Anne' ones, designed for artists or people who liked being in the neighbourhood of artists. There is no evidence that the Board of Works initially aimed for this type either of architecture or of client, but they certainly accepted it and by 1878 were forcing deviants into a 'Queen Anne' uniform.

The sites along the Embankment were probably more expensive than any available artists could afford and were all developed as very large houses built by rich people with artistic inclinations. Artists, on the other hand, settled thickly along Tite Street, both in individual studio houses and in blocks of studio flats. The architects employed in both streets included Shaw, Godwin, Bodley, R. P. Spiers (by now producing 'Queen Anne' in spite of his outburst at the Architectural Association in 1875), Arthur Blomfield, Hungerford Pollen, and R. W. Edis. The first houses were designed individually for clients who intended to live in them, but a certain amount of speculative housing appeared very early on. On the Embankment numbers 9–11 were developed as a speculation by J. W. Temple, of the Shaw Savill Line, in conjunction with Norman Shaw, who was his cousin, and numbers 4–6 by Gillow's the furniture manufacturers, with E. W. Godwin as their architect. In Tite Street, number 33 was erected as a block of studio flats by Jackson and Graham, a high quality furniture shop in Oxford Street, to the design of R. W. Edis. This incursion into small-scale property development by enlightened businessmen and progressive shop-owners was a new feature in the building world, and produced houses that competed favourably with those designed for individual clients—not surprisingly, since both groups employed the same architects. But traditional speculative housing arrived as early as 1878, when an architect, Frederick Beeston, and his relation, Francis Butler, began to fill the gaps in Tite Street with much less distinguished 'Queen Anne' houses.[4]

Late Victorian development on and around the Cadogan estate, which was ultimately to cover acres of Chelsea with 'Queen Anne' houses, large, small, good, bad, and indifferent, started in 1876–8 with the extension of Pont Street westward across Sloane Street and the laying out of Cadogan Square on what had been the grounds of Prince's Club. The land was developed by the Cadogan and Hans Place Estate Company, an example of yet another recent arrival on the London building scene, the limited-liability development company. The architectural character of the new development probably owed more to the directors of the company than to Lord Cadogan and Smith's Charity, who were the ground landlords. The company's Chairman was Colonel W. T. Makins, whose brother had employed J. J. Stevenson for his house in Palace Gate in 1873, and who was shortly to employ him himself to design his house in Lowther Gardens in 1877–8. Not surprisingly, it was laid down by the Company that all new housing had to be of red brick, and two substantial slices of it were designed by J. J. Stevenson.[5]

Other architects employed included Shaw, George Devey, Ernest George, J. J. Stevenson's former partner A. J. Adams, and William Young, the latter passing through a 'Queen Anne' phase in a career that was to lead to the War Office and Glasgow Municipal Chambers. Lesser-known architects employed included G. T. Robinson and W. A. Niven. A few of the houses were designed for occupation by individual clients, but the majority were built in blocks by different building firms as speculations. Among the latter were Stevenson's 42–58 Pont Street and 63–79 Cadogan Square for Pink and Son and Holland and Hannen, houses by Devey and G. T. Robinson for Trollope and Sons, and houses by Shaw, Adams, and Niven for Pink and Son.[6]

The area rapidly assumed a character suitable to its position, poised between aristocratic Belgravia and artistic Chelsea. The first occupants varied between upper class and upper middle class, between rich and very rich, and between gently artistic and mildly philistine. Shaw,

69. Detail of 6 Chelsea Embankment.
By E. W. Godwin, 1876–8.

Stevenson, and others catered for the artistic; the more conventional element was catered for
by architects like Niven, who proclaimed that in his designs 'the quaintness of the so-called
Queen Anne style is studiously avoided'.[7] In effect this meant that his houses, and others on the
estate, especially the many houses designed by G. T. Robinson, were recognizably influenced by
'Queen Anne', but were a little stodgier, and a little closer to genuine Queen Anne or Georgian.
The public failed to differentiate and thought of the area as a 'Queen Anne' one. The style's
appearance in so well-heeled a neighbourhood was impressive evidence that it really had arrived,
and probably did as much as anything else to release the flood of 'Queen Anne' that followed in
the 1880s.

      The west side of Cadogan Square and (though some are grievously mutilated) the houses
69, 70 along Chelsea Embankment are the two most impressive surviving conglomerations of 'Queen
Anne'—for those, at any rate, who prefer their festive opulence to the diminutive prettiness of
Bedford Park. They set the tone for 'Queen Anne' terrace houses. These, although always trying
to be individual, were all clearly related to each other. Their common starting-point was the need
to be as different as possible from the stucco-faced housing of the previous generation. Stucco
was, of course, unthinkable, red brick an essential; stone dressings were little used until the
1890s. The typical London house plan, with staircase to one side and L-shaped drawing rooms
on the first floor, tended to be avoided, sensible and useful though it had proved itself to be.
Architects tried to find plots wider or deeper than was usual, and experimented with changes of
level, differences of ceiling height, and the use of top-lit staircases and internal light wells. The
more variety on skyline or façades, the better. Much of the variety came from the detailing.

70. Looking along the west side of Cadogan Square.

Houses were delicately prettified with carved brick panels by firms such as John M'Cullock of   71, 72
Kennington, ornamental plasterwork by Walter Smith of Lambeth and others, and wrought
ironwork by Thomas Elsley or Alfred Newman.

Variety and delicacy often had to be achieved in the teeth of the District Surveyor, and of
building regulations limiting the size and materials of projections. Shaw's oriels on Marcus
Stone's house in Melbury Road were only allowed because they were made of concrete.[8] The
regulation requiring window frames to be set back behind the building face was nicely calculated
to sabotage the delicacy which was an essential part of 'Queen Anne'. Clever architects did what
they could by chamfering the jambs or using other devices; the fact that most architects were
less enterprising explains the dreariness of most later 'Queen Anne' terrace houses.

Studios and Flats

Apart from the traditional hierarchy of London houses—free-standing in the roomier suburbs,
semi-detached and terraced towards the centre—'Queen Anne' had to deal with a number of
recently developed housing types, especially studio houses, flats, and studio flats. All of them had
existed before the 'Queen Anne' movement got under way, but to the problems of adaptation of
all of them it produced attractive and original solutions; and as studios were, by definition,
'artistic', and flats were considered progressive, it was not surprising that for ten or fifteen years
the bulk of buildings of this type were 'Queen Anne'.

Among them much the most publicity went to the artists' houses. They were recognized as
a new phenomenon of the age; numerous magazine articles were written about them; they
were the subject of a book by Maurice B. Adams, *Artists' Homes* (1883), based on his articles in
the *Building News*, and occupied pride of place in Mrs. Haweis's *Beautiful Houses* (1882). At first
sight it might seem strange that artists had to wait until the mid-nineteenth century for a specific
building type to be evolved for them. Various factors contributed to its appearance. The new
enthusiasm for art among the middle classes released an impressive amount of money into the
art world and enabled very considerable numbers of artists to live on the same scale as successful
barristers and businessmen, instead of in rented accommodation in unfashionable areas. Pre-
Raphaelitism brought daylight into painting and made studios lit by large areas of glass an
essential for most painters. Victorian theories of functional expression meant that any self-
respecting architect, when designing a house for an artist, had to make the big studio windows
a dominating element in the design. And artists, like the rest of the middle classes, became house-
proud and house-conscious, and ceased to be satisfied with utilitarian studios built in the gardens,
or tacked onto the backs, of houses bought off the peg.

But too much can be made of artists' houses as a separate phenomenon; basically, they were
a variant on other prosperous middle-class houses built by the artistic, with the artist receiving
in his studio replacing the hostess receiving in her drawing-room. Maurice B. Adams's remark, in
the Preface to *Artists' Homes*, that 'the public looked, with reason, to Artists to show them how
best to profit by the lessons learned from the first workers in our modern Art Revival' allotted
them a pace-setting role which was not really justified. A few artists, like Whistler, were architectural pioneers, and a few, like Millais, built houses that expressed their own tastes and
personality; but most artists' houses, including all the many designed by Shaw, were built in
the 'Queen Anne' style after it had already become established, and expressed the personality of
the architect rather than the artist.

To aspiring artists and hostesses on the make artistic houses were useful forms of advertisement, at once evidence that they had already arrived, and tools for further advancement. The
artists' world in London was a highly competitive one; however quickly the numbers of people

◁   **71, 72.** Details of 68 Cadogan Square, Chelsea.
By Norman Shaw, 1877–8.

73. (*Top*) Studios in Park Road, Hampstead. By T. K. Green, 1879.

74. (*Bottom*) Albert Hall Mansions, Kensington. By Norman Shaw, 1879–81.

ready to spend money on art were increasing, they were immediately counter-balanced by the numbers of artists springing into existence to cater for them. Competition was set into especially frenzied action on 'Show Sunday', the Sunday before the opening of the annual Royal Academy exhibition each May. On that day artists kept open house to the public, and the public flocked round the studios to see what was available. An artistic and prosperous exterior, an impressive ascent to the studio, and the final discovery of the artist surrounded by his pictures in a richly tasteful setting all helped in the bid for custom.[9]

From the 1870s onwards artists without the means to build their own houses could rent a studio or studio flat especially tailored to their needs. An apartment block of studios was built in King Henry's Road, Belsize Park, in about 1870; Luke Fildes had a studio there before moving to his Norman Shaw house in Melbury Road.[10] The block has been demolished, but is unlikely to have been 'Queen Anne' in style. 'Queen Anne' first appeared in this context in the studio flats designed by Godwin and Edis in Tite Street in the late 1870s and early 1880s. After that studios proliferated, both piled up one above the other and strung out horizontally. The accommodation attached to them could vary from a couple of small rooms to a sizeable house, but the uniform was almost always 'Queen Anne', though frequently in its most utilitarian form: huge windows criss-crossed by a grid of white-painted wooden glazing bars, a Flemish gable on the skyline, and very little else.[11]   73

Studio flats were only a specialized variant of residential flats, which appeared at much the same time. The first big block of flats in London was Queen Anne's Mansions in Queen Anne's Gate, but in spite of the name their style was far from being 'Queen Anne'. A year or two later the Albert Hall Mansions Company Limited took a lease from the 1851 Exhibition Commissioners of a site overlooking Kensington Gardens, next to the Albert Hall. Their first design did not please the Commissioners who brought in Norman Shaw in 1879, first as a consultant to improve the original design, and finally to produce a new one of his own. The result was so superbly confident   74 and competent that innumerable blocks of more-or-less 'Queen Anne' mansion flats quickly followed its lead in the 1880s, although they seldom approached the panache of Shaw's design.[12]

Houses by Norman Shaw

Apart from Albert Hall Mansions, between 1873 and 1881 Norman Shaw designed at least eighteen sizeable 'Queen Anne' houses, as well as considerable numbers of smaller houses, especially in Bedford Park. In 1888 William Morris was to write with approval of Shaw's 'elegantly fantastic Queen Anne houses at Chelsea',[13] and the description could equally well be applied to the whole group. Some were built as speculations, some for individual clients, some were terrace houses, some were free-standing, some were for artists, others were for businessmen. The differences were superficial; their similarity of materials, size, and style make them a unified group. As examples of the way in which an architect, at the height of his powers and creative abundance, selected a comparatively limited number of elements, played variations on them with inexhaustible resourcefulness, and, in doing so, so obviously enjoyed himself and set out to give enjoyment to others, the houses are unparalleled in English architecture except, perhaps, by the steeples of Wren's City churches. Wren's steeples are pure fantasy, with no functional purpose, except to advertise the whereabouts of the churches beneath them. Shaw's houses had to be lived in, but his genius could combine sense with nonsense and make fantasy work for his clients rather than against them. His chimneys drew, his drains worked, in his oriels and ingle-nooks children could curl up with a book or intimate groups draw out of the noise of a party.[14]

All the houses were in London or its suburbs, except for the house at Chigwell, which was within commuting distance of London and was built for a City businessman. The clients, in those

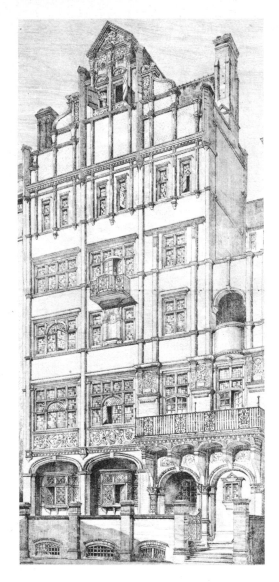

76. A sunflower at 196 Queen's Gate.

75. 196 Queen's Gate, Kensington. By Norman Shaw, 1874–6.

houses which were purpose built, were typical both of Shaw and 'Queen Anne'. They included only one aristocrat, the Hon. William Lowther, of Lowther Lodge. His wife was the last arrival among four high-minded and artistic hostesses who lived on Kensington Gore, the others being Lady Marion Alford, Lady Ashburton, and Lady Somers. Mrs. Lowther was an amateur artist, and her mind was so high that, according to one of her guests, 'at some of her entertainments it was not easy to tell where society ended and high thinking began'.[15]

75, 76, 77   Around the corner from Lowther Lodge, under the stylish Flemish gable of Shaw's 196 Queen's Gate, lived J. P. Heseltine, a rich stockbroker, an amateur engraver, and one of the most discriminating of late Victorian collectors. Shaw's clients on Chelsea Embankment included G. Matthey, a successful engineer, and Wickham Flower, a solicitor with artistic tastes. A. Savill, at Chigwell, was a partner in Shaw's family shipping line. Laurence Harrison, of Cadogan Square, was another stockbroker (and brother to Frederic Harrison). Jonathan Carr, of Tower House, Bedford Park, was an enlightened property developer.

Of the five artists for whom Shaw designed London houses in this period (in addition to the house which he built for himself), Edwin Long and Frank Holl, on Fitzjohn's Avenue, were already Academicians; Luke Fildes and Marcus Stone, in Melbury Road, and George Boughton, on

77. Looking up the front of 196 Queen's Gate.

79. Farnley House,
15 Chelsea Embankment.
By Norman Shaw, 1877–9.

Campden Hill, were all anxious to get into the Academy and well aware that a fashionable house by Shaw would help them on their way. Frank Holl's was the last of the group to be built, and the only one whose design suggests that Shaw was beginning to be bored with 'Queen Anne'. He was, indeed, about to move on to other things; but he returned to 'Queen Anne' a few years later with Kate Greenaway's house on Frognal (1885), and a country house for the Hon. Francis Baring at Banstead Wood (1884), both charming and original designs.

The elements of Shaw's London houses had all been used already, by Shaw or other architects in the 'Queen Anne' circle. But Shaw had the ability to use and re-use them in constantly different combinations, so that each new design had the freshness of a new creation: one can still sense, through the pages of late Victorian building magazines, the feelings of amazement and delight evoked among his contemporaries as year by year each new glittering drawing showed that he had done it yet again.

In his compositions Shaw rang all the changes from total asymmetry to complete, or almost complete, symmetry. At one end of the scale is his own house in Ellerdale Road and at the other his Chelsea Embankment houses (with the exception of G. Matthey's Cheyne House), in particular Wickham Flower's Swan House. The differences grew out of the different characters of the Embankment and Ellerdale Road. Swan House (which was designed in 1875) is a terrace house with other houses to either side, so that all the passer-by ever sees is the entrance front; the site is a flat one along the river, and the dominant feature of the house is the long drawing room filling the whole length of the façade and placed up on the second floor to get a better view of the river. It was a site and a plan that suggested formality and Shaw abandoned himself to the pleasure of almost complete symmetry, though with a different window pattern for each floor; the only deviation is in the position of the great chimney-stack, and this is scarcely noticeable except from across the river.[16]

78, 79

◁ **78.** Old Swan House, 17 Chelsea Embankment.
By Norman Shaw, 1875–7.

ARTISTS' HOMES Nº 24. MR NORMAN SHAW'S HOUSE. ELLERDALE ROAD. HAMPSTEAD.
R NORMAN SHAW. R.A. ARCHITECT.

80. 6 Ellerdale Road, Hampstead. By Norman Shaw, 1874–6.

81. Studio house for Marcus Stone, 8 Melbury Road, Kensington. By Norman Shaw, 1875–6.

Shaw's own house, on the other hand, (designed in 1874) occupied a corner site with its   80
main front sloping sharply downhill from east to west; the site worked against symmetry and
Shaw went along with it and produced a design whose whole strength and originality lies in the
contrast between the left- and right-hand sides. But, as always with Shaw, this contrast grows
out of the plan; the different floor levels and window treatment of the left-hand section express
the fact that it contains the great dining-room, the highest and biggest room in the house.

More usually in Shaw's 'Queen Anne' houses, however, elements of symmetry are skilfully
played against elements of asymmetry. His two houses in Melbury Road, for instance (both
designed in 1876), are nice examples of asymmetry within symmetry and symmetry within
asymmetry, looking at each other across the road, so that the two houses form a contrasting but
obviously related pair.[17] The difference is conditioned by the fact that both houses have north-
facing studios, with the result that the studio of the Marcus Stone house looks on to the street and
that of the Luke Fildes house on to the garden. The street front of the Marcus Stone house is   81
dominated by its studio. This is expressed externally by a row of three oriel windows under (in
the original design) three tile-hung gables. The combination of these gables and oriels with the
front door, which is under the middle oriel, is so strong that the front gives a first impression of
being symmetrical; but in fact everything else—the ground-floor fenestration, the corner chimney-
stack, the wing—is asymmetrical, as is the side elevation. The Luke Fildes house drops back from   82, 83
the road on three planes, in the last of which a tall window and a balcony show the whereabouts
of the studio; on the garden side its five huge windows introduce a strong element of symmetry,

82. (*Right*) Studio house for Luke Fildes, 31 Melbury Road, Kensington. By Norman Shaw, 1875–7.

83. (*Below*) Elevations and plans of 31 Melbury Road.

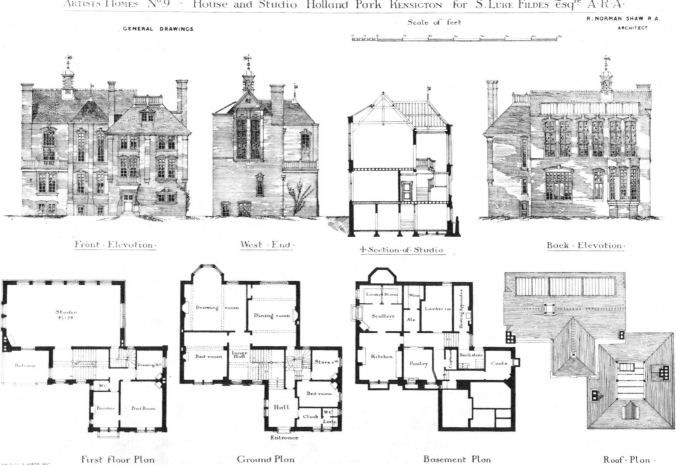

ARTISTS' HOMES Nº 9 · House and Studio Holland Park Kensington for S. Luke Fildes esqre A·R·A·

GENERAL DRAWINGS

Scale of feet

R. NORMAN SHAW R.A.
ARCHITECT

· Front · Elevation ·   · West · End ·   ✝ Section · of · Studio   · Back · Elevation ·

First floor Plan   Ground Plan   Basement Plan   Roof · Plan ·

but from the street the house gives a first impression of an irregular and almost rambling design. Closer inspection shows that the entrance block is, from the first floor up, basically a symmetrical pavilion of elegant artificiality, from its two pairs of paired windows to the railed-off platform surmounting the hipped roof. But a final examination shows that within this symmetry there are a number of small deviations; the pair of windows over the entrance, for instance, which let on to a balcony, have minor variations in their glazing from the adjoining pair; the main chimney-stack is symmetrical as regards the fenestration beneath it, but asymmetrical as regards the hipped roof.

Bay or oriel windows are prominent in almost all the houses. It is worth looking at their variations as examples of Shaw's resourcefulness. He used three main types: the 'Sparrowe's House' type, with curved sides and a flat front, all glazed with leaded lights and with the central light arched; the eighteenth-century shop-window type, glazed continuously with small lights and wooden glazing bars; and the ordinary brick bay window, either three-sided or five-sided.

The variations and combinations are endless. Sparrowe's House windows could come with or without pargeting, or pediments above the central light; the arch could be omitted; the leaded lights could be replaced with eighteenth-century glazing bars; the windows could come singly or in sets of three, and be run through two or three floors or confined to a single storey; they could dominate a façade with huge billowing expanses of glass or be reduced to miniature lanterns delicately skied up in a gable, as at 72 Cadogan Square. Brick bay windows could be lit by openings 84 divided by stone mullions, as in the George Boughton house, or by segmental leaded openings framed with brick mouldings in the early eighteenth-century manner; the latter could be glazed with small-paned sashes, as in 68 and 72 Cadogan Square, or with leaded casements, as in Ellerdale Road; the bay could be surmounted by balconies of wrought iron or white painted wood. One type of window could be contrasted with another, as in Ellerdale Road, where a three-storey Sparrowe's House oriel starting at the first floor is set against a bigger and bolder brick bay going down to the ground; or one type could be run into another, as at 68 Cadogan Square 84 where a three-storey brick bay is changed, at ground-floor level, into a wooden oriel with white painted glazing bars of Georgian shop-front type. It was typical of Shaw that the more fragile and delicate-looking element comes beneath the stronger one, so that it gives an impression of being suspended from, rather than supporting, the brickwork above it. A similar device is used at Swan House, where the second and third floors overhang the lower half of the house by several feet, and three Sparrowe's House windows are suspended beneath the overhang; a final touch of elegance and fantasy is given by alternating elongated sash windows in the floor above with immensely elongated oriel windows; their contrast in shape and style from the oriels beneath them nicely expressed the fact that they lit the long drawing-room, used for formal entertaining, whereas the more homely Sparrowe's House oriels lit the family living-room on the floor below.

A final conceit which Shaw quite often indulged in was what might be called false oriels, that is, windows projecting only a few inches from the wall surface. There are several of these at Lowther Lodge, projecting quite boldly and carried up through the cornice to become pedimented 41 dormers; similar projecting windows at the Luke Fildes house are only one brick deep; at Ellerdale Road the central light of a Sparrowe's House oriel has been flattened against the upper storey and hung from the coved cornice like a flag.

The interiors of Shaw's 'Queen Anne' houses are notable for two features, the varied and carefully contrived routes from front door to drawing-room or studio, and the ingenious way in which, in some of the houses, rooms of different heights are packed together on different levels. At Swan House the staircase well spreads out to twice its original size when the stairs finally emerge on the second-floor gallery, outside the drawing-room; at the Marcus Stone house the main run of the staircase goes right through the house from front to back, transferring the visitor in the process from the low entrance hall to the spacious and lofty upper staircase well leading

Hovses·in·Cadogan·Sqͬ·Chelsea·
R·Norman·Shaw·RA·ARCHITECT·

84. 68 and 72 Cadogan Square, Chelsea. By Norman Shaw, 1877–9. As built the houses were separated by another, designed by A. J. Adams.

to the studio. The low inglenook and coved roof of the drawing-room are neatly fitted under the slope and the half-landings of the staircase, and another half-landing leads to an intermediate floor of lower bedrooms. This use of half-landings to give access to rooms of different heights to those on the main floors had appeared in London houses from at least the 1860s; Shaw, in some though by no means all of his 'Queen Anne' houses, developed it much further, and expressed instead of disguising it on the external elevations, in order to achieve effective contrasts of fenestration.

Such a contrast, as already discussed, is very evident on the external elevations of Shaw's own house in Ellerdale Road, which is perhaps his most notable exercise in this particular vein. His play with levels enabled him to fit the lofty dining-room and the low and much more intimate drawing-room on the same floor and make the house centre on their contrast in character. The detailing of both rooms was typical of 'Queen Anne' eclecticism; fortunately, drawings and photographs survive to show their original appearance.[18] The drawing-room, one of the most   **85** successful and original of 'Queen Anne' interiors, was divided into sections by screens of stumpy columns; in the centre was a marble chimney-piece of late eighteenth-century type, but fitted with a low overmantel for china and lined with gay contemporary tiles; above it was a plaster-work frieze of Elizabethan character; the joinery of the screens was, if anything, early eighteenth century in inspiration, but given an individual twist; the furniture was mainly eighteenth century but there was a spinning-wheel by the fire-place. The big dining-room (which was used as a   **86** dining-living-room) had an 'Old English' inglenook, stamped leather on the walls, bolection-moulded panelling, much oriental porcelain, and a strong French Renaissance element in the exposed beams of the ceiling and the detailing of the internal window over the inglenook. This gave onto Shaw's own personal sanctum, a minute studio approached from the dining-room by its own staircase, with views down into the dining-room through the internal window, and over the whole of London from little external windows to either side of the chimney-breast. Shaw had, of course, a separate office in Bloomsbury Square, but it was in this little hideaway that he drew the preliminary designs and worked out the details for all his amazing series of buildings.

85, 86. The drawing-room and (*right*) dining-room in Shaw's own house in Ellerdale Road, Hampstead.

Pink shews Red Brickwork.
Red shews Gauged Brickwork.

FRONT ELEVATION.

BACK ELEVATION.

87. Designs by J. J. Stevenson for 44 (originally 185) Pont Street, Chelsea, 1876.

88. A detail from over the door of 77 Cadogan Square, Chelsea. By J. J. Stevenson, *c.* 1881.

Houses by J. J. Stevenson

In moving from the houses of Norman Shaw to those of J. J. Stevenson one experiences a marked change in temperature. Stevenson described 'Queen Anne' with a quotation as 'simple and homely',

> Not too great or good
> For human nature's daily food.[19]

Shaw's Marcus Stone house was also described by Maurice B. Adams as 'quiet and homely'[20] but in spite of this, and the spinning-wheel in Shaw's drawing-room, one suspects that Stevenson had a more genuine taste for the unassuming. The dash and sparkle of Shaw's best buildings suggest an inheritance from his n'er-do-well Irish father. With Stevenson one is always conscious, through the fashionable 'Queen Anne' trimmings, and in spite of one's knowledge of his own jaunty social manner, of a Lowland Scots background—sensible, prosperous, and a little staid.

Stevenson's 'Queen Anne' houses can be approximately divided into three groups: the London terrace houses designed for or through the Makins family; the free-standing houses designed for his own family, or for artists and dons in London, Cambridge, and Oxford; and Ken Hill, his only 'Queen Anne' country house. His later terrace housing, at Kensington Court, Park Street in Mayfair, and Buckingham Palace Road, were designed when 'Queen Anne' was being injected with new elements and turning into something rather different; in Stevenson's case, the results were not especially interesting.

Almost all the earlier terrace houses derive from the formula of Stevenson's own Red House in Bayswater. The Red House (1871–3) and the similar house designed for H. F. Makins in Palace Green (1873) have already been described in Chapter III. For or through the latter's brother, W. H. Makins, chairman of the Cadogan and Hans Place Estate Company, Stevenson designed two adjoining houses in Lowther Gardens, off Exhibition Road, Kensington, and two large blocks of houses in Cadogan Square and Pont Street. The Lowther Gardens houses were completed by 1878, in which year they were illustrated in the *Building News*; the larger of the two was built as Colonel Makins's own house, and incorporated his initials, the smaller (though still far from small) house was built and sold as a speculation. In Chelsea, numbers 42–58 Pont Street were designed and built in 1876–8; the block filling the south side of Cadogan Square (numbers 63–79) was already projected in 1879, but the first half seems not to have been built until about 1881–3, and the rest not finished until 1886. The Pont Street houses were described in the *Building News* of 17 January 1879, soon after their completion; like earlier speculative

87

89

89. 63–73 Cadogan Square, Chelsea. By J. J. Stevenson, *c.* 1885–6.

housing in the 1850s and 1860s they were offered for sale ready decorated, with tasteful colour schemes executed by 'Mr. Chevalier of Westbourne Grove'.[21]

Stevenson's answer to the problem of designing a block of nine adjoining houses was to keep the plans, sizes, and floor levels the same but give each house a slightly different façade. It was a new solution for speculative terrace housing in London or, as far as I know, anywhere else, and was to be widely imitated; but it was not a very felicitous one. Unless developed with the ebullience of Ernest George, who in Harrington Gardens a few years later made each house wildly different from its neighbour in every way, it meant that the rhythm of the houses was confused by their architecture instead of accentuated by it; the varieties in the detailing fight against the regular lines of the windows. Shaw, faced with a similar problem on a large scale at Albert Hall Mansions and E. J. May, working on a small scale in Priory Gardens, Bedford Park, went in for a regular rhythm, with much more effective results.

90, 91   The best of Stevenson's terrace houses are the pair in Lowther Gardens, largely because there are only two of them; one sets off the other, without the total effect becoming confused, and on their (originally) island site they form a single sculptural mass. Their composition is typically 'Queen Anne'. Asymmetry on the Exhibition Road frontage is combined and contrasted with symmetry round the corner, but into this symmetry is inserted a picturesquely off-centre entrance to the Makins house: a balustraded flight of steps leads up to a little porch playfully
92   tucked under one of the two boldly projecting arches which support the first-floor balcony. It was a piece of detailing understandably admired and sketched at the time. Stevenson's detailing in general, his gaily broken pediments, panels of swags or foliage in brick or terracotta, fan-lights, delicate wrought-ironwork and intimately arched porches, is always agreeable, even
88, 93   when the architectural effect as a whole is disappointing.

90, 91. 1–2 Lowther Gardens, Kensington
and (*below*) plans of 1 Lowther Gardens.
By J. J. Stevenson, *c.* 1877–8.

92. (*Right*) The entrance to 1 Lowther Gardens.

93. Detail of 1 Lowther Gardens, Kensington, by J. J. Stevenson, *c.* 1877–8.

Even so it is a relief to turn to the second group of Stevenson's houses, designed on detached sites to suit the tastes of clients who were usually his relatives or friends, rather than artificially 94–98 varied as bait for prospective buyers. The group contains at least seven houses. Southgarth, in Westoe village, South Shields, a few miles from the Jarrow Chemical Works, was designed in about 1874–5 for his brother Archibald. In 1876 he designed a studio house in Melbury Road for Colin Hunter, a Scottish seascape-painter recently arrived from Glasgow. In 1881 he designed two adjoining (but detached) houses on St. John's College land, 27 and 29 Banbury Road, Oxford. No. 29 was for his brother-in-law, T. S. Omond, the bursar of St. John's; Omond probably IV introduced him to Thomas Hill Green, the Balliol philosopher, who was the client for 27. One suspects that his work for Green led him to Alfred Marshall, the economist, who moved from Balliol to Cambridge in 1884, and employed Stevenson to design Balliol Croft, in Madingley Road, Cambridge, in about 1885. In 1883 he had designed the largest and (even before recent alterations) least interesting house in the group, 1 Fitzjohn's Avenue, Hampstead, for Gavin Anderson, one of his Orient Line cousins. In about 1890 he converted the Old Granary, on the Backs at Cambridge, for Charles Darwin's son, George. All these are documented; two more houses in Cambridge, 5 and 6 Selwyn Gardens, can be attributed to him with reasonable confidence. They

94. (*Left*) 27 Banbury Road, Oxford. Designed for
T. H. Green by J. J. Stevenson, 1881.

95. (*Below*) Studio house for Colin Hunter,
14 Melbury Road, Kensington. By J. J. Stevenson,
1876–8. (Demolished.)

96. Balliol Croft, Madingley Road, Cambridge. Designed by J. J. Stevenson for Alfred Marshall, *c.* 1885.

were first occupied, in the late 1880s, by two Trinity dons: A. W. Verrall, an eminent classical scholar, and James Ward, a pioneer of psychology. Their windows have identical detailing to windows at Balliol Croft, and Mrs. Verrall had been friends with Mrs. Marshall since they had been at Newnham together.[22]

Unassuming, but never dim, pleasantly irregular but never quaint, these houses are amongst the most agreeable products of the 'Queen Anne' movement. At Southgarth the irregularity of the fenestration is pulled together by the big gable and boldly projecting oriel, at the two houses
94 in Banbury Road by the dominating hipped roof, crowned with wooden balustrades and great chimney-stacks linked by arches; the first-floor bay window supported by iron columns on the first floor of T. H. Green's house appears to be a deliberate reminiscence of the similar window at Rossetti's house in Cheyne Walk.[23] This low and easy-going house designed for Colin Hunter
95 in Melbury Road must, before its destruction in the last war, have made an agreeable contrast to Shaw's more fanciful pair up the road.[24] The two houses in Selwyn Gardens are delicate and
98 pleasing designs, with sensitively irregular fenestration and a reticent sprinkling of brick mouldings and pilasters. The smallest, cheapest, and most original house in the group is Balliol Croft.
96 A dormer window is pushed to one end of its roof like a little turret, a timber veranda lets out of a first-floor study, a miniature bay window projects from the drawing-room, and the roof slopes down the back of the house almost to the ground; there is no ornament and no fuss, but
97 the result is entirely delightful. The Old Granary, with its first-floor veranda (obviously related to that at Balliol Croft) sticking out above the Cam, is equally full of character.[25]

97. The Old Granary,
Silver Street, Cambridge.
By J. J. Stevenson, *c.* 1890.

98. 5 Selwyn Gardens,
Cambridge. Probably by
J. J. Stevenson, *c.* 1888.

It is worth taking a closer look at Stevenson's clients at Balliol Croft and in Banbury Road, for they were ideally progressive 'Queen Anne' material, even if they exuded more light than sweetness. T. H. Green was the son of a Church of England clergyman, but himself a Christian who rejected all dogmatic theology.[26] He was at Rugby with Henry Sidgwick, who became a close friend. In 1871 he married the sister of John Addington Symonds, the historian of the Renaissance. From 1860 until his early death in 1882 he was a tutor at Balliol College, and as such figures prominently as 'Professor Grey' in Mrs. Humphry Ward's *Robert Elsmere*. Although he published comparatively little, his influence as a teacher can scarcely be over-estimated. He was amongst those who provided the serious-minded middle classes of the later nineteenth century with a new religion of undogmatic but deeply felt theology combined with dedication to the service of others. Among those he influenced were Arnold Toynbee, whose teaching was to lead to the foundation of Toynbee College as an institution where educated people could help the inhabitants of the East End of London without patronizing them; and Canon Scott-Holland and Bishop Gore, whose Christian Social Union converted a substantial portion of the High Church movement to socialism. Green himself was one of the first members of the University to take a prominent part in local politics, as a citizen rather than a don; he sat on Oxford City Council from 1876 until his death, and took a prominent part in the foundation of Oxford Grammar School; he passionately resented all forms of snobbery, which he thought the cancer of English society. He was a committed Temperance advocate, belonged to every Temperance organization in Oxford, and set up a coffee tavern in 1875. He was a shy and not at all an easy character but his complete integrity and basic goodness inspired great affection; his funeral cortège was attended through the pouring rain by over 2,000 mourners. It is a tribute to the elasticity of 'Queen Anne' that it could cater for Green as well as for aesthetic hostesses; Stevenson gave him exactly what he needed, a comfortable middle-class house with no frills but plenty of quality; sadly, he died before he could move into it.

Alfred Marshall is generally recognized as the father of modern economics. The *Principles of Economics* and most of his other books and articles were written in his first-floor study at Balliol Croft. He married Mary Paley, whom we met a few chapters back embroidering her tennis dress with pomegranates in her room at Newnham, where she was one of the first students. The Marshalls were socialists and had only one servant—an adventurous set-up for a Victorian professor and his wife. They had no children; the modest unpretentiousness of Balliol Croft suited them to perfection. Alfred Marshall exerted considerable influence on its design. The study was on the first floor because he 'thought that in Cambridge it was as well to live as far from the ground as possible'; he originally wanted it on the second floor, but Stevenson persuaded him to come down a storey. He insisted that the dining-room and sitting-room should be capable of being run together for entertainments, and designed the fittings for the little kitchen, likened to 'a ship's cabin'. For visitors 'the unvarying character of the surroundings—upstairs the books and nests of drawers containing manuscript, downstairs the Michelangelo figures from the Sistine Chapel let into the furniture, and at the door the face of Sarah the maid—had a charm and fascination for those who paid visits to their Master year after year, like the Cell or Oratory of a Sage'.[27]

Stevenson was probably more at home in donnish than country-house circles; his country-house commission at Ken Hill[28] came to him because a family with a very similar background to his own had made enough money to adventure into the landed gentry. Edward Green's family motto 'Waste not' hints at the origin of the family fortune, which came from 'Green's Economizer', an ingenious device for re-channelling the steam which escaped from industrial boilers. The Greens, like other Victorian industrialists, patronized contemporary artists, and their collection included pictures by Spencer Stanhope and by Whistler's friend Thomas Armstrong. It was almost certainly Armstrong who recommended them to employ Thomas Jeckyll, an interesting artist on

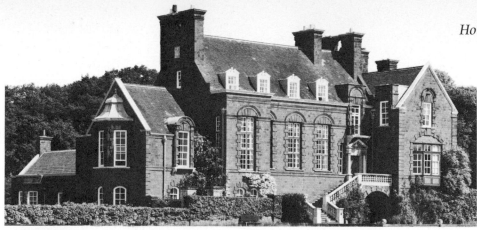

99. Ken Hill,
Snettisham, Norfolk.
By J. J. Stevenson,
1879–81.

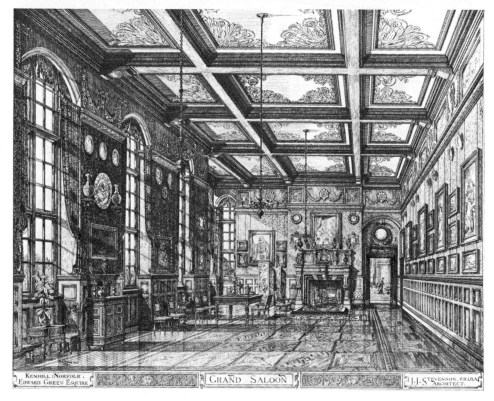

100. The hall or saloon
at Ken Hill. From a
drawing by A. J. Adams,
1880.

the fringe of the Whistler–Rossetti circle, to design furniture for the house they rented outside Wakefield from the 1860s; and it was probably Armstrong who put them in touch with Stevenson, when they decided to build a country house of their own.

Ken Hill is a beautiful example of the 'Queen Anne' approach, of what Goodhart-Rendel called the 'Gothic game played with classical counters', Stevenson took the plan of a typical medieval hall-house, adapted it for nineteenth-century use, and translated all the details into eighteenth-century idiom. The main rooms are raised up on, so to speak, an undercroft, in fact containing kitchens, servants' rooms, and smoking-room; the screen passage becomes the entrance hall, the medieval great hall becomes a living-hall in the Shaw–Nesfield manner, and the solar beyond it a drawing-room decorated in the Adam style. The wing to the right of the entrance contains the dining-room and main bedrooms, the bachelors were tucked away under the roof above the hall. The result is an enjoyable and original design, but one that bred no imitations, probably because it was too far removed from the accepted Victorian image of a country house. The *Building News* commented that it was 'picturesque enough and quaint, but not very like a gentleman's house'.[29]

99

100

Houses by Other Architects

During the 1870s Philip Webb drew further and further apart from the 'Queen Anne' architects. This was partly because 'Queen Anne' had become fashionable and Webb had an instinctive dislike of being fashionable; but it was also because the cleverness and conscious prettiness of many 'Queen Anne' buildings was repugnant to him. His assistant, George Jack, later wrote that 'he frequently impressed upon me the value of the Commonplace';[30] what he aimed at was honest traditional building. Moreover, he had always disliked copying, especially copying ornament; the increasing repertory of pretty period details which was appearing in 'Queen Anne' buildings was not at all to his taste, however great the skill with which they were mixed together, or the originality of the final result. He expressed his point of view in a letter to his friend and client Percy Wyndham, written in 1886. Wyndham had written to Webb describing Clouds, the house in Wiltshire which Webb had designed for him, as 'the house of the age'. Webb replied: 'There are two classes of houses which would rightly come under the title. The first is the majority one, the natural style of a "shoddy period", of which the houses in Tyburn, Belgravia, Victoria Street, etc., and their kind in the country, give the type which might be called Victorian. The second is the non-natural class, of which the mediaeval style is represented by the Law Courts, the scholastic by the British Museum, the showy by the Club houses, and the dilettante-picturesque by the so-called Queen Anne style. All these styles are exceedingly artificial, and have been run to death by fashion.'[31]

The design of Clouds develops out of those of Webb's buildings of the 1860s which were built before G. P. Boyce's house in Glebe Place. It was as though Webb were deliberately disassociating himself from the 'Queen Anne' movement and his own former association with it. Probably the last of his buildings which can reasonably be described as 'Queen Anne' is Smeaton
101   Manor in Yorkshire, one of Webb's most attractive works, designed for Lowthian Bell's son-in-law Major Godman in 1877, and built in 1877–9. The house is 'Queen Anne' in its predominantly but not completely eighteenth-century character, its mixture of symmetry with asymmetry and of hipped roof with gables, its bold chimney-stacks and its combination of different window rhythms on different floors. But it has no elaborate period ornament or strikingly picturesque detailing; it is 'Queen Anne' with the quaintness and the frills left out.[32]

101. Smeaton Manor, Yorkshire. By Philip Webb, 1877–9.

Like Webb, Nesfield also faded from the 'Queen Anne' scene in the 1870s, but for different reasons. It was not that he reacted against 'Queen Anne' but that, either because of ill health or for other reasons that remain obscure, he produced less and less work—practically none at all from 1880 until his early death in 1888. His last known 'Queen Anne' buildings were a Flemish-gabled house in Westcombe Park, Greenwich, designed for Garrard in 1879, and Loughton Hall in Essex, designed for the Revd. J. W. Maitland (whose sister was married to his cousin) in 1878.[33] The latter has huge gabled bay windows pushing up in front of its capacious hipped roof on the entrance side, and a garden front which is completely symmetrical except for the off-centre cupola and chimney-stack. It is a lively and genial design, but shows the influence of Shaw much more strongly than Nesfield's earlier 'Queen Anne' work. It suggests, as was in fact the case, that Shaw was on the way up and Nesfield, though still a force to be reckoned with, was on the way down.

102

Of Gilbert Scott's old pupils Bodley designed a distinguished, if not startlingly original, house on Chelsea Embankment in 1876 for the Hon. John Charles Dundas, M.P., for whose sister-in-law he had recently designed his ecclesiastical masterpiece, the Church of the Holy Angels at Hoar Cross. No. 3 Chelsea Embankment[34] has a handsome symmetrical front (but with an off-centre cupola), is rich in brick pediments and Flemish gables, and is built of brown stock bricks with red-brick dressings in the manner revived by Stevenson. Robson was increasingly absorbed by his work for the London School Board, but in about 1876 designed an agreeable group of red-brick houses with Flemish gables on the east side of Wandsworth Common, one of them for Miss Peddie; a few years later he was responsible for another group near to Nesfield's house in Westcombe Park, Greenwich.[35]

103, 104

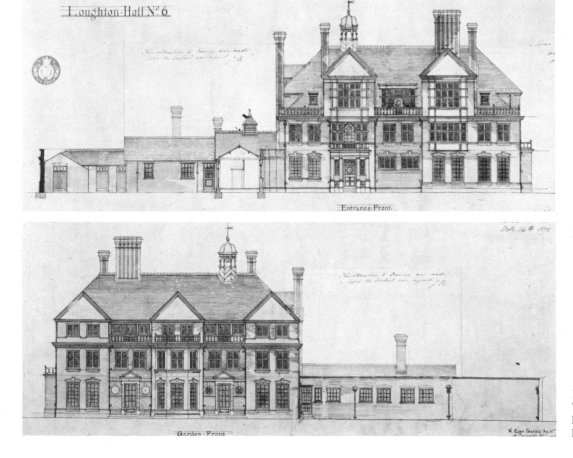

102. Designs by W. E. Nesfield for Loughton Hall, Essex, 1878.

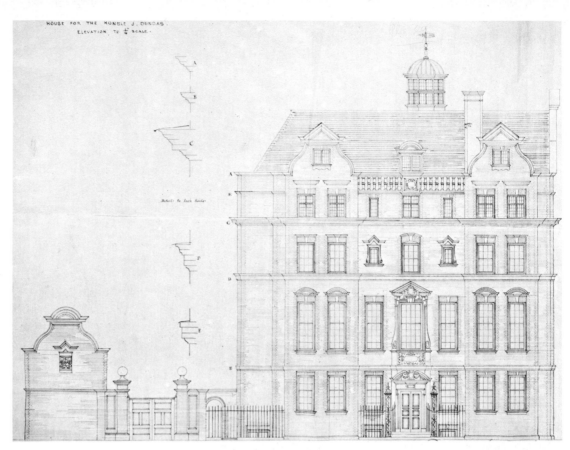

103. Design by G. F. Bodley for 3 Chelsea Embankment, 1876.

104. The oriel window at 3 Chelsea Embankment.

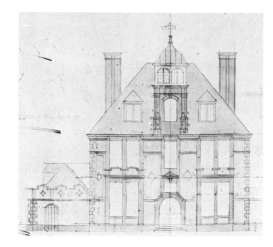

105. (*Left*) Design by G. G. Scott, jun., for houses in Salisbury Street, Westbourne Park, Hull, 1876.

106. (*Below*) Two of Scott's Salisbury Street houses.

G. G. Scott, junior, was especially active in the mid 1870s, when he produced a group of 'Queen Anne' designs of the greatest charm. The best of them, an enchantingly dainty little house for Arthur H. Whipham of Middlesbrough, designed in 1874–5, was unfortunately never built, but the working details were adapted for a modest vicarage at Woolton Hill, near Newbury, designed and built in 1874–7. A slightly more elaborate new wing was added to the vicarage at Pevensey in 1876–7.[36] In 1876 Scott designed a remarkable group of houses along the west side of Salisbury Street, in Westbourne Park, Hull.[37] His client was his cousin, John Spyvee Cooper, a solicitor in the firm of Scott and Cooper, who were the agents for the Westbourne Park estate; one of the houses was for Cooper himself. The houses are built to a variety of designs, all with prominent hipped roofs but some free-standing, some semi-detached, some with Flemish gables, others with little domed turrets (from which the domes have been removed). They are built in a distinctive combination of Portland cement panels framed with rubbed red brick; it results in a gay and unusual uniform of red and white, reminiscent of Scott's earlier two-coloured stripings at Garboldisham and Leamington.

III

105, 106

107. Manor Farm, Frognal, Hampstead, designed by Basil Champneys for himself, 1879–80.

108. House by Champneys in Branksome Park, Bournemouth, *c.* 1878.

109. St. Chad's, Grange Road, Cambridge. Probably by Champneys, *c.* 1880.

110. Design for a house in Grove Park, Kent. By Ernest Newton, 1879.

Champneys was also designing houses in the later 1870s and 1880s. They did not radically develop on his earlier manner but were still full of character and charm. A big house in Branksome 108 Park, a select suburb of Bournemouth, was a typical example of his style; it was built about 1878 for James Rhoades, but has unfortunately been demolished in recent years.[38] His own house in Hampstead, built about 1879–80, fortunately survives. Its name, Manor Farm, sums up rather 107 too exactly the spuriously rural element in 'Queen Anne'; but it is an extremely pleasing building, dominated by a huge hipped roof which rises up behind shaped gables to a little belvedere platform (from which the balustrade was removed a few years ago), with a brick chimney-stack at each corner. The kitchen, instead of being hidden away in a basement or back yard, was allowed a prominent window on the ground floor next to the front door—an example of a modest but undeniable relaxation of mid-Victorian snobbery in keeping with the spirit of 'Queen Anne'.[39]

A little batch of Champneys houses survives relatively unaltered at South Ascot. They were built in about 1884–6 by the Ascot and Sunninghill Estate Company in which Champneys had a financial stake.[40] Another house, rather grander than anything at South Ascot, that has all the appearance of being by Champneys is St. Chad's, in Grange Road, West Cambridge. The fact 109 that it was built (in about 1880) for a Trinity College don, the Revd. Robert Burn, supplies a possible connection with Champneys, and the house, especially on its garden front where weatherboarded gables project over bay-windows of Sparrowe's House type, has a welcoming prettiness that is very suggestive of him.[41]

From the 1870s Shaw's former assistants, including Edward Schroder Prior (1852–1932), William West Neve (1852–1942), Mervyn Macartney (1853–1941), Edward John May (1853–1941), and Ernest Newton (1856–1922) were beginning to set up in independent practice. They all started very much under Shaw's influence, however much they later developed away from it. May's work at Bedford Park is described in Chapter VII. Early work by Ernest Newton could be 110 seen in abundance at Grove Park, an estate near Eltham belonging to the Earl of Northbrook,

111. The Red House, Byron Hill Road, Harrow. By E. S. Prior, 1883.

where from 1879 onwards he designed a public house and a good deal of housing. The result must have been the prettiest and most accomplished of the various estates built under the influence of Bedford Park in the 1880s, but little of it has survived. Prior's early work includes, in addition to his housing at West Bay in Dorset (for which see Chapter VIII), an interesting group on Byron Hill Road, Harrow, the Red House of 1883, and its slightly later neighbour, Byron Cross, which has been demolished. Both were recognizably in Shaw's 'Queen Anne' manner, but Byron Cross, with an ingeniously irregular plan, and the Red House, with an up-and-down roof and oriels or bays of different shapes and sizes projecting in all directions, already showed signs of the whimsicality that was to typify Prior's later houses.[42]

A row of houses by T. E. Collcutt, in Nightingale Lane, Wandsworth, is a slightly unusual example of the numerous 'Queen Anne' houses being designed by other architects. It dates from about 1879 and shows the idiosyncrasies of the client, a sanitary engineer called Jenning; the houses are built of a mixture of glazed brick and shiny washable terracotta, and were provided with all the most up-to-date sanitary and ventilating fittings.[43] More conventional 'Queen Anne' designs, by Collcutt, J. D. Sedding, A. J. Adams, John Belcher, Arthur Cawston, Batterbury & Huxley, George Sherrin, George Vigers, and other architects, stud the pages of the building journals in the later 1870s and the 1880s; almost all of them are agreeable and many must still be in existence and awaiting identification. So must others by local men picking up London fashions, such as W. L. Sugden of Leek, or Asahel P. Bell and George Freeth Roper of Manchester. Sugden's work in and around Leek (already referred to in Chapter IV) includes a good many

112. House in Portland Street, Leek, Staffordshire. ▷
Probably by W. L. Sugden, *c.* 1885.

113. House in Westoe,
South Shields, Durham.
By Henry Grieves, 1882.

houses, some of them rather pedestrian exercises in the Norman Shaw manner, others (by or attributable to Sugden) with entertainingly eccentric detailing. The area in the vicinity of Newnham College, Cambridge, is thick with 'Queen Anne' houses, some apparently by London architects (such as the houses in Selwyn Gardens and Grange Road attributed to Stevenson and Champneys) but the majority by Cambridge men such as T. H. Fawcett.

Another minor centre of 'Queen Anne' is South Shields in Durham. Here J. J. Stevenson, whose brothers lived in South Shields and ran the family chemical works there, provided a link with London, in the same kind of way as Morris and Shaw provided one in Leek. Stevenson's former clerk of the Works, T. A. Page, set up on his own in South Shields in the 1870s and did much work in and around the town. But one of the best examples of 'Queen Anne' in the area is by an otherwise obscure architect, Henry Grieves. He was responsible for the wing, ending in
113   a Flemish gable and oriel window, which a local shipowner, T. B. Barker, built on to Winterbottom House to contain a picture gallery in 1882.[44] The house is one of those along the long tree-lined village street of Westoe, on the edge of South Shields, next door to the 'Queen Anne' house which Stevenson had built for his brother Archibald a few years earlier; it is one of a number of biggish houses, most of them more or less 'Queen Anne', which the Victorian plutocracy of South Shields slotted in between the pleasant eighteenth-century houses which had previously lined the street.

114. Unexecuted design by Ernest Newton for Fremington House, Devon, 1882.

115. Dunley House, near Dorking, Surrey. By Ernest George and Peto, 1887.

The houses described in this chapter have almost all been in, or on the edge of, towns. There were comparatively few 'Queen Anne' country houses. Apart from those already described, three examples are worth a brief mention. Woodcote Hall in Shropshire (1876) is by Frederick Pepys Cockerell, a fringe member of 'Queen Anne' circles, a charming and lively man, but not a very good architect. Woodcote seems to be the result of an attempt to make 'Queen Anne' sufficiently important for a country house by leaving out the style's more fanciful elements and putting the accent on symmetry; the result is a fairly straightforward imitation of seventeenth-century houses of the type of Raynham or Swakeleys. Two later country houses, Fremington House near Barnstaple in Devon, by Ernest Newton (1882), and Dunley House near Dorking, by Ernest George and Peto (1887), are more in the spirit of 'Queen Anne' in their asymmetry and genial mixture of motifs from different periods; but the design for Fremington was never carried out.[45]

114, 115

'Queen Anne' failed to make more than a marginal impact on the country house world for three main reasons. It was not considered dignified enough; its image was too much a middle-class one; and it was thought of as a town style, for no very good reason except that the first 'Queen Anne' buildings to come to the public notice had been in London. Yet a few more houses like Bodrhyddan, Ken Hill, Smeaton, Loughton, Dunley, or Fremington would have provided a welcome relief to the eternal Gothic or Elizabethan considered suitable for the later Victorian landed classes.

VI   Fitting Out the House Beautiful

Furnishings

The outside of a 'Queen Anne' house had a consistency of style which was not to be expected inside. The outside used an architectural vocabulary which, however eclectic its origins, had coalesced into a language that was immediately recognizable; not only were its elements comparatively limited, but they were put together in a distinctive way. There was no equivalent or equally limited vocabulary for the interior, and no attempt was made to create one. The aim was to produce a harmony less of style than of treatment; ideally, the interior of each house expressed the artistic personality of its owners.

In effect this almost always resulted in various shades of eclecticism, discriminating in intention if not always in effect. Contemporary fashion limited the range, but it was still a very wide one. The hall and dining-room might be more or less Jacobean, the drawing-room more or less 'Adams', the billiard- or smoking-room more or less Moorish. Although a few decorators went in for 'period' interiors that aimed at historical accuracy, the accent was usually on the more or less. Elements from other styles would be introduced, the proportions subtly, or not so subtly, varied, the walls hung with contemporary art wallpapers, and the windows curtained with contemporary art fabrics.

The eclecticism of the decorations was usually out-trumped by the even greater eclecticism of the contents, new and old. Among the old might be Japanese prints, screens, and fans, blue and white china both oriental and Dutch, Hispano-Moresque plates, Turkish tiles, Persian carpets, Chelsea and Worcester porcelain, and English eighteenth-century portraits and furniture, the latter vaguely classified as either 'Chippendale' or 'Sheraton'. Among the new were art furniture, fabrics, tiles, and ceramics of every description, in addition to pictures in fastidiously artistic frames, by Whistler or Burne-Jones for the more advanced, by Marcus Stone, G. H. Boughton, or W. Q. Orchardson for those who still wanted their pictures to tell a story.

All this could easily get out of hand. The widespread belief that Victorian interiors were unbelievably cluttered with junk is due to the fact that nearly all photographs of Victorian interiors date from the 'Queen Anne' period or later; mid-Victorian rooms were not nearly so crowded. But ideally clutter was kept under control by the fastidious eye of the owner; a unity of the spirit harmonized all the different shades of eclecticism, and a unity of colour prevented one room from jarring with the next. Although every room was usually given a different colour scheme they were all based on the same principles. Primary colours, or, even worse, bright coal-tar mauves and magentas were fastidiously avoided. Rooms were decorated in a wide variety of tertiary colours, subtly blended together. Mrs. Haweis's description of the drawing-room in G. H. Boughton's house on Campden Hill (designed by Norman Shaw in 1876) suggests the effects aimed at: 'The mantel-piece, very prettily designed to enclose in its crannies innumerable cups and vases, is painted in two yellows, like the primrose. . . . The *ensemble* of the room is decidedly mother-o'-pearl like.'[1] In general, the slightly precious language and deliberately old-fashioned type-face of *Beautiful Houses* accurately catches the atmosphere of artistic interiors of the period.

116

To help fit them out, a mass of art manufacturers and art firms came into existence, providing everything the artistic housewife could wish for. Much of what they had to offer was designed by architects, for the philosophy of the 'Queen Anne' movement demanded that architects should be artists, who could turn their hands to any form of design. Webb designed furniture and glass for Morris and Company; Shaw designed furniture for his friend Aldam Heaton; Collcutt designed

V.

Mr. 𝕭𝖔𝖚𝖌𝖍𝖙𝖔𝖓'𝖘 *Houſe.*

ONE of the moſt charming houſes in *London* is that built, decorated, and inhabited by *G. H. Boughton. Mr. Boughton* has brought from *America* a certain elegance of ſtyle in living which has not yet become common on this ſide of the

116. Chapter-heading from *Beautiful Houses*, by Mrs. Haweis, 1882.

furniture for Collinson and Lock; Godwin designed wallpaper for Jeffrey and Company and furniture for Gillow and Company, Collier and Plucknett, and William Watt and Company; R. W. Edis designed furniture for Jackson and Graham; Maurice B. Adams designed a wide range of different fittings for the Burmantofts Faience Company of Leeds, in addition to furniture for William Watt and Company and other firms; Thomas Jeckyll designed metalwork for Barnard, Bishop and Barnard; E. R. Robson contributed designs to his father's furniture firm; Bodley, Garner and G. G. Scott, junior, set up the firm of Watts and Company, which made furniture, wallpaper, textiles, and metalwork.

Whether the resulting products (both those designed by architects and others) can be described as 'Queen Anne' is really a matter of semantics. They drew inspiration from the whole English decorative tradition from the fifteenth to the early nineteenth century, from Greece and Japan, from the Italian Renaissance and from contemporary aesthetic fashion, as expressed, for instance, in pomegranates and sunflowers. In so far as all these elements (even, occasionally, the Greek ones) can be found in 'Queen Anne' buildings, almost every new object that an aesthetic lady was likely to buy for her house can also be described as 'Queen Anne'. But if, as seems reasonable, the description is confined to those objects in which elements derived from seventeenth- and eighteenth-century England predominate, however freely treated, the field immediately contracts to a small circle within the vast range of 'art' goods. Very roughly speaking, this is how the term tended to be used at the time; but attitudes were so easy-going, and the term 'Queen Anne' anyway such a ridiculous one that it was possible for almost any art object produced during the 1870s and 1880s to be described as 'Queen Anne'.

A good deal of 'Queen Anne' furniture in the more limited sense is illustrated in contemporary furniture catalogues or building periodicals. Sometimes the pieces are illustrated individually, sometimes a whole room is shown, with chimney-piece and wall-decorations to match the furniture. Complete rooms designed by the architect J. D. Sedding for T. Knight and Son, decorators

117. Designs by E. W. Godwin for William Watt, *c.* 1877, including a 'Queen Anne' cabinet.

124   and builders, are illustrated in the latter's *Suggestions for House Decoration* (1880); the illustrations include a number of colour plates which give a good idea of the greys, greyish-blues, bluish-greens, and browns which in the 1870s drove out the bright primary colours of the mid-century. There

118, 119   are further complete rooms by R. W. Edis in his *Decoration and Furniture of Town Houses* (1881) a treasury of interior design of all varieties, by Edis and others. 'Queen Anne' designs by Godwin

117   are illustrated in William Watt's furniture catalogue, 'Queen Anne' designs made by Maurice B.

120, 121   Adams for Robertson Sons of Alnwick and others in the *Building News*. The immense catalogue put out by Shoolbred and Company of Tottenham Court Road is rich in 'Queen Anne' of every

125   variety and very variable quality.[2]

There are a number of favourite motifs in this furniture, including broken pediments, chinoiserie glazing or fretwork, turned balusters either in Renaissance or vernacular seventeenth-century manner, and legs either spindly and 'Sheraton' or curving and 'Chippendale'. All are mixed up with complete abandon and disregard of scholarly correctness. A major new function which furniture designers had to cater for, and for which the eighteenth century supplied no precedent, was the display of bric-à-brac, the array of pots, plates, feathers, and fans which were *de rigeur* for every artistic house. Two new types of furnishing appeared as a result, the over-

122   mantel with its innumerable shelves and brackets, sometimes incorporating a central mirror or clock, and the display cabinet, combining glass-fronted cupboard with open shelves and ledges, and at times rising as high as the dado, at times the whole height of the wall.

On the whole 'Queen Anne' furniture is disappointing; Godwin's 'Queen Anne' furniture,

117   for instance, has none of the distinction and originality of his Anglo-Japanese designs. Although the same kind of eclecticism was at work as in the architecture, the 'Queen Anne' furniture within seldom achieved the delicacy and originality of the 'Queen Anne' façades without; too often it just looked like eighteenth-century furniture which had gone wrong. But there are exceptions.

Domestic Iron and Brass Work ·

made by Thomas Elsley ·

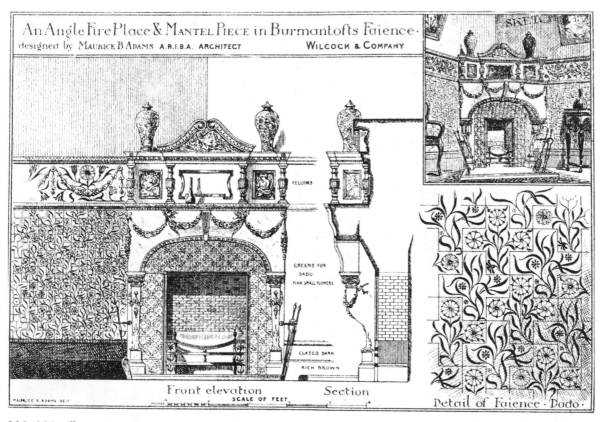

118, 119. Illustrations from *Decoration and Furniture of Town Houses,* by R. W. Edis, 1881.

120. (*Right*) Drawing-room cabinet designed by Maurice B. Adams and made by William Watt, 1883.

121. (*Below*) Cabinet sideboard designed by Maurice B. Adams and made by Robertson and Sons, 1883.

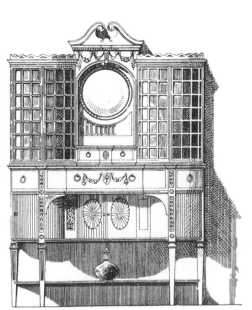

122. Model bedroom designed by R. W. Edis for Jackson and Graham, and shown at the International Health Exhibition, 1884.

123. A lady's china cabinet and writing table designed by T. E. Collcutt, 1884.

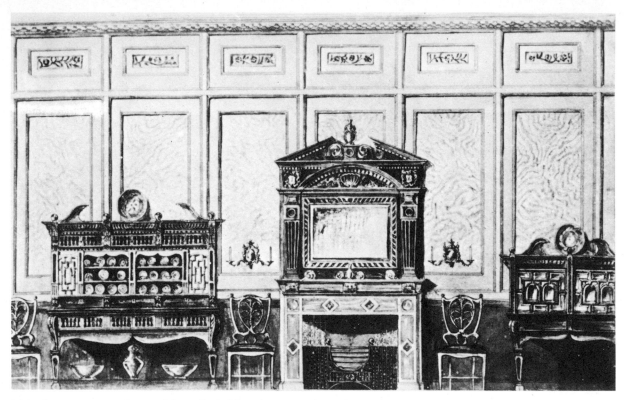

124. Specimen room designed by J. D. Sedding for T. Knight and Son, *c.* 1880.

Some pieces are designed with engaging asymmetry, like miniature versions of 'Queen Anne' houses. Some of the built-in furniture, by Edis and others, exhibited at the Health Exhibition in 1884 had considerable charm, besides being suitably progressive.[3] And sometimes the element of exaggeration takes off into fantasy and the towering display cabinets, bulging with glass fronts, bristling with shelves, loaded with bric-à-brac, and towering up to the ceiling seem like the central shrine of some forgotten cult. In contrast to such formidable objects light-weight 'Queen Anne' chairs, in the Morris 'Sussex' tradition, can have an amazingly attenuated and spindly elegance.[4]

'Queen Anne' was not of course confined to furniture. In addition to the Japanese-inspired grates designed by Thomas Jeckyll for the Norwich firm of Barnard, Bishop and Barnard, which were much in demand in artistic households, delicately pretty basket-grates of more or less eighteenth-century type were manufactured by Morris and Company, by Coalbrookdale, and by Thomas Elsley, the latter a metal-worker much patronized by 'Queen Anne' architects. There are Elsley grates decorated with typical 'Queen Anne' broken pediments and framed by de Morgan tiles in the bedrooms of J. J. Stevenson's Ken Hill.[5] Downstairs, in the dining-room, a silver centre-piece presented to the daughter-in-law of the owner, Edward Green, on the occasion of her marriage in 1885, is an especially lavish example of the innumerable pieces of more or less Georgian-style silver produced in the late nineteenth century. They have been largely neglected by art historians as reproduction work of no interest, but it seems likely that research would distinguish between straightforward copies and pieces that were examples of creative eclecticism in the 'Queen Anne' manner. An attractive example of the latter in the sphere of ceramics is the 'Countess' service made by Doulton's in the 1880s, odd pieces from which are frequently to be found in antique shops and even junk stalls. Although its basic motif, of Adam-style medallions joined by swags, is clearly of eighteenth-century inspiration it has a spindly individuality which ties it unmistakably to its period.

120, 121, 123

126

118, 127

125. (*Left*) 'Queen Anne' asymmetry. Cupboard by J. Shoolbred and Co., from a catalogue of *c.* 1889.

126. Three designs for chairs from *Fashionable Furniture*, 1881.

127. A grate made by Thomas Elsley, *c.* 1880, at Ken Hill, Norfolk.

128. *In the Shade,* by Marcus Stone, 1879.

129. *Her First Dance,* by W. Q. Orchardson, 1884.

A gently entertaining, if never very high-powered side-product of the 'Queen Anne' movement was the genre picture in eighteenth- or early nineteenth-century dress, examples of which
first began to proliferate in the 1870s. They were produced by artists such as J. S. Lucas and
G. D. Leslie, but their best-known purveyors were Marcus Stone and Stevenson's friend William
Quiller Orchardson.[6] Marcus Stone's pictures tended to have outdoor settings, with a speciality
128   in sentimental tea parties held in old-world gardens. W. Q. Orchardson preferred interior scenes,
129   with ball-rooms as his speciality. Both artists had started by painting medieval subjects but moved
on to the eighteenth century at much the same time as 'Queen Anne' became fashionable; it is
amusing to contrast the Tudor fancy-dress of Orchardson's *The Duke's Antechamber* (1869) with
the Georgian fancy-dress of *The Queen of Swords* (1876–7), and Stone's *Edward II and Piers
Gaveston* (1872) with his *An Appeal for Mercy* (1876). Marcus Stone changed his style of painting
to suit his house; the year in which *An Appeal for Mercy* was painted was the year in which
Norman Shaw designed him a fashionable new 'Queen Anne' house in Melbury Road.

Picture-books

But the best advocates for 'Queen Anne' were to be found in the nursery. The picture-books of Walter Crane, Kate Greenaway, and Randolph Caldecott were secret persuaders, more accomplished than the pictures of Stone and Orchardson and more effective than anything J. J. Stevenson or Basil Champneys ever wrote. Like little aesthetic bombs they scattered sweetness and light beyond the nursery into every corner of the house. Parents appreciated them as much as, and probably more than, children. An application of Crane or Greenaway, in particular, would rapidly shine up the taste of the most philistine of fathers; and dedicated aesthetes, in no need of improvement, fell on them with delight as a means of conditioning their children. It was typical of the difference between generations that parents of the 1850s looked for books that would make their children good, and parents of the 1870s for ones that would make them artistic. Ellen Terry relates how her children Edith and Gordon Craig 'were allowed no rubbishy picture-books, but from the first Japanese prints lined their nursery walls, and Walter Crane was their classic. If injudicious friends gave the wrong sort of present, it was promptly burned. . . . This severe training proved so effective that when a doll dressed in a violent pink silk dress was given to Edy, she said it was "vulgar".' This was in the early 1870s, when Edith was about three years old.[7]

Walter Crane was the first of the three to illustrate children's books. His career and opinions were an exact expression of the *Zeitgeist*. He was born in 1845, the son of a provincial portrait painter. He was apprenticed to a wood engraver in London and in 1863 began to work for Edmund Evans, the best colour printer of the time. In the mid-1860s he read J. S. Mill, Darwin, and Herbert Spencer, and 'decided for Free Thought'. He was, if anything, a radical in politics, and at the time of the Reform agitation of 1867 attended political meetings to listen to Bright, Dilke, and Fawcett. In the early 1880s he became an active Socialist; in the 1860s, 'though . . . by no means without political feelings and sympathies, my real world was a dream world, a cloister, or quiet green garden, where one only heard afar and dimly the echoes of the strife of the great world'.[8] His gods were Rossetti, Morris, and Burne-Jones, but to begin with he adored them from a distance.

Crane's first work for Edmund Evans consisted in designing pictorial covers for the cheap yellow-back novels published by George Routledge and sold on railway book stalls. In 1865 he began to contribute to Routledge's series of illustrated '6*d* toy books', also printed by Evans. The first nine books illustrated by him were nothing out of the ordinary. In 1867 a lieutenant in the navy, recently back from Japan, presented him with a collection of Japanese prints.[9] They took a year or two to affect his work, but once they did the results were revolutionary. There is an amazing contrast between *Grammar in Rhyme* and its successor *Annie and Jack in London*, both published in 1869. Both show scenes of contemporary Victorian life. The illustrations to *Grammar in Rhyme*, charming though they are, are in the idiom of mid-Victorian book illustration. *Annie and Jack in London* has been hit by Japan. Colours are simplified, shading is reduced to a minimum. Yet the people remain ordinary middle-class people in ordinary middle-class settings, with a complete absence of artistic accessories. The result of this bourgeois story seen through semi-Japanese eyes is altogether delightful. 130

In about 1870 Crane got to know Basil Champneys, who was living in Queen Square, in the same house as Crane's artist friend Ellis Woolridge. Morris and Company had moved into a house a few doors away in 1868. Crane saw William Morris for the first time through Ellis Woolridge's window, 'a sturdy figure clad in snuff-brown, with an oak stick in his hand, and a soft felt hat on'. He first met him at the end of 1871, at 1 Palace Green, having dinner with George Howard, who had become Crane's friend and patron. Through George Howard he also got to know Philip Webb, Burne-Jones, and numerous other artists.[10] He was now well launched

And Papa and Mamma took them
  home the same day,—
They were glad to go home, and yet
  wanted to stay;
But the train went quite fast, and it
  seemed a nice change
To be back in their own home, where
  nothing was strange;

And always they reckon'd that
  seeing these sights
Was a thing to remember—a week of
  delights;
And, though they may see them all
  many times more,
They'll never enjoy them so much, I
  am sure.

130. A page from
Annie and Jack in London,
1869, illustrated by
Walter Crane.

into the circles from which 'Queen Anne' was emerging. His children's books begin to show their influence from about 1870.

Between then and 1874 Crane produced about twenty-four picture-books for Routledge and Evans, mostly illustrating old fairy-tales or rhymes, but including a few pictorial ABCs.[11] All of these showed 'Queen Anne' influence, and 'Queen Anne' was predominant from about 1872. The books can reasonably be described as 'Queen Anne' not only because they show fashionable 'Queen Anne' accessories but because they are based on the same recipe as 'Queen Anne' buildings: a free selection of seventeenth- and eighteenth-century elements, mixed with a little of almost everything else, including details from Japan, to produce a final result that is completely original.

V, 131   The 'Queen Anne' accessories are very charming. Cinderella and the Little Pig sit by fireplaces lined with art tiles, and Cinderella's kitchen has a sage-green dresser lined with blue and white china. Jack Spratt and his wife sit on light-weight 'Queen Anne' chairs eating out of blue

131. 'This little pig stayed at home', from *This Little Pig*, 1871, illustrated by Walter Crane.

So Silverlocks, in sudden terror flying,
Reached home; and when the Nurse the
        story hears,
She says, "You are in luck, there's no
        denying,
To get away in safety from

THREE BEARS."

132. A page from *The Three Bears*,
c. 1872–3, illustrated by
Walter Crane.

132   and white china on a light-weight table. The three bears have a border of sunflowers round their house and a blue-green 'Queen Anne' staircase. The Princess Belle Étoile holds a peacock feather fan and sits in a bay window equipped with leaded lights and roundels of stained glass, which might have been designed by Norman Shaw.

The eclecticism can be amazingly elaborate. Cinderella in full Victorian rig dances with an eighteenth-century prince surrounded by courtiers some of whom have full-bottomed wigs and others robes patterned with sunflowers, while the attendants are in heraldic jerkins, like the

133   knaves in a pack of cards. In the *Frog Prince* the King, in chain mail and medieval dress, sits in an elaborate neo-classical chair in the style of Thomas Hope; his daughter is elegantly neo-classical, one of his guests has a full-bottomed wig and peer's robes of the early eighteenth century and the servants wear medieval jerkins; the table is Elizabethan and there is a row of blue and white plates on the dresser. Crane had an especial fondness for neo-classical dress and furniture,

134   which reached its culmination in the courtship scene in *Beauty and the Beast*. Beauty's boudoir is sumptuously neo-classical, except for the wallpaper which resembles a Morris one; she sits on an extravagant neo-classical sofa in a dress and hair-do to match (but holding a Japanese fan) and entertains the Beast, who is dressed like a seventeenth-century cavalier, splendid in top boots and lace ruffles.[12]

THERE was an honest gentleman, who had a daughter
     dear ;
His wife was dead, he took instead a new one in a year ;
She had two daughters—Caroline and Bella were their names ;
They called the other daughter Cinderella, to their shames,
Because she had to clean the hearths and black-lead all the
     grates ;
She also had to scrub the floors, and wash the dinner plates.
But though the others went abroad, did nothing, smiled, and
     drest,
Yet Cinderella all the time was prettiest and best.
The King who ruled in that country, he had an only son,
Who gave a ball to all the town, when he was twenty-one ;
And Caroline and Bella were invited, and they said,
"Cinderella shall leave scrubbing, and act as ladies' maid."

V. A page from *Cinderella* illustrated by Walter Crane, *c.* 1872–3.

VIA. (*Top*) 'Two little girls at tea', from Kate Greenaway's *Under the Window*, 1879.

VIB. (*Bottom*) An illustration from *Froggy Would a-wooing go*, by Randolph Caldecott, 1878.

And then the Fairy raised her wand, and touched the shabby
gown—
It turned to satin, trimmed with lace, and jewels, and swans-
down.
Her face was clean, her gloves were new, her hair was nicely
curled,
And on her feet were shoes of glass, the neatest in the world.
"Now, Cinderella, you may go; but take care to return
Before the clock strikes twelve, or else you'll see your carriage
turn
Into a pumpkin once again, your horses into mice;
Your coachman, footmen, will become rat, lizards, in a trice,
And you yourself the cinder-girl will once again become;
So mind that when the clock strikes twelve you must be safe
at home."

She promised, and with joyful heart she gained the palace
hall,
And danced, and laughed, and looked indeed the fairest of
them all.
The King's son danced with her, and praised her lovely shape
and air;
All treated her as if she were the greatest lady there:
But in good time she slipped away, and waited safe at home,
In kitchen corner sitting till her sisters back should come;
And when they came they told her all about the stranger fair,
And what she wore, and how she looked, and how she did
her hair.
Next night another ball was held—the sisters dressed, and
went,
And pretty Cinderella, too, by Godmother was sent.

133, 134. Walter Crane illustrations from *Cinderella*, *c.* 1872–3, and *Beauty and the Beast*, *c.* 1873–4.

The result is rather overpowering; most of the illustrations in the picture-books are a good deal simpler, but even the elaborate ones are kept in control by Crane's Japanese technique. There is little sense of depth or movement, but great strength and feeling for pattern; the figures are like a series of flat overlays silhouetted one against the other. This technique of overlay, Japanese in origin, becomes more explicit when lettering and pictures are combined. On the covers of the shilling toy books, title and author's name are in two rectangular panels with concave sides

135. A page from
Walter Crane's
*Alphabet of Old
Friends, c.* 1873–4.

overlapping each other and superimposed on a decorative background. In the *Alphabet of Old Friends* the pages are divided up asymmetrically into rectangles, with superimposed circles which

135   sometimes overlap the divisions between the rectangles; the rectangles contain drawings, elements of which, like the branch of a tree or the feathers of a bird, at times break out into neighbouring rectangles.

Crane's picture-books create a world of their own, which must have been strange, delightful, and fascinating for the children of the period, but was also extremely sophisticated. Crane claimed that they made him little money but 'I had my fun out of them, as in designing I was in the habit of putting in all sorts of subsidiary detail that interested me, and often made them the vehicle of my ideas in furniture and decoration'.[13] It was not surprising that, from 1875, architects and manufacturers came to him for decorative designs. By the end of the 1870s a 'Queen Anne' house was liable to have a Walter Crane frieze in the drawing-room, and Walter Crane tiles and wallpapers throughout the house, as well as Walter Crane books in the nursery.

136. 'Lavender's Blue' from *The Baby's Opera*, 1877, illustrated by Walter Crane.

Routledge and Evans's picture-books were published at 6*d* and 1*s*; they were expensive to produce and although they sold in large quantities made little money. The series was discontinued in about 1875, and in 1877 the same partnership tried a new format, in the shape of Walter Crane's *The Baby's Opera*. This was a thicker volume of illustrated songs for children, selling at 5*s*. It was an immediate success, and in the end sold over 40,000 copies. It was followed next year by *The Baby's Bouquet*, in a similar format. The two books combined text (and music) with pictures on the same page, in the manner pioneered by Crane's *Alphabet of Old Friends*, but there was a noticeable change in character. The colours were softer, the decorations were daintier and sweeter; in the picture-books there had been little blank space but now decorations were silhouetted against white borders, like the figures on a Greek vase. Children had been comparatively rare in the picture-books, except in the *Alphabet* where, under E, Elizabeth, Elspeth, Betty, and Bess processed across the page, in bonnets, high-waisted frocks, and sprigged aprons. In the *Baby* books children proliferated; quaint little figures in bonnets, mob-caps, aprons, or knee-breeches danced, chased, and played over page after page.

In the 1880s Walter Crane's work deteriorated. The colours became even softer, the designs much less strong; though the result is pretty enough it is flabby compared to his earlier work. Meanwhile his thunder had been stolen by a rival illustrator; a certain amount of bitterness can be read through the lines (and the silences) of his autobiography. At the end of 1878 Routledge and Evans produced *Under the Window* by Kate Greenaway.

136

137. 'Polly, Peg and Poppety', from Kate Greenaway's *Under the Window*, 1878.

VIA

137

138, 139

Kate Greenaway (1846–1901) had been working as a professional artist for ten years when she hit the jackpot with *Under the Window*. She had made a small reputation designing Christmas cards for the Belfast firm of Marcus Ward and Co., before she brought a collection of little drawings of children, with accompanying verses written by herself, to show to Edmund Evans. He was so impressed that he signed her up immediately and, to Routledge's horror, printed 20,000 copies of the resulting book. Evans was right, however; *Under the Window* sold about 100,000 copies, and its successor *Kate Greenaway's Birthday Book*, published in 1880, had a first printing of 150,000, in English, French, and German. The two books were followed by a steady flow of picture-books, illustrated stories, and almanacs; although her sales were affected by imitations and the Kate Greenaway craze gradually subsided, she remained popular until her death. In 1885 she built a house and studio for herself designed, almost inevitably, by Norman Shaw. It was equally in keeping that Elizabeth Garrett Anderson was her friend and doctor, and Thackeray's daughter Anne one of her intimates.[14]

Under the Window had an extraordinary reception. It reduced the elderly Ruskin to a state of almost drooling appreciation, and provoked a series of increasingly embarrassing letters from him which continued for twenty years. The poet and critic Austin Dobson wrote that 'since Stothard, no one has given us such a clear-eyed, soft-faced, happy-hearted childhood; or so poetically apprehended the coy reticences, the simplicities, and the small solemnities of little people. Added to this, the old-world costume in which she usually elects to clothe her characters lends an arch piquancy of contrast to their innocent rites and ceremonies. . . . there is a fresh pure fragrance about all her pictures as of new gathered nosegays.'[15]

This description is wholly accurate; and if it is a little cloying, so is Kate Greenaway. Many people, when looking through her books, must find revulsion from so much sweetness and quaintness fighting with admiration for her extraordinary skill. In her way she is a minor master. Like Crane she creates a world of her own; the fact that it is a very much simpler world perhaps

138, 139. Two illustrations by Kate Greenaway
for *Little Ann*, by J. and A. Taylor, 1883.

explains her even greater success. She had been a suburban child, living at Hoxton and Highbury, but spending happy holidays on remote farms in Nottinghamshire. In her books she recreated a Londoner's vision of an ideal country childhood from which every possible sting had been removed, a childhood transformed by the passage of time and heavily conditioned by Walter Crane. Although Kate Greenaway claimed that her children were based on memories of children in the old-fashioned country villages where she spent her holidays, they were actually drawn from models dressed in clothes which she made herself; and the resulting children, together with their rustic backgrounds, were remarkably like those previously drawn by Crane in the *Alphabet of Old Friends* and *The Baby's Opera*.

140. An illustration from *Sing a Song for Sixpence*, illustrated by Randolph Caldecott, 1880.

But quaint children had only been one of Walter Crane's lines; Kate Greenaway produced almost nothing else. Few of her books have any narrative content; in many of them the pictures are accompanied by her own pretty little rhymes. Under perpetually cloudless skies, in untouched rural villages or old-fashioned gardens, never cross, never cruel, seldom crying, never creased, children cavort, toddle, play games, or pretend to be grown-ups with absurd solemnity. One may wonder to what extent Victorian children really enjoyed Kate Greenaway, but their parents certainly found her irresistible; she portrayed exactly the kind of children they would like to have. They set about producing them, and in no time aesthetic nurseries and playgrounds were full of children dressed up in Kate Greenaway clothes; the children obligingly acted up to the dress and provided their parents with just the right kind of drolly grave remarks or toddling adventures to relate to other parents over the tea-tables in 'Queen Anne' drawing rooms.

Kate Greenaway's clothes, though mainly early nineteenth century in type, are eclectic in typically 'Queen Anne' fashion. Her hats, for instance, vary from mob-caps and ribbons of early eighteenth-century type, through late eighteenth-century straw hats to the huge early nineteenth-century bonnets for which she was especially famous. The dresses under the hats are normally high-waisted ones of early nineteenth-century type (with the boys' clothes to match) but include late eighteenth-century overskirts; all the various elements are combined with no attempt at period accuracy. Unlike those of Walter Crane, the settings in which the children play are never elaborate; the village streets are lined with modest vernacular houses of vaguely seventeenth- or eighteenth-century type; the gardens are of the kind known at the time as 'old-fashioned'. The colours are soft and silvery, following the tendency in Crane's *Baby's Opera*, but carrying it even further. The use of blank space, already noticeable in the *Baby's Opera*, is brilliantly developed; a single little child is marooned in the centre of an otherwise blank page, or a drawing is balanced asymmetrically against a verse, with space flowing all around, with altogether different effect from Crane's much tighter compositions.

VII

140   Blank space is used with equal skill in some of the illustrations of Randolph Caldecott.[16] But Caldecott's illustrations are far more boisterous and superficially philistine than Kate Greenaway's; perhaps that is why the fourteen picture-books which he produced between 1878 and his early death in 1886 proved, in the long run, the most successful series produced by Routledge's gifted trio. Caldecott was a keen horseman, and lively hunting scenes feature prominently in several of his books. But however much these may seem the work of a jolly no-nonsense sort of fellow, Caldecott was in fact more of an aesthete than Kate Greenaway; before he turned to children's

141. 'The wondering neighbours ran', from Goldsmith's *Elegy on the Death of a Mad Dog*, illustrated by Randolph Caldecott, 1879.

books he had been painting compositions in the Japanese manner, experimenting in sculpture (he carved the capitals in Leighton's Arab Hall), and collaborating with his friend Thomas Armstrong in decorating the dining-room of Bank Hall in Derbyshire with panels of birds and flowers and wistful neo-classical scenes which are the quintessence of aestheticism.[17]

His children's books, though less sweet than Kate Greenaway's and less obviously sophisticated than Walter Crane's, are just as much a product of 'Queen Anne' eclecticism, besides showing a highly developed sense of decoration. His subject-matter ranges from the Middle Ages to the early nineteenth century, and though there is less superficially 'Queen Anne' bric-à-brac than in Walter Crane's books, where it appears it is inserted with great wit and panache; especially charming are his frogs in *Froggy Would a-Wooing Go*, dressed in early nineteenth-century outfits and sitting on spindly chairs before an Adam-style chimney-piece sporting an immense peacock feather.

141

VIB

142. Frontispiece from *Abroad*, illustrated by Ellen Houghton and Thomas Crane, 1882.

Caldecott, Greenaway, and Crane were much imitated. Kate Greenaway was especially incensed by J. G. Sowerby's and H. H. Emmerson's *Afternoon Tea* (1880), a close but at the same time flaccid imitation of her work which must have been excessively irritating. But both Sowerby and Emmerson were to do better things. In 1884 Emmerson, who had studied in Newcastle under William Bell Scott, collaborated with another Northumberland artist, J. T. Dixon, in producing a lavish manuscript volume to commemorate the visit of the Prince and Princess of Wales to Norman Shaw's Cragside. In addition to numerous illustrations showing different episodes in the visit, the book was embellished with delightful decorations in the manner of Walter Crane.[18] In

IN THE CORNER.

143. 'In the Corner', from *At Home*, illustrated by J. G. Sowerby and Thomas Crane, 1881.

1881 Sowerby collaborated with Walter Crane's brother Thomas on *At Home*, an illustrated series of verses on the life of a family of children. It was so successful that it was followed in the next year by a sequel, *Abroad*, showing the same family on holiday. *At Home* is especially charming; the family is an ideal 'Queen Anne' one, living in a 'Queen Anne' house complete with Japanese screens, spindly furniture, old-fashioned flowers, and even a 'Queen Anne' bathroom and kitchen. The book is dedicated in verses of appropriate whimsy, the first couplet running

142

143

> To all who love the little folk
> Their little ways, their little talk . . .

144. Woodcut by E. V. Boyle, from her *Days and Hours in a Garden*, 1884.

The Old-fashioned Garden

One of the forgotten accompaniments of the 'Queen Anne' movement is the 'Queen Anne' or 'old-fashioned' garden. It has been squeezed out of memory by popular mythology, which portrays William Robinson, followed by his disciple Gertrude Jekyll, as the man who rescued gardening from the horrors of bedding-out, and introduced the golden age of the flowering shrub and the herbaceous border.

The story is in fact a good deal more complicated. There were two main traditions of mid-Victorian gardening: the formal Italianate garden, with terraces, gravel paths, stone balustrades, garden ornaments, and parterres patterned with bedded-out flowers, as popularized by Barry and W. A. Nesfield; and the 'gardenesque' garden, as popularized by Loudon. The latter was a development of the picturesque garden of the eighteenth century, with eighteenth-century meanders tightened to highly stylized curves and wriggles, and eighteenth-century lawns brightened up by yet more bedded-out flowers.

Robinson reacted against bedding-out and the formal garden; he accepted the gardenesque tradition, but aimed to make it more 'natural'. The 'Queen Anne' gardeners reacted against both bedding-out and the gardenesque; they accepted, and enjoyed, formality, but only the modest formality of the 'old-fashioned' gardens of the late seventeenth and early eighteenth centuries. They preferred clipped hedges and topiary to temples and balustrades, and borders of 'old-fashioned' flowers to parterres of bedded-out ones. The two schools pursued largely independent courses until, in the 1890s, two books by J. D. Sedding and Reginald Blomfield publicized the 'Queen Anne' tradition in its most architectural form, and were immediately attacked by Robinson with vitriolic fury.[19] It was left to Gertrude Jekyll and Lutyens to reconcile the two approaches.

The 'Queen Anne' garden was inspired more by painters, poets, and architects than by professional gardeners. This was one reason why Robinson disliked it; and indeed it could be argued that its flowers were chosen more as symbols of old-fashioned values than for themselves. Its origins stretch back well before Robinson's time, to Tennyson and to the first Pre-Raphaelites and their associates. The garden in Tennyson's song, 'A spirit haunts the years last hours', where

> Heavily hangs the broad sunflower
> Over its grave i' the earth so chilly;
> Heavily hangs the hollyhock,
> Heavily hangs the tiger lily;

introduces three flowers which at that time had been pushed out of fashionable gardens by calceolarias, lobelias, and begonias. Walter Howard Deverell's *The Pet* (1852–3) has a garden in the background, said to have been painted from his own garden at Kew, in which straight gravel paths are lined with grass borders and long beds filled with drifts of tangled flowers. In Arthur Hughes's *Fair Rosamund* (1854) there are somewhat similar flowers along a straight path, lined with low clipped borders; in the foreground is a bower of irises, ivy, and old-fashioned roses.[20]

Fair Rosamund's garden is ostensibly medieval but there must have been many quiet unfashionable Victorian gardens that resembled it. At the Red House in the early 1860s William Morris and Philip Webb attempted to combine an old-fashioned garden with something that approached rather nearer to the gardens shown in medieval illuminations. Morris had already sketched out his idea of a medieval garden in the *Story of an Unknown Church*, published in 1856: 'At the edge of the lawn, near the round arches, were a great many sun-flowers that were all in blossom on that autumn day; and up many of the pillars of the cloister crept passion-flowers and roses . . . in the garden were trellises covered over with roses, and convolvulus, and the great-leaved fiery nasturtium; and specially all along by the poplar tree were there trellises, but on those grew nothing but deep crimson roses; the hollyhocks too were all out in blossom at that time, great spires of pink, and orange, and red, and white, with their soft, downy leaves.'[21] At the Red House existing orchard trees were carefully preserved, there were wattle-fence enclosures smothered in roses, and roses, jasmine, and passion flower were trained to grow up the house walls.[22] At Cloverley, later on in the 1860s, Nesfield or his clients planted an orchard round the dovecot which terminated the garden elevation of the house.

A revived taste for clipped hedges and topiary also dates from the 1860s, with Rossetti in the thick of it. There were topiary hedges at Morris's Red House. In 1866 Rossetti's letters enthusiastically described a visit to an old-fashioned topiary garden at Brickwall House, Northiam, in Sussex of which he took the trouble to obtain photographs. On the same tour he was so delighted with a complete topiary arm-chair which he found in a cottage garden that he bought it and transplanted it to Cheyne Walk, where it promptly died.[23] At about the same time Warrington Taylor, in one of his letters to E. R. Robson, mounted a violent attack on Liverpool City Council for sponsoring a 'gardenesque' garden. The letter was sparked off by the current competition for the layout of Sefton Park, Liverpool, in which it was stipulated that the layout had to be of that kind. Taylor's reason for hating 'gardenesque' is interesting; it was because it pretended to be natural. 'It will not have design, human design, but wants an imitation of God's work by a man, that is, a landscape garden. . . . If they want a garden and park let them have one showing its human origins, by design, as in Kip. . . . old English gardens, parks—a place more or less like Versailles, broad allées, clipped hedges, grand avenues, shrubberies, woods with grand straight walks on them . . . No—they prefer to be cads, Philistines, tradesmen.'[24]

In 1868 and 1869 Frederick Walker painted two water-colours showing old-fashioned gardens, both of which were exhibited at the Old Water-Colour Society and attracted much attention. Both were bought by William Graham, who for many years was the close friend and principal patron of all the later Pre-Raphaelites and their circle. *Lilies*, painted in 1868, was based on the garden of Mr. Heywood Hardy at Goring, with some additions from Tennyson's garden at Freshwater; it showed a lady in eighteenth-century dress (anticipating Walter Crane by a few years) admiring a row of splendid tiger-lilies in an old-fashioned garden of mixed flowers and box edges. *A Lady in a Garden, Perthshire* (1869), sometimes called *Stobhall Garden*, was painted in the seventeenth-century garden at Stobhall in Perthshire, which Graham was renting at the time, and where both Walker and Rossetti came to stay. The water-colour showed similar planting to that in *Lilies*, but with the additional feature of spires of yew or cypress symmetrically planted at the corners of the flower-beds.[25]

By 1870 the revival of the old-fashioned garden was well under way, and the form it was to take for the next fifteen years had been more or less worked out. The typical layout was formal but not grand, with clipped hedges, sometimes with trellised walks and bowers, and with enclosing walls up which climbing plants flowered in profusion. Flower-beds tended to be lined with a low

145

145. *Lilies*, by
Frederick Walker, 1868.

edging of clipped box, and the flowers were all 'old-fashioned' ones, sometimes discovered in
cottage gardens and lovingly transplanted. Sunflowers, lilies, and poppies, being both old-fashioned
and highly fashionable, were much in evidence; so were rows of standard roses, growing out of
the lawn. Flowering cherries introduced an exotic Japanese note. Often an orchard, or a vegetable
garden in which vegetables were mixed with borders of flowers, was incorporated into the layout.
Like 'Queen Anne' houses, old-fashioned gardens had a widely eclectic background; like them
they were deliberately unscholarly; like them they expressed a reaction against what seemed the
glare and vulgarity of modern fashion in favour of the gentler and more human values which
their owners found in old-fashioned things.

A garden of this type is charmingly commemorated in a sonnet by Rossetti's friend William
Bell Scott, from his sonnet-sequence *The Old Scotch House*. The sonnets were written and illustrated in about 1874, and describe Penkill, in Ayrshire, where Rossetti came to stay and Bell
Scott was the yearly summer visitor of the owner, Miss Alice Boyd. Penkill had been an old,
semi-derelict house; Miss Boyd and her brother enlarged and remodelled it, and recreated the
gardens during the 1860s and '70s. One of the accompanying engravings shows a corner of the
146   garden, and the relevant sonnet runs as follows:

> The old house garden grows old-fashioned flowers
> Sheltered by hedges of the close yew tree
> Through which, as Chaucer says, no wight may see;
> The sunflowers rise aloft like beacon towers,
> Their large discs fringed with flames; and corner bowers
> There are of mountain-ash, and the wild rose;
> Short-lived, blue star-flowers that at evening close
> Spring there; sweet herbs and marigolds in showers;
> Gilly-flowers too, dark crimson and nigh white;
> Pied poppies, and the striped grass, differing still
> In each long leaf, though children ever will
> Believe in finding two shall match aright;
> The paths are edged with box grown broad and high
> At evening sheltering moths of various dye.[26]

146. An illustration by William Scott to his sonnet-sequence *The Old Scotch House,* *c.* 1874.

In 1875 the *Saturday Review* published an article on 'Queen Anne's Flowers' by Stevenson's cousin, Mrs. Loftie. It deserves a long extract:

It is often amusing to trace a fashion as it percolates downwards. By the time it has reached the far away sleeping country villages, something quite new and entirely opposite is the rage among the upper ten thousand. Cottagers would try to fill their little plots with geraniums and calceolarias . . . Meanwhile my lady at the Court is hunting the nursery grounds for London Pride and gentianella to make edgings in her wilderness, and for the fair tall rockets, the cabbage roses, and the nodding columbines which her pensioners have discarded and thrown away. The disappointed gardener at the Court sees the border which he had destined for the last new and most hideous pattern of ribbon bordering turned into a lovely pattern of lilies and larkspur, penstemon and phlox, all allowed to grow at their own sweet will amongst hardy and sweet scented shrubs.

We rejoice heartily, so far as the science of gardening is concerned, at the new turn of the wheel which has given us back those dear old flowers. Queen Anne has come into her own again, and the train of faithful and enthusiastic subjects with whom she has returned bring in their hands proud turncap lilies and stately hollyhocks to plant against a background of moulded brick or melancholy yew. They troop into the panelled rooms of her houses, bearing in their hands creamy white vases filled with lavender and lupin, which they place on emaciated tables to harmonize with the dove coloured curtains and the straight lines of the uncomfortable sofas. They plant passion flowers round the porticoes and train the musk roses, despised but yesterday, to mingle with the ghostly juniper, and to blush on the inhabitants looking at them through the square-paned windows . . .[27]

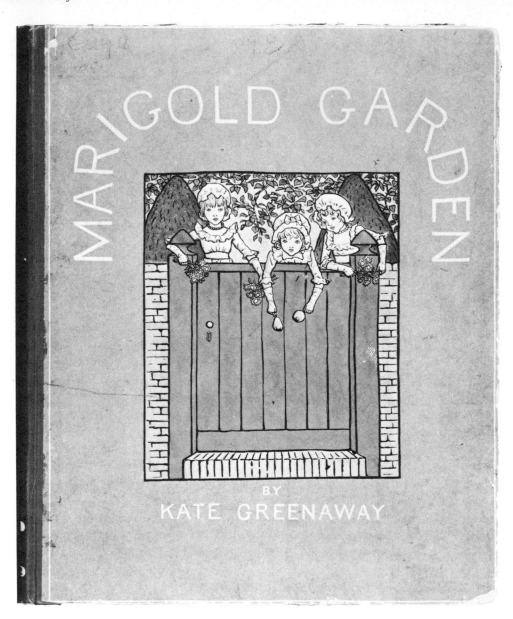

147. The cover of
Kate Greenaway's
Marigold Garden, 1885.

Old-fashioned gardens proliferated during the 1870s and 1880s. Many of the later Pre-Raphaelites and their circle had them. The Morrises created one at Kelmscott, which Morris and Rossetti first rented in 1871; Burne-Jones had one at the Grange, in Fulham; when William Blake Richmond moved to Beaver Lodge, Hammersmith, in 1870, he made a garden with 'long grass walks with borders on each side, in which great scarlet poppies made vivid spots of colour, and blue irises and white rear their stately heads, and lilies and delphiniums and many other old fashioned plants grow at their will'.[28] Old-fashioned gardens and flowers abound in the drawings of Walter Crane and Kate Greenaway. Little Red Riding Hood's grandmother, as depicted by Crane, has one; the title of Kate Greenaway's *Marigold Garden* underlines her passion for clipped hedges and old-fashioned flowers; a whole book was given over to the latter in Walter Crane's *Flora's Feast* (1889), one of the most decorative and popular of his later publications. Bedford Park acquired a Natural History and Gardening Society in 1883 of which, inevitably, 'a special object' was 'to revive active interest in the cultivation of simple and old-fashioned flowers'.[29]

VIA

147

148. The old-fashioned garden at Hardwick Hall, Derbyshire, laid out by Lady Louisa Egerton, *c.* 1870.

Many gardens of this date, or their remains, must survive, probably often credited with a spurious seventeenth-century origin on the one hand, or thought to date from thirty years later, on the other. The gardens at Hardwick Hall in Derbyshire are often mistaken for seventeenth- or eighteenth-century ones; Reginald Blomfield was taken in as early as the 1890s.[30] In fact they were laid out in the 1860s or 1870s, within original Elizabethan walls, by Lady Louisa Egerton, daughter of the 7th Duke of Devonshire; she was one of the few of George Howard's relations with whom he maintained a close friendship after he and his wife had given up smart society in favour of their friends among artists and intellectuals.[31] The main garden at Hardwick is divided into four parts by cross-shaped alleys of clipped yew or hornbeam. The alleys meet in a central space where alcoves are cut into the hedges to hold lead statues of the early eighteenth century. Of the four subdivisions two originally contained vegetable gardens mixed with flowers; one contained an orchard; one was a green lawn planted with trees. There were long walks along the perimeter, with borders under the walls, and old-fashioned roses climbing up the Elizabethan walls.

148

A garden of about the same date survives in modified form at Blickling in Norfolk. It was inserted by Constance, Lady Lothian, one of the most celebrated of artistic Victorian *grandes dames*, into a formal layout dating from the eighteenth century. Lady Lothian built a half-rectangle of brick terraces in more or less seventeenth-century style, punctuated with trellised alcoves for climbing plants. She laid out the space enclosed by the terraces with topiary work and box-trimmed flower-beds, grouped around stone eighteenth-century vases and terms. Bedding-out was sedulously avoided; in 1885 Augustus Hare wrote enthusiastically of Lady Lothian's 'splendid herbaceous garden'.[32]

At Kinmel, in the 1870s, Nesfield introduced a large formal garden of brick terraces and topiary work, much of which still survives. Old photographs show the huge old-fashioned garden formerly at Bodley and Garner's Hewell Grange, Worcestershire, a neo-Jacobean mansion designed for the Earl of Plymouth in 1884.[33] Another interesting garden of the period, at Huntercombe Manor, near Maidenhead, was laid out from 1871 onwards by Mrs. E. V. Boyle. Mrs. Boyle was an artistic upper-class lady very much in the style of Lady Lothian. She was a friend of Tennyson and Leighton, and one of the two women (the other was Louisa, Marchioness of Waterford) whom Rossetti proposed as members of an abortive sketching club in 1854. She illustrated books under the pen-name E.V.B.; she laid out the gardens at Huntercombe in old-fashioned style, and related her experiences in 1883 in a series of articles in the *Gardener's Chronicle*, which were republished in the following year as a book called *Days and Hours in a Garden*. This was illustrated with her own charming little vignette woodcuts, of sunflowers, pyramid-cut yews, gate-piers, and straight walks lined with trimmed hedges.[34]

149. The garden at Hewell Grange, Worcestershire, from a late nineteenth-century photograph.

VII. Illustration by Kate Greenaway from *A Day in a Child's Life*, 1881.

VIII. St. Michael and All Angels, Bedford Park. By Norman Shaw, 1879.

All these were considerably larger than the average old-fashioned garden. Their size was not necessarily an advantage. Old-fashioned gardens were never in the grand manner, and tended to be as crowded with bushes and little flower-beds as a 'Queen Anne' drawing-room was with bric-à-brac. The effect of this in, for instance, the great open space before the garden front of Blickling was certainly fussy if by no means without charm; as often happened with 'old-fashioned' gardens, the layout has been simplified and smoothed out in this century. The style was probably better adapted for gardens on a smaller scale; research into old photograph albums should bring to light many examples which have long since been altered or swept away, and enable a better appraisal to be made of one of the most intriguing side-products of the 'Queen Anne' movement.

150. *Two Lovers Whispering by an Orchard Wall.* One of a set of stained-glass roundels of *The Round of Life* by C. E. Kempe, made for the Wood House, Epping, Essex, *c.* 1898, possibly from earlier designs.

VII   Two 'Queen Anne' Communities

Bedford Park

At the end of the 1870s Bedford Park became the best-known symbol both of the aesthetic movement and of 'Queen Anne'. Light gushed out of it; its sweetness was almost overpowering. As Moncure Conway put it: 'Angels and ministers of grace! am I dreaming? Right before me is the apparition of a little red town made up of quaintest Queen Anne houses.'[1] A 'Queen Anne' church, a 'Queen Anne' art-school, shop, club, and inn, and nearly five hundred 'Queen Anne' houses were set amid green fields and along tree-lined avenues. Almost every house was equipped with a suitably progressive or artistic family. Children in Kate Greenaway clothes bowled their hoops along the street on their way to co-educational school. Fashionable ladies rode out from the West End to stare at all these odd people; parties of architectural students came on pilgrimages, as one of them later put it 'much as students today visit the latest experiments in concrete and glass'.[2] The whole complex survives today, miraculously untouched except for the loss of the art school and a few houses. It is internationally famous as 'the first garden city'. So indeed it was, but more by accident than intention.

Its founder, Jonathan T. Carr (1845–1915), is a mysterious figure.[3] He wrote no books or autobiography, his private papers have disappeared, and his financial speculations have never been properly unravelled. He was the son of a City cloth merchant, whose Radical politics and a share of whose business he inherited; his sister was an art student at the Slade; his brother, J. W. Comyns Carr, was a well-known art critic and dramatist, and from 1877 one of the directors of the Grosvenor Gallery. He married Agnes Fulton, the daughter of a civil engineer who lived at Bedford House, an eighteenth-century building in the fields between Chiswick and Acton. The house had twenty-four acres of land attached to it; the property included two other eighteenth-century houses, fields, orchards, and an arboretum planted by Dr. John Lindley, a botanist who had owned Bedford House in the early nineteenth century. It was only a few yards from Turnham Green station, from which the City could be reached in thirty minutes. Bedford Park originated when Jonathan Carr or his father-in-law decided to develop the land for building.[4]

The extent of Carr's original intentions, or of his contacts in 1875, when the project was born, are not known. He certainly envisaged an estate of houses of good architectural quality for middle-class people of modest means. There is no evidence that at this stage he was planning to create a community or a garden city; if he had been, it seems unlikely that he would have called it Bedford Park, for 'Park' was a popular suffix for suburban developments and had genteel rather than progressive connotations. There is not even any evidence that he was originally thinking in terms of 'Queen Anne'. His first architects, E. W. Godwin and the firm of Coe and Robinson, were a curiously ill-assorted pair. H. E. Coe had been in Scott's office long before the 'Queen Anne' generation; in 1857 he had won the original Foreign Office competition with a French Renaissance design, only to be supplanted by his old master. He was a safe and competent architect, but well behind the van of fashion. Godwin, on the other hand, was one of the liveliest and most adventurous architects in England. It is not certain to what extent Carr realized this; he is said to have selected Godwin not because he knew him but because he had come across an engraving of Godwin's parsonage at Moor Green, Nottinghamshire, published in the *Building News* of 16 March 1874, and had thought it just the kind of house he was hoping to build. It is a little hard to believe that the connection was as accidental as this anecdote indicates. Apart from other possible contacts Godwin must have known Carr's brother Comyns Carr, for they moved in the same aesthetic circles, were both friends of Whistler, and both interested in the drama as well as art.[5]

Once Godwin was involved, Bedford Park was almost bound to become architecturally interesting. Apart from being a man of immense talents himself, he put Carr in touch with the progressive architectural circles supported by the *Building News*. His own connection with Bedford Park was a short one, but Carr moved on from him to Maurice B. Adams, the editor of the *Building News*, and to Norman Shaw, one of its favourite architects. By 1877, if not before, Carr had become an enthusiast for 'Queen Anne' and the aesthetic outlook that went with it. Bedford Park became a scaled-down counterpart of the Chelsea Embankment and the Cadogan Estate, adapted for people with much more modest incomes. Architecturally it went over completely to 'Queen Anne'. The street-names reflected the architecture. The first road to be built on had been named, non-committally, 'The Avenue'; many of the ones that followed were given names with eighteenth-century associations such as Queen Anne's Grove, Queen Anne's Gardens, Addison Road, Marlborough Crescent, Blenheim Road, and Woodstock Road.

Too much and too little can be made of the layout, which has at various times been presented as progressive or uninteresting, when in fact it was neither. It was based on three main roads, The Avenue, Woodstock Road, and Bath Road, converging from the north, east, and north-east on a point adjacent to Turnham Green station. The other roads were, approximately speaking, laid out on grids based on one of these three roads, so that there were irregularities and changes of direction wherever one grid merged into another. Moreover, neither The Avenue nor Woodstock Road (which followed the line of an older lane) was entirely straight, and there were plenty of T-junctions. So there was variety instead of a simple grid, and almost all the roads were closed at the end by a view of trees or houses. Existing trees were kept wherever possible; the line of some of the roads is said to have been adjusted to fit the trees. The houses all had gardens, usually a small one in front and a rather larger one at the back.

All this was agreeable (if a little monotonous) but not especially revolutionary. There was no shortage of other suburban building estates of the 1850s and 1860s laid out with trees and gardens on an irregular street plan. Research would probably produce examples of estates which preserved existing trees. A more unusual feature was that none of the houses had basements. In the 1870s this was still out of the ordinary for middle-class London housing, even of a modest nature. Basements seem to have been absent at Bedford Park less out of consideration for servants, than for reasons of health. At the congress of the Social Science Association in 1875 Dr. B. W. Richardson had made a considerable impression by proposing a 'City of Health' in which basements were forbidden and houses were limited to four storeys and were normally to have only two.[6] According to an article of 1883 in the *Bedford Park Gazette* basements in Bedford Park were left out following on Dr. Richardson's recommendations; very few of the houses were over three storeys and many only had two. However, the houses ignored Richardson's more revolutionary proposals, which included flat roofs, top-floor kitchens, glazed brick surfaces internally instead of wallpapers, and communal smokeless chimneys.

It is widely believed that Carr went bankrupt over Bedford Park. The reputed aftermath was picturesquely retailed by G. K. Chesterton: 'He lived for the rest of his life with the bailiff as his butler. He and his equally impoverished brother would spend long hours playing cards together, and getting highly excited when three shillings changed hands.'[7] The stories are probably exaggerated. Carr started developing Bedford Park as a private individual, possibly in partnership with his father-in-law. He later bought another eighty-nine acres, making a total of 113 acres. In 1881 he sold the whole estate (saddled with a mortgage of £200,000) to a new Limited Liability Company, Bedford Park Ltd. Although he was its managing director he had no financial stake in it; in 1886 it got into difficulties, the company was wound up, and the undeveloped land sold off, but by then Carr's interests had shifted to a new project. This was the purchase of

151. 1 The Avenue, Bedford Park, by E. W. Godwin, 1876. It was one of the first houses to be built on the estate.

the Kensington Court estate, and its development, from 1883 until about 1890, with housing mostly designed by J. J. Stevenson. By 1884 Carr had also bought and sold the land on which Whitehall Court was later to be built.[8] He did not go bankrupt in the 1880s, although he may have done so later. His numerous speculations certainly never gained him a solid fortune, and there is some reason for thinking that the other members of his family were embarrassed by him; it may be that the description of him as 'genial and optimistic' is a euphemism for 'specious and not altogether honest'.[9] But he lived on in his house at Bedford Park, as an undisturbed and benevolent patriarch, until a few years before his death in 1915.

The first few houses on the estate were built in 1876, on The Avenue. Godwin had provided two prototype designs: No. 1 The Avenue, designed for a corner site, was a revised version of his Moor Green parsonage; the other design, which was repeated in alternation with houses by Coe & Robinson along the southern half of the Avenue, was a completely new one. Coe & Robinson's houses were agreeable designs but, apart from a few small panes in the upper lights of the windows, there was little of 'Queen Anne' about them. Godwin's houses lay somewhere between Butterfield and fully fledged 'Queen Anne'; although they were cheap and simple the corner design, in particular, was full of character and quality. But when they were illustrated in the *Building News* their planning was bitterly criticized and compared unfavourably to that of Coe & Robinson's houses.[10] Godwin was accused of impractical kitchen planning and bad placing of doors, and of skimping his stairs and passages to provide bigger living-rooms. Carr seems to have agreed with the criticisms, for Godwin did no more work on the estate, although his corner site design, modified and slightly enlarged, continued to be used on it.

Godwin and Coe & Robinson disappeared together and were replaced by Norman Shaw, who was described as 'Architect to the Estate' on an advertising poster of 1877. Five prototype designs for detached or semi-detached houses by him were illustrated in the *Building News* in

151

152, 153

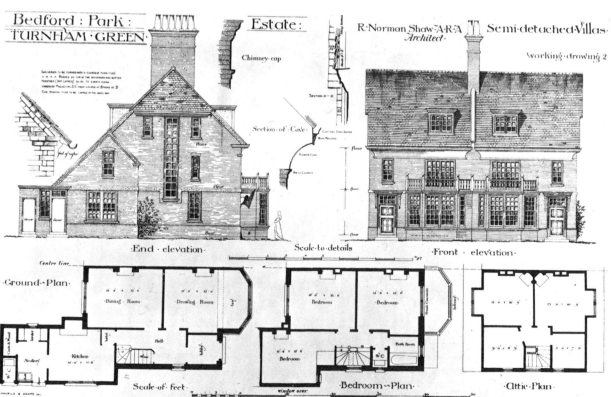

152. (*Top*) Designs by Norman Shaw for Bedford Park, illustrated in the *Building News* of 21 December 1877.

153. (*Bottom*) Another Norman Shaw design, from the *Building News* of 16 November 1877.

154. Tower House and Queen Anne's Grove, Bedford Park. From a lithograph by M. Trautschold, published 1882.

155. The Vicarage, Bedford Park. By E. J. May, *c.* 1881.

154 1877 and 1878. In addition he designed Tower House, Jonathan Carr's own big free-standing house in a big garden, in 1878, the parish church of St. Michael and All Angels in 1879, and a terrace containing the Tabard Inn, a co-operative store for the estate, and a house for its manager, in 1880.[11] A number of other design-types on the estate can be attributed to him with some confidence. But in 1879 or 1880 he resigned from his position as architect (apparently in a state of some exasperation with Carr, possibly for financial reasons) and recommended E. J. May (1853–1941) as his successor.

155   May, who had been in Nesfield's office, designed many houses in Bedford Park. He was almost certainly also responsible for the club which was built next to the garden of Tower House in 1878, although it was published in the *Building News* as by Shaw. Maurice B. Adams, by now editor of the *Building News*, designed the Chiswick School of Art, in Bath Road, which was opened

156, 157 in 1881, a house for J. C. Dollman in Newton Road, and the Parish Hall, next to the church. He constantly publicized Bedford Park in articles and engravings in the *Building News* and

156. Two houses, including studio house for J. C. Dollman, Newton Road, Bedford Park. By Maurice B. Adams, c. 1880.

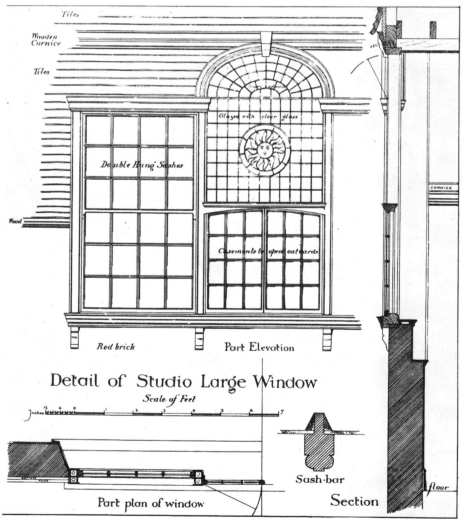

Tiles

Wooden Cornice

Tiles

Glazed with clear glass

Double Hung Sashes

Wood

Casements to open outwards

Red brick   Part Elevation

Cornice

Sash-bar

Section   floor

Detail of Studio Large Window

Scale of Feet

Inches

Part plan of window

157. A detail of the Dollman house

158. Bath Road, Bedford Park. From a lithograph by B. F. Berry, published 1882.

eventually came to live there himself in about 1883. Finally, an otherwise unknown William Wilson (of Norfolk Street, Strand) adapted Godwin's designs and provided designs of his own for 7 Queen Anne's Gardens (for T. M. Rooke, the painter) and probably for other houses, including the south side of Blenheim Road.[12]

    In addition to the occasional one-off house, and a few short terraces of individual design, Godwin, Shaw, May, Adams, and Wilson provided between them a stock of about thirty prototype designs, for detached or semi-detached houses, which were used all over the estate. Instead of one design being confined to one street, the designs were mixed up together in different combinations, so that every street is full of variety. But the general effect is a unified one, because May, Adams, and Wilson, although capable designers with an individuality of their own, were all strongly under the influence of Norman Shaw.

    It was Shaw who created the architectural character of Bedford Park, one which delighted and surprised the visitors who, emerging from Turnham Green station, felt themselves to be in a village or small country town where nothing had happened for at least a hundred years. In fact none of the houses bore more than a superficial resemblance to anything built in the seventeenth or eighteenth centuries; their apparent artlessness concealed a great deal of sophistication. One small house-front, for instance, could contain from three to six different types of window and one window several different types of glazing; however simple the elements were in themselves, the end result was far more complex than anything likely to be found in a genuine old village street. What Shaw had done was to scale down and simplify the eclectic style which he had worked out for his Chelsea, Kensington, and Hampstead houses to fit the modest price-ceilings on which Bedford Park was based. In the interests of economy he used comparatively few shaped or Flemish gables, and even those he kept simple, but a great many ordinary straight-sided ones; ornament was confined to a brick sunflower in a panel, or occasional pilasters or shaped and pedimented brick surrounds to doorways; there was no expensive wrought-ironwork, but an

158

157

159. A Norman Shaw house in Priory Avenue, Bedford Park.

160. Railings in Priory Avenue, Bedford Park.

160   abundance of wooden railings, balconies, and verandas. The villagey feeling was accentuated by
the use of tile-hanging, and of a certain amount of rough-cast rendering; Shaw seems to have
been the first architect to revive the latter material in the suburban context in which it was later
159   to proliferate.

The planning of the houses, whether by Shaw or the other architects, was unadventurous.
However artistic they might be, the inhabitants of Bedford Park accepted contemporary middle-
class standards. Within the comparatively small space available no attempt was made to experi-
ment in a degree of open planning; each house had to have at least a separate drawing-room
and dining-room, and if possible a separate study; the living-rooms tended as a result to be
uncomfortably small, and many of them have been knocked together in recent years. E. J. May
seems to have been the only one among the architects to venture even as far as to have sliding
doors between dining-room and drawing-room in some of his houses.

Prospective tenants were allowed to choose their own wallpapers, which were installed for
them by the estate workmen. The three most popular brands (no doubt with Carr and Shaw's
encouragement) were those produced by Morris, Jeffreys, and Woolams, the three most aesthetically progressive suppliers of wallpaper at the time.[13] The furniture tended to go with the wallpapers; as the *Lady's Pictorial* put it, in an article on Bedford Park published on 24 June 1882:
'those who pin their faith to massive mahogany and plate glass fly from it as from a spot bewitched.
The word horsehair has never been breathed within its precincts, gas is almost tabooed and the
odour of pot pourri supersedes that of eau de Cologne.'

161   Of the public buildings Shaw's Tabard group of old-fashioned inn, old-fashioned shop, and
old-fashioned house in a row together is an extraordinarily clever design which sums up the
essence of Bedford Park—its prettiness, its liveliness, and its preciosity. The church of St. Michael

161. Water-colour by T. M. Rooke of the Tabard, Bedford Park, designed by Norman Shaw, 1880. It is probably a sketch for the inn-sign.

162. St. Michael and All Angels, Bedford Park. By Norman Shaw, 1879.

162, VIII

and All Angels is more unusual. On the whole 'Queen Anne' architects, while arguing that Gothic was unsuitable for nineteenth-century houses accepted its suitability for churches. 'Queen Anne' churches (and even chapels) are a rarity and St. Michael and All Angels makes one regret it.[14] It is entirely 'Queen Anne' in its approach, but the Gothic element is much more in evidence than in Shaw's secular buildings. Shaw's starting-point was probably the King James Gothic of the seventeenth century. Approximately speaking, the stonework at St. Michael's is Gothic and Perpendicular and the woodwork derives from the seventeenth and eighteenth centuries—including the cupola that rides on top of the deep-eaved roof and used to echo the cupola on the roof of Carr's Tower House across the road. The combination is completely successful; several decades later it was to give ideas to Ninian Comper, but for the time the weight of Anglican convention was too great for it to be imitated.

May's club-house and Adams's School of Art underline the fact that May was a better architect than Adams. The club-house is an interesting design. Although it employs the 'Queen Anne' vocabulary, the strong contrast between its two halves and their sleek uncluttered lines give it a toughness that anticipates some buildings of the later nineteenth century. The Chiswick School of Art, which was destroyed in the war, had a rather clumsy combination of Sparrowe's House oriels and Flemish gables. The design was amended by Shaw, who wrote to his assistant Lethaby that 'Bedford Park is convulsed about the design for the School of Art—and bloodshed is imminent'.[15] So Shaw instructed Lethaby to raise the central gable and redesign the porch. The letter is interesting in that it shows that Shaw had a watching brief over all the Bedford Park designs.

The Architectural Association, always alert for architectural novelty, came out to have a look at Bedford Park in March 1877. This was before Norman Shaw had appeared; Carr showed them round the eighteen completed houses, and told them that he intended to build 600.[16] Nothing was said about the club, church, stores, and inn, but by the time the *Building News* wrote an editorial on Bedford Park on 9 November 1877, the club and church had been projected, and the idea of having an inn, stores, and college of art must have followed shortly after. It was by no means unusual—rather the opposite—for property developers to provide a church, shops, and a public house on an estate, but a club and a school of art were a different matter. Moreover the church, stores, and inn were, each in their own way, different from their equivalents in a conventional middle-class suburb. The church was bizarre in its design and extravagantly Ritualistic in its liturgy; the stores were co-operative; the public house was an 'old-fashioned inn' rather than a contemporary gin-palace, had an inn-sign painted by T. M. Rooke, one of the colony painters, and was lined with tiles by Walter Crane and William de Morgan. Some time between March and November 1877 Carr must have begun to think in terms of creating more than a housing estate. By 1880 descriptions of Bedford Park were beginning to refer to it as a 'quarter', a 'village', or a 'colony'.

161

According to Moncure Conway, who was one of the first tenants, 'each institution has appeared in response to a definite want. It was not in consequence of any original scheme that the co-operative stores, the club, or the Tabard Inn were built.'[17] That Bedford Park developed in the way it did was due to the type of people it attracted. It provided the only 'Queen Anne' houses of moderate size and price as yet on the market. As soon as they were available they were immediately filled, not only by ordinary middle-class people in search of a cheap but respectable address (although there were a good many of those) but also by middle-class people with the artistic or progressive tastes which went with 'Queen Anne'. It was the latter who coalesced with the architecture to give Bedford Park its character; it was to cater for their needs and ideals that the club and co-operative stores were built; it was because of their principles that only something as unlike a conventional Victorian pub as the Tabard was acceptable. Their consciousness of being a special kind of person living in a special type of house, of being missionaries of progress in the wastes of suburbia, combined with the publicity (and not a little ridicule) showered on them by the press to give them a strong feeling of corporate identity.

The early residents of Bedford Park included artists, actors, writers, revolutionaries, and progressives of every variety.[18] Among the artists were T. M. Rooke, a pupil of Burne-Jones and protégé of Ruskin, who lived with his old mother (habitually dressed in peacock blue) in a house in Queen Anne's Gardens; F. Hamilton Jackson, who came from the Slade School to run the School of Art; H. M. Paget, who started up a Voluntary Fire Brigade; C. J. Haité, known for his 'excessive reverence for the sunflower', who was a talented designer of wallpapers and fabrics as well as a painter; Joseph Nash, water-colourist; J. C. Dollman, book illustrator; and J. B. Yeats with his two young sons, Jack and W. B. Yeats. Architects were represented by Maurice B. Adams, E. J. May, and, for a year or two in the 1880s, by C. A. Voysey, who later designed 14 South Parade, Bedford Park, in an idiom deliberately in contrast to the pretty red-brick houses around it. Among people connected with the stage were Sir A. W. Pinero, the dramatist, William Terriss, the actor, who had been at school with Jonathan Carr, and William Bancroft, presumably a relation of the better known Squire Bancroft. Among the writers was John Todhunter, whose efforts to revive poetic drama were much admired by W. B. Yeats as a young man, and whose *Helena in Troas*, when produced in London with costume, décor, and direction by E. W. Godwin, was one of the aesthetic sensations of 1885.

Other residents included York Powell, Icelandic scholar, friend of William Morris, and Professor of History at Oxford; Charles Loch, Secretary of the most progressive of Victorian philanthropic bodies, the Charity Organization Society, and close friend of Octavia Hill, the founder of the National Trust and sponsor of the Kyrle Society; Canon J. W. Horsley, the chaplain of Clerkenwell prison, who devoted himself to the reclamation of burglars and invited them to stay with him (one of them is said to have described the Bedford Park balconies as 'uncommon 'andy'); Dr. Gordon Hogg, who was active in local government, a member of the first Middlesex County Council, and employed E. J. May to design him a house with something approaching an air-conditioning system;[19] Moncure Conway, an American-born clergyman who knew a great many well-known people and whose chapel in South Place provided late Victorian agnostics with religious uplift conveniently divorced from God; John O'Leary, the Fenian revolutionary fresh from a nine-year prison sentence;[20] and Sergius Stepniak, anarchist and author of *Mother Russia*, who was run over by a train and killed when absent-mindedly walking across a local level-crossing, consulting his notes as he walked.

With such residents it was not surprising that the atmosphere at Bedford Park was consciously progressive and aesthetic; that the shadow of the sunflower fell on the green lawns; that Japanese lanterns glowed in the shrubberies in the summer evenings; that tennis was played on Sunday mornings as well as afternoons; that the club was open to women as well as men, and alternated lectures on such subjects as co-operative workshops with meetings to press for women's suffrage or to debate Education or Dress Reform. Jonathan Carr, with his red tie blazing, hurried round the estate, showing parties of new arrivals the effect of the wallpapers already up to help them in their choice. Ellen Terry, John Bright, and Henry Fawcett were to be seen at garden parties at Tower House. Young ladies in aesthetic dress lovingly painted sunflowers in the School of Art. York Powell steered his friends on a tour of inspection, in which he would comment on the abundance of children and 'point with pride to their good looks and condition, explaining that they came of parents who had married, like himself, young, and for love, and imprudently'.[21]

Powell also remarked that unlike Oxford, where 'they dress for dinner, which I loathe', Bedford Park went in for 'camaraderie, without giving of banquets or dressing up to eat them'. But however much Bedford Park disliked dressing for dinner, it loved dressing up for parties. Fancy-dress parties and the forming of societies were its main recreations. The societies included the Ladies' Discussion Society, the Musical Society, the Conversazione Club, the Amateur Dramatic

163

MRS. ACHLIN.—Spanish Fortune Teller, red and blue skirt, blue jacket,
red handkerchief tied round head.

MISS ROGERS.—Crimson petticoat, figured paniers and
saque, one red rose in muslin hat, and an ostrich feather.

MISS ROGERS.—Pale blue satin skirt with pompadour
panier and bodice, rich lace on fichu and sleeves, and muslin
hat with blue and salmon-pink flowers in it.

THE MASTERS CARR in white suits: one as a little baker, and the other as a *marchand des*
confitures.
MISS CONNIE KING.—Soft, yellow silk dress, with deep lace collar, black mittens and stockings.

MRS. GOULD. — White nainsook muslin
dress trimmed with lace, and white wig.

MRS. WILSON.—Blue flannel petticoat,
bodice and panier of arabesque sateen.

MRS. BURRIDGE.—Brown and light blue flowered dress, with hat to match.
MRS. KING.—Handsome dark slate-coloured silk petticoat, overdress of rich brocade a
hundred years old, and miniature of the same date, cream-coloured lace at neck and
sleeves, white wig, small silk hat with lace trimmings.

163. Fancy dress worn at the Bedford Park fête. From the *Lady's Pictorial* of 24 June 1882.

Club, the Lawn Tennis Club, and the Natural History and Gardening Society. Most of these met at the club, which had a reading-room, tennis-courts, facilities for both sexes, and a big hall for meetings, parties, and plays. The fancy-dress galas mostly took place in the club; after one of them the young men, having danced until dawn, concluded by playing tennis in their fancy-dress until breakfast. 'The tradesmen and others moving about at that hour', concluded Moncure Conway, 'no doubt supposed it was only some new Bedford Park fashion.'

Tradesmen and others probably did not distinguish between different types of crankiness in Bedford Park, but the society there was not quite as cohesive as the publicity it received tended to suggest. It is possible to separate out a section which was ritualistic and probably voted Conservative and a section which was agnostic and probably voted Liberal. The two showed their colours when two rival schools were founded in Bedford Park, both in 1884. The Bedford Park High School advertised itself as being 'organized on a Christian basis'; the High Church Beresford-Hope was chairman of its council, on which the Bedford Park residents included Maurice B. Adams (who was also a churchwarden at St. Michaels) and Canon Horsley. The Bedford Park School was co-educational, and non-denominational (although religious teaching of a suitably undogmatic nature was given to those whose parents asked for it); among its Governors were Miss Buss, founder of the North London Collegiate, and two members of the London School Board; the local directors included Professor York Powell, who was certainly an agnostic, and Dr. Gordon Hogg.[22]

To outsiders both groups probably seemed equally eccentric. From about 1880, once Du Maurier, Gilbert, and others began to make everyone talk about aesthetes, Bedford Park inevitably received a great deal of publicity and numerous visitors: so many aesthetes, or reputed aesthetes, living together were too good to be missed. Some of the publicity was supplied by Bedford Park residents or sympathizers. Moncure Conway wrote a long article on it in *Harper's Magazine* of

164. *A visit to Turnham Green.* Bedford Park sketches by T. Raffles Davison, 1880.

March 1881; Walter Hamilton devoted a chapter to Bedford Park in his book *The Aesthetic Movement in England*, published in 1882; a group of Bedford Park artists produced a set of gay and pretty lithographs in the same year. This type of publicity was naturally sympathetic to the colony; Moncure Conway described it as 'Thelema', a Utopia in brick and paint, and saw its club-house and societies as an unconscious movement towards 'that co-operative life that animated the dreams of Père Enfantin and Saint-Simon.' The architectural periodicals were equally favourable about its architecture. Apart from the many illustrations and articles published in the *Building News* T. Raffles Davison sketched it for the *British Architect* and gave titles to his sketches, such as 'a shady dormer', 'a peep between the trees' and 'a cosy porch' which sums up the effect Bedford Park tended to have on visually sympathetic visitors.[23]

164

But much of the publicity made fun of it, not always with affection. *Youth*, on 6 April 1883, for instance, described the superior smugness of a Bedford Park mother and daughter encountered in a railway carriage, and commented 'I had heard of this aesthetic colony, of course, and found that I had by no means been wrong in imagining that Tennyson must have had them prophetically in his mind's eye when he wrote the line "They think the cackle of their burg the murmur of the world".'

'The Ballad of Bedford Park', which was published in the *St. James's Gazette* of 17 December 1881, was much more genial. It has been widely quoted but no book on the 'Queen Anne' style could omit it:

In London town there lived a man
  a gentleman was he
Whose name was Jonathan T. Carr
  (as has been told to me).

'This London is a foggy town'
  (thus to himself said he),
'Where bricks are black, and trees are brown
  and faces are dirtee.

'I will seek out a brighter spot,'
  continued Mr. Carr.
'Not too near London, and yet not
  what might be called too far.

''Tis there a village I'll erect
  with Norman Shaw's assistance
Where men may lead a chaste correct
  aesthetical existence.'

With that a passing 'bus he hailed
  (so gallant to be seen)
Upon whose knife board he did ride
  as far as Turnham Green.

'Oh, here we are,' said Mr. Carr.
  'No further will I roam;
This is the spot that fate has got
  to give us for our home.

' 'Tis here, my Norman, tried and true,
  our houses we'll erect;
I'll be the landlord bold and you
  shall be the Architect.

'Here trees are green and bricks are red
  and clean the face of man.
We'll build our houses here,' he said,
  'in style of good Queen Anne.'

And Norman Shaw looked up and saw,
  and smiled a cheerful smile.
'This thing I'll do,' said he, 'while you
  the denizens beguile.'

To work went then, these worthy men,
  so philanthropic both.
And none who sees the bricks and trees
  to sign the lease is loth.

'Let's have a store,' said Jonathan.
  Said Norman, 'So we will,
For naught can soothe the soul of man
  like a reasonable bill.'

'A Church likewise,' J. T. replies.
  Says Shaw, 'I'll build a Church,
Yet sore, I fear, the aesthetes here
  will leave it in the lurch.'

'Religion,' pious Carr rejoined,
  'in Mon-Cure Conway's view,
Is not devoid of interest
  although it be not true.

'Then let us make a house for her,
  wherein she may abide,
And those who choose may visit her,
  the rest may stay outside.

'But lest the latter should repine
  a tennis ground we'll make
Where they on Sunday afternoons
  may recreation take.'

Then each at t'other winked his eye
  and next they did prepare
A noble Clubhouse to supply
  with decorations fair.

With red and blue and sagest green
  were walls and dado dyed,
Friezes of Morris there were seen
  and oaken wainscot wide.

Thus was a village builded
  for all who are aesthete
Whose precious souls it fill did
  with utter joy complete.

For floors were stained and polished
  and every hearth was tiled

And Philistines abolished
  by Culture's gracious child.

And Abbey (he the artist,
  malicious little wretch)
Said it made him feel like walking
  through a water-colour sketch.

And Jonathan and Norman
  found so much work to do,
They sold out to a Company
  to put the business through.

Now he who loves aesthetic cheer
  and does not mind the damp
May come and read Rossetti here
  by a Japanese-y lamp.

While 'Arry' shouts to 'Hemmua':
  'Say, 'ere's a bloomin' lark,
Thems the biled Lobster 'ouses
  as folks calls "Bedford Park."'

Although by the mid 1880s Bedford Park was beginning to lose its news value, until in the 1890s it became decidedly *passé*, its influence was enormous and continued to operate long after parties of students had ceased to go on pilgrimage there. A number of housing estates were built in its shadow in and around London during the 1880s. They must have caused a little aesthetic fluttering in their neighbourhoods, even if they never acquired the cultural coherence of Bedford Park. Ernest Newton's houses and pub at Grove Park and Champneys's houses at South Ascot have already been mentioned in Chapter V. Streatham Park, which was being laid out in 1880, suggests the hand of Ernest George, whose family lived in Streatham; the houses in Telford Park, its rather dimmer neighbour, were designed in the same year by E. J. Tarver for 'Messrs. Sutton and Dudley', and Voysey actually left Bedford Park to go and live in one for a few years.[24] In 1883–4 the *British Architect* consistently plugged the Bush Hill Park estate near Enfield. Here houses mostly by T. Tayler Smith and a hotel by E. J. May were all to be much in the Bedford Park manner and built along roads with suitably aesthetic names, such as Village Road and Queen Anne's Grove, Place, and Gardens. But the estate was a financial failure, May's hotel and many of the houses were never built, and only a thin echo of Bedford Park survived the inroads of later suburbia.[25] What was built was little if any better than the work on a dozen or so other building estates in and around London. For during the 1880s the Bedford Park vocabulary was being taken up by speculative builders and put to every kind of use, literate and illiterate, enterprising or pedestrian.

The Garden Cities and Garden Suburbs came a little later, and have been described often enough. Although other elements went into their making, the Bedford Park ideal of a green setting in which like-minded people could lead a co-operative life in like-minded houses was very strong in them (but the pub was usually left out). More generally, the Bedford Park flavour lingered on, together with many elements of the Bedford Park style, in almost every suburban development built in the British Isles from about 1900 to the last war and beyond. Its influence extends to suburban house-names. Walter Hamilton recorded that at Bedford Park 'even the names on the doorposts have a touch of poetry about them', and quoted 'Pleasaunce, Elm Dene, Kirk Lees, Ye Denne' as examples.

Tite Street, Chelsea

Tite Street was much too small a neighbourhood to support a church, stores, and club-house as at Bedford Park (although, almost by accident, it had its own theatre).[26] But for a few years it was just as much of a community. It had a distinctive life-style, a distinctive architecture, and a distinctive colony of artists. It had its links with Bedford Park. Both communities tended to exhibit at the Grosvenor Gallery; E. W. Godwin, Tite Street's favourite architect, designed stage-sets and décor for John Todhunter, the Bedford Park poet; one can envisage Ellen Terry going from a Bedford Park garden party to a Tite Street soirée given by Whistler or Oscar Wilde.

She would have had a livelier time in Tite Street. Its Bohemian swans were several cuts above Bedford Park's artistic geese. Admittedly Frank Dicey, John Collier, Frank Miles, Archibald Stuart-Wortley, and Carlo Pellegrini were no better artists, though possibly better company, than T. M. Rooke or J. C. Dollman. But Whistler, Wilde, Sickert, and Sargeant make even the best of Bedford Park seem second or third rate. Bedford Park liked to think of itself as rather daring; but what a squawking in aesthetic drawing-rooms there would have been if the morals of Tite Street had been practised in Bedford Park, or if Godwin's raw-boned studios had been introduced among Shaw's sweetly pretty little houses. Late Victorian society made fun of Bedford Park, but had no difficulty in digesting it. Tite Street was more than it could stomach. Artistically, it made Whistler a bankrupt; architecturally, it emasculated Godwin's designs; morally, it sent Miles to a lunatic asylum and Wilde to prison.

Whistler dominated Tite Street. By the mid 1870s he had moved out of the orbit of Rossetti; Rossetti, busy doping himself to death with chloral at Kelmscott or Cheyne Row, was a spent force, and Whistler had replaced him as the artistic leader of Chelsea. Most contemporary English artists regarded him with open dislike. His cockiness, his caustic tongue, and his openly expressed contempt for almost every accepted English master, must have been very irritating to the Establishment. But for those who had eyes to see he was, as George du Maurier put it in his earlier and less conventional days, 'the great genius and innovator'.[27] His genius as a painter was reinforced by his brilliance as a personality; with his mistresses, his smart friends, his epigrams, and his dashingly dandyish clothes he exuded Bohemian chic.

In 1877 Whistler, the most daring painter in England, joined forces with Godwin, the most daring architect.[28] Whistler, who was then living at 2 Lindsay Row (now 96 Cheyne Walk), signed an agreement with the Metropolitan Board of Works, on 23 October 1877, to build a studio house on a double plot in Tite Street, close to the river. He commissioned Godwin to design it. It was to contain two studios; one of them had to be very large, since he planned to start an atelier. In addition, admirers or friends of Whistler, including a number of the well-connected young men with artistic aspirations for whom he had an especial fascination, took up other plots along the street and employed Godwin as architect. Whistler may have encouraged them to do both.

The first to follow him were Archibald Stuart-Wortley and Carlo Pellegrini, for whom Godwin designed a double studio house opposite Whistler's site in 1878; a month or two later Frank Miles took a plot a little further up the street. Archibald Stuart-Wortley (1849–1905) was the nephew of Lord Wharncliffe and the son of an M.P. and former Solicitor-General; he studied under Millais, became a professional painter of sporting scenes, and, by the mid-1870s, had moved from the Millais to the Whistler orbit. His friend Pellegrini was better known by his pseudonym of 'Ape', under which he drew cartoons of contemporary celebrities for *Vanity Fair*; he, too, came under Whistler's influence, to the detriment of his career; he gave up his profitable cartoons in favour of landscapes in the Whistler manner, which nobody bought.[29] Frank Miles was a well-connected young man, just down from Oxford; he had numerous rich relations (the Miles family had been

Bristol merchants and bankers since the eighteenth century) and was boosting a small private income by drawing pallid pictures of society beauties in aesthetic poses, with considerable success. Before he moved, Miles had been sharing rooms in Salisbury Street, off the Strand, with his Oxford friend Oscar Wilde, who came with him to Tite Street. The exact nature of their relationship is unlikely to be established; it was probably homosexual, but also socially useful to Wilde who, although very ambitious and already making his mark on London society, had little money and no social connections; Frank Miles had both.[30]

By the time they moved in, in the summer of 1880, the Tite Street scene had been largely reorganized. Whistler had barely settled into his house before the Ruskin libel case blew up, in November 1878, followed by his bankruptcy in May and the sale of his house in September. Whistler vanished to Italy for a year. Meanwhile the short-lived Pellegrini–Stuart-Wortley partnership had also broken up. In 1879 Stuart-Wortley commissioned a new house from Godwin, just for himself, further up the street. The reason for the move remains obscure; it may have been because he had already set up with Eleanor (Nelly) Bromley, an actress much favoured by young aristocrats, although he did not marry her until 1883. The original house was sold in August 1879 to the Hon. Slingsby Bethell, a Clerk in the House of Lords, and presumably also an amateur artist. Bethell had previously been interested in the possibility of building a tower of studio flats to Godwin's designs on the site next to Whistler's; this project now fell through and instead Jackson & Graham, an Oxford Street furniture shop, built a block of studios on the same site, to the design of R. W. Edis. Edis also designed a single studio house next door, for Frank Dicey, a portrait painter and another member of the Whistler circle.[31]

Whistler had returned to England in November 1880. He moved into one of the Edis studios in May 1881 and lived there until 1885. Sickert came as his student in 1882. The Tite Street gang re-assembled round him; it was probably at about this time that he, Miles, and Wilde did a song-and-dance act together in an amateur sketch called *The Grasshopper*.[32] But at the end of 1881 Wilde went off to America, and on his return set up independently of Frank Miles. In 1884 he married, and moved back to Tite Street. He had no money with which to build a house, and instead leased one of the dimmer Tite Street ones, in a row of commercial 'Queen Anne' houses put up as a speculation by an architect Frederick Beeston in partnership with his relative Francis Butler, who was a solicitor. But Wilde brought in Godwin to decorate the interior for him.

Whistler left Tite Street again in 1885 but moved back in 1887. Godwin had died the year before, but before his death had at last managed, in about 1884–5, to get his tower of studios built, although to a different design and on a different site, next door to Frank Miles's house. Whistler moved into one of the studios in June 1888, married Godwin's widow in August, and finally left Tite Street on March 1890. Three years previously, in circumstances that remain obscure, Miles had suddenly been removed to a lunatic asylum near Bristol, where he died in 1891. By then Wilde's friendship with Whistler had long ago collapsed; it had been unable to survive Wilde's ceasing to be Whistler's protégé and becoming his rival. The early 1890s saw him at the height of his fame, but in 1895 came his trial, imprisonment, and bankruptcy. The contents of his house in Tite Street were sold for the same kind of knock-down prices as Whistler's belongings had fetched when the White House had been sold sixteen years previously.

Two other artists in Tite Street deserve a brief mention. John Collier, later to become famous for his 'problem' pictures, lived in a 'Queen Anne' studio in the mews off Tite Street; it had been built for him in 1878 by his father, Sir Robert Collier (a successful lawyer, later created Lord Monkswell) at the back of his own house, which was on the Embankment. Both house and studio were designed by Phené Spiers.[33] In 1879 John Collier married the daughter of T. H. Huxley and after moved into one of two houses, each of different design, built on the river side of the Frank Miles house on Butler and Beeston land but designed in 1881 by Frederick S. Waller & Sons of Gloucester.[34] He seems not to have known Whistler. John Singer Sargeant arrived in

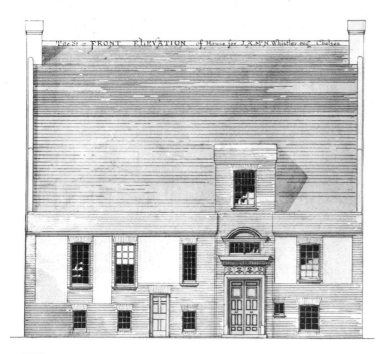

165. The first design for J. M. Whistler's White House, 35 Tite Street, Chelsea. By E. W. Godwin, 1877.

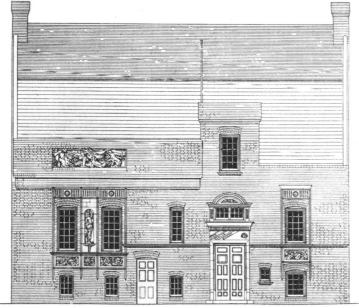

166. The final design for the White House 1878. (Demolished.)

Tite Street in 1885 when he took one of the Edis studios; in 1901 he absorbed Frank Dicey's house as well, and kept both house and studio until his death.[35]

Godwin's houses in Tite Street had as controversial and confused a history as his clients. Whistler's house was not, in fact, his first commission in the area; in 1876 he had designed Nos. 4, 5, and 6 Chelsea Embankment (on the corner of Tite Street) as a speculation for Gillow's of Oxford Street. They were handsome houses liberally sprinkled with oriel windows, like most of the Chelsea Embankment houses, and still noticeably under the influence of Webb and Norman Shaw.

The first design for Whistler's White House was much more original. Its big studio window faced north, on to the garden, so that the street front was dominated by the vast expanse of the studio roof, covered in green slates and broken only by a single small window. Under this were

165

two storeys of windows of different sizes and arrangements, reflecting the rooms and floor levels behind them, and punctuated by the front and back doors.

This irregular arrangement of doors and windows was, in fact, very deliberately composed. The pattern of the windows was carefully balanced and was superimposed on a related and very gentle pattern of white and red rectangles, obtained by rendering portions of the brick wall. The delicate asymmetry and pregnant use of blank spaces suggested that Godwin in his architecture, like Whistler in his pictures, had profited from his enthusiasm for Japanese art. The designs can be seen as the architectural equivalent of one of Whistler's 'arrangements of line, form and colour'. Doors, windows, roof, and wall provided the form; a few very sparing mouldings provided the line; the green roof, red and white wall, and the blue door provided the colour. The upper window projected against the blankness of the roof like the head against the blank wall in Whistler's portrait of Carlyle.

In so far as the exterior of the house adapted the brick detail and sash windows of a London terrace house to express its internal arrangements, on good Gothic Revival principles, and even in so far as it showed signs of Japanese influence, it could also be seen as an extreme development of the 'Queen Anne' point of view. But its startling simplicity and avoidance of any of the pretti-nesses and quaintnesses by now associated with 'Queen Anne' was more than the Metropolitan Board of Works could digest. The situation was not unlike that which had developed between Webb and the Office of Woods and Forests over his house for George Howard nine years pre-viously; but by now the type of house which Webb had anticipated was entirely acceptable, while Godwin's architecture was not.

Having got his design from Godwin, Whistler started to build it, without bothering to get the necessary clearance from the Works and General Purposes Committee of the Metropolitan Board of Works. The Board's architect, George Vulliamy, visited the site and found that the walls had already gone up ten to twelve feet. Vulliamy was the nephew of Lewis Vulliamy, the architect, and had been one of Charles Barry's best assistants; he was a capable man but his standards were those of an earlier generation. He was obviously startled by the design, and realized that his committee would be even more startled. But at this stage he behaved very well. In his report to the committee he described the design as presenting 'some novel features' and concluded 'the appearance of the building is unusual, but I do not think the Board can with-hold its approval upon that account. The building is intended for a particular purpose and the peculiarity of the design is due to its being constructed in a manner adapted to that purpose.'[36]

His committee disagreed with him. 'On the motion of Mr. Roche seconded by Mr. Runtz' they rejected the design. An amended one submitted on 28 January 1878 was also rejected. All this time Whistler was continuing to build. On 11 February Vulliamy reported that 'not with-standing my repeated notifications to Mr. Whistler' the building was nearly completed. On 25 February the Board's solicitor informed the committee that it had the right to take back the site and keep the deposit. But as 'the only objection which the Board have is that the elevation is of an ugly and unsightly character' he suggested that the committee content itself with threaten-ing to take up its rights unless Whistler agreed to make whatever alterations it required.

166   Whistler had to give in, but he went down fighting. At Vulliamy's suggestion Godwin made a number of alterations to the façade. The amended designs were passed on 18 March. They showed the parapet raised and filled with a panel of sculpture, a statue in an alcove inserted between two of the windows, the front door enriched and the main first-floor windows given decorative brick surrounds, which were carried down to frame the upper half of the ground floor windows. The latter arrangement may have been suggested by the somewhat similar treatment of the windows in Stevenson's Lowther Gardens, which were then in course of erection. The whole façade was now to be rendered white and 'The White House' inscribed over the door; this was the first recorded appearance of the name.

The surrounds were added immediately, but two months later the sculpture had still not been inserted. The committee accordingly withheld the lease. On 20 and 23 May Whistler sent off two furious letters. The new tenants were pressing to move into his house in Cheyne Walk; 'the consequence will be that I shall be turned into the street'. The delay in providing the sculpture was because 'one must of course wait the time of such men as Mr. Boehm, Mr. Leighton or Mr. Watts—unless indeed the Board elects after all to stultify itself by accepting any kind of work that could be done by the nearest stonecutter'. Withholding the lease was 'a proceeding whose wanton cruelty and unexampled vexatiousness no court of law could countenance'. Unless it was granted within twenty-four hours he would communicate with his solicitor. 'The bearer waits your answer.'[37]

This was too much for the committee; on 27 May they agreed to grant the lease subject to a covenant that the remaining work had to be done within a year. It never was. Whistler's failure to carry it out was due less to Messrs. Leighton, Watts, and Boehm's refusal to be hurried than to his own lack of money. He was already pawning his unsold pictures; in 1878 his disastrous libel suit against Ruskin precipitated bankruptcy in 1879, followed by sale of the White House to Harry Quilter. Quilter made a number of alterations and filled the blank panels with majolica; the house was demolished in the 1960s.

Meanwhile Godwin had submitted designs for two more Tite Street houses to the Metropolitan Board of Works. One of these was passed and the other and more interesting one had the same trouble as Whistler's. The designs for the Pellegrini–Stuart-Wortley house were passed by the committee on 3 June 1878, and it was built immediately afterwards. Its main features were two large studios set at right angles to each other on the top floor; they both had prominent partly-glazed roofs of double pitch and huge studio windows which rose into the roofs like dormers and were surmounted by Flemish gables.[38] It was probably these 'Queen Anne' trimmings, combined with a rather whimsical tower and dove-cot on the back elevation and, perhaps, with Stuart-Wortley's good connections which carried the design past the committee.

Frank Miles was less fortunate with his house. When Vulliamy saw the drawings he exclaimed 'Why this is worse than Whistler's'; and yet Godwin thought it 'the best thing I ever did'. One can see what both of them were getting at, for it was a startlingly original design. As the site was on the other side of the street to the White House, the studio window had to be on the street front. Frank Miles wanted balconies on the front, for he was an enthusiast for flowers (he introduced a number of Japanese varieties to England) and there was no garden or outlook at the back. Godwin incorporated windows, door, roof, and balconies into what was virtually an abstract composition of interlocking rectangles; it was a composition in colour as well as form, made up   167 of the green of the slates, the alternating red and pale yellow of the brick work, and the many colours of flowers and foliage, which were designed to spill out of the balconies and soften the right-angles of the masonry and windows. Rich terracotta ornament was shown on the porch and balcony front, perhaps in a vain hope of conciliating the committee.

The design came up on 5 August 1878. Seven of the committee voted for it, and seven against; the chairman then used his casting vote to reject it. 'Who are they who dare to sit in judgement on my work?' Godwin burst out a few months later. 'What "judgement" have retired farmers and cheesemongers, who never drew a line nor saw a drawing till yesterday?' He presented a revised drawing on 30 September, and it was accepted. As he put it 'I introduced a number of reminiscences of a visit to Holland, and the thing was pronounced charming'.[39]

What in fact he had done was to soften the design by giving it 'Queen Anne' trimmings.   168 The studio windows were given a Flemish gable and the door a moulded brick surround with pediment and scrolls. The balustrade of the studio balcony was changed into a light wooden one in the Japanese manner, supported on a projecting brick oriel. A little less than half of the ground floor was pushed forward to the frontage of the oriel, so that the two merged together; the flat

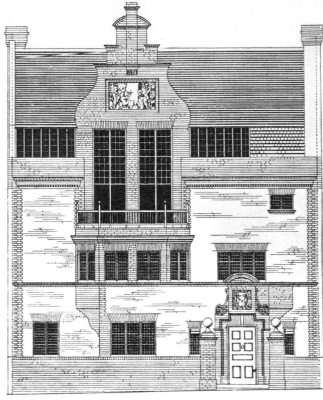

167. (*Above left*) The first design for the Frank Miles house, 44 Tite Street, Chelsea. By E. W. Godwin, 1878.

168. (*Above right*) The final design for 44 Tite Street, 1878.

169. (*Right*) The staircase, 44 Tite Street.

170. (*Far right*) The studio inglenook, 44 Tite Street.

roof of the projection was presumably designed to take flowers. The result was no longer revolutionary, but it was a sophisticated and original design. Inside, the staircase has delicate Japanese-style balustrading, originally unpainted, with brass-capped finials of the type that Godwin was   169
using in his furniture designs of this period. In the studio is a deep and capacious inglenook similar to the one which Godwin had designed for the White House; with its 'Queen Anne' framing and Japanese benches and Jeckyll grate it was an appropriate den for an aesthetic artist.   170

Godwin made designs for three more Tite Street houses in the summer of 1879, only one of which was ever built or, probably, ever likely to be built. But all three were clearly calculated to appease the committee; Godwin's taste for rectangularity was softened by ornament and picturesque additions. In August 1879 he designed, for the site next to the Frank Miles house, a 'studio and cottage for Miss Rosa Corder' which was published in the *British Architect* of 3 October 1879. On 14 May 1880 the *British Architect* published an engraving of the south side of Tite Street, showing Godwin's second house for Archibald Stuart-Wortley, Edis's house for Frank Dicey, Godwin's studio tower for Slingsby Bethell, and Godwin's White House. Of these   171
the Stuart-Wortley house was enriched by tile-hung gables more 'Old English' than 'Queen Anne'; the studio tower had 'Queen Anne' detailing and an octagonal corner cupola that was to be much imitated by designers in the 1880s and 1890s, in America as well as England; the Rosa Corder house was a variant on the original Frank Miles design, prettified, not to its advantage, by the addition of a cupola and a good deal of quaint detailing around the studio window.

Rosa Corder was a painter of race-horses, and the subject of one of Whistler's best portraits. She was also the mistress of Charles Augustus Howell, one of the most curious of the figures moving in Pre-Raphaelite and aesthetic circles. He had a buccaneering disregard for all accepted

171. The south side of Tite Street, as depicted in the *British Architect*, 14 May 1880.

Victorian standards of morality and respectability which much endeared him to both Rossetti and Whistler. As Rosa Corder neither owned the site nor is likely to have had the money with which to build a house, the design was probably a kite flown to attract a client. The Bethell studio tower was another project that never materialized. But the Stuart-Wortley house was passed by the Metropolitan Board of Works committee on 6 October 1879, and was in course of building at the time of publication of the *British Architect* engraving.

Godwin succeeded in getting a studio tower built in Tite Street in the end, but on the other side of the road. The 'Rosa Corder' site had, in fact, been leased in 1878 to an admiral's widow, Mrs. Bagot, who seems to have had difficulty in raising the money with which to build on it. In January 1882, she finally submitted designs; the fact that the Metropolitan Board of Works committee turned them down suggests that they may have been by Godwin. In 1883 she succeeded in buying the freehold of the site, which released it from the Board's aesthetic control. Tower House was built on it to Godwin's designs shortly afterwards; there is a possibility that he had bought or leased the site from Mrs. Bagot and was his own client.[40] The result was a remarkable and original building. Four huge multi-paned studio windows were piled one above the other, with eight storeys of little single windows to one side of them. The detail was very simple but what there was was 'Queen Anne'; the shallow arches above the windows were carved with sunflowers.

Tower House is still there, but the upper storeys have been mutilated. Frank Miles's house next door has been comparatively little changed, although some of the small panes have been removed; even the interior retains much of the original detail. The two Stuart-Wortley houses and Whistler's White House have all been demolished. Ironically, in contrast to the wholesale destruction of Godwin's work in Tite Street, every single one of the far less interesting houses by R. W. Edis, Frederick Beeston, and F. S. Waller survive.

172. Tower House, 46 Tite Street, Chelsea. By E. W. Godwin, *c.* 1884.

VIII   The Architecture of Enjoyment

'Queen Anne' by the Seaside

'Queen Anne' was well equipped to become a holiday style. Its red and white trim and fondness for balconies, oriels, and cupolas gave it an appropriate air of gaiety; its eclecticism and tendency towards exaggeration had to be developed only a little further for it to take off into fantasy. The results, when 'Queen Anne' goes crazy, can be exceedingly enjoyable, but it does so less often than one could have wished. It was a style that was based on visual fastidiousness; moreover, deep layers of earnestness tended to lurk under the surface brightness and sophistication of its patrons. Among the upper echelons of 'Queen Anne' there was built-in reaction against anything that could be thought either frivolous or vulgar; lower down the scale it was only occasionally that a local builder or minor architect was both sufficiently inspired and sufficiently uninhibited to kick over the traces. But between the extremes of fantasy and dullness is a great mass of holiday 'Queen Anne' architecture that is both gay and pretty. Most of it is unrecorded and much of it is decaying; fashion has passed it by, and its paint blisters and its wood rots beneath the salt-loaded breezes.

Most Victorians on holiday were not only, or even mainly, looking for enjoyment; they were in search of health as well as pleasure. Resorts were classified as either bracing or relaxing; in the late nineteenth century it was more fashionable to be braced than relaxed. A north exposure was considered especially bracing; the two most fashionable late Victorian resorts, Westgate-on-Sea and Cromer, not only faced due north but gloried in it.[1]

Westgate owed its success to two causes: its proximity to Margate and its reputation for healthiness. Margate had been one of the most select seaside resorts of the early nineteenth century but by the mid-century it was becoming vulgarized. Its fashionable clientele detached themselves from the crowd and retired to Westgate, in much the same way as the fashionable French retired from Trouville to Deauville; except that, once they got there, the French built a casino and the English built a golf course. Westgate never acquired a pier, deliberately prevented its promenade from joining on to Margate's, and prided itself on its freedom from 'hawkers, niggers, hurdy-gurdies and the general rowdy element that is so great a draw back to some of our English watering-places'.[2] All these proliferated at Margate but being next door to it seems to have done Westgate no harm; its clientele probably got an agreeable kick out of the thought of all that vulgarity being kept at bay just down the road.

Until 1865 Westgate consisted of nothing but fields and sand-dunes. In that year the owner of the land, Mr. H. D. Mertens, commissioned Charles N. Beazley, an architect, to make plans for laying out the site for building; he also managed to bring the railway to the area, but achieved little else and in 1868 sold the property in disgust to Mr. W. Corbett. Corbett made the roads, built the sea wall and the drainage system, established gas- and water-works, and began to build houses; at about the same time an architect called John Taylor, who was creating a settlement of bungalows next door at Birchington, built a small group of bungalows at Westgate.[3]

One of these was bought by Erasmus (later Sir Erasmus) Wilson. Wilson was a successful doctor who had made a fortune out of speculating in railway shares. His main claims to fame are that he brought Cleopatra's Needle to London and persuaded the English to take a daily bath. He also deserves to be considered one of the founders of Westgate, for his enthusiastic advocacy of its bracing qualities did much to make it popular. At a meeting held in September 1880 to discuss improving the drainage system, Wilson claimed that 'somehow or another it

173. Waterside, Westgate-on-Sea, Kent. By Ernest George and Peto, 1880.

has entered into the minds of the public that Westgate is the most healthy place, if not in England, at least within easy reach of the metropolis'. The doctors agreed with the public, and Prescott Hewett 'one of our most distinguished surgeons' was amongst the many who sent patients to recuperate there.[4]

During all this time C. N. Beazley[5] had maintained his connection with Westgate. A plan by him engraved in 1872[6] shows an ambitious layout of terraces and squares, but by 1879 only two of the squares and a few rows of villas had been built. The houses, most of which were probably designed by Beazley, were of white brick, gabled, gothic, and a little grim. Change was in the air, however; the resort was becoming fashionable, and its architecture was about to go over to red brick and 'Queen Anne'.

In 1880 the visitors included the Earl of Clarendon, the Marquis and Marchioness of Bath, the Marchioness of Tweedale and her nieces, Mrs. Astor, Captain and Lady Blanche Hozier, Mr. and Lady Clementine Mitford, Lady Evelyn Campbell, Lady Fairbairn, Lady Rose Weigall and her artist husband, W. Q. Orchardson, Luke Fildes and his family, and Dr. Andrew Clark, perhaps the most select doctor in London.[7] At that period such a combination of the fashionable and the artistic inevitably meant 'Queen Anne'. It arrived in the same year. 1880 is the date on Waterside, the house which Ernest George designed for W. H. Peto, brother of his new partner H. A. Peto. George was a rising architect who had not yet developed the Flemish terracotta style which was finally to establish his reputation. His house at Westgate was a delicate variation on the 'Queen Anne' manner of Norman Shaw.[8]

173

174. (*Above left*) Exbury House, Westgate-on-Sea. Built for A. B. Mitford, later Lord Redesdale, *c.* 1880.

175. (*Above right*) House on the front at Westgate. By C. N. Beazley, 1883.

176. Ellingham, Westgate-on-Sea.

In the same year or shortly afterwards Algernon Bertram Mitford built Exbury House on the plot next to Waterside. Mitford was an ex-diplomat who had become Secretary of the Office of Works; he was interested in Japanese art and was a friend of Whistler, who gave him as a referee when leasing the site of the White House.[9] His architect at Westgate is not known, but it may have been Beazley. On 22 September 1883 a house designed by Beazley at Westgate   175 was illustrated in the *Builder*. It shows that Beazley had gone over from Gothic to 'Queen Anne'; but it was a 'Queen Anne' of his own concoction, a mixture of metropolitan fashion with the local seaside tradition.

A. B. Mitford's Exbury House combines Norman Shaw mannerisms—tile-hanging, a gable   174 undercut by a bay window, a smaller gable tucked into one corner of a bigger one—with a two-storey veranda projecting flush to the bay window. Two-storey verandas were by then a common-place in seaside towns, but the detailing of the one at Exbury House was something new. Its spindly supports and rails suggest Japanese influence, as does the glazing of the windows. It is an elegant unassuming little house, very much what the rich of the time described as a 'cottage'. In the course of the 1880s the sea-front and broad peaceful roads of Westgate filled up with numerous similar houses, all too many of which have been demolished. Most of them were probably designed by Beazley, who was now permanently resident in Westgate. Few, if any, had Japanese elements; some showed the influences of earlier Victorian *cottages ornés*; but as a group they have an immediately recognizable character which can reasonably be described as 'holiday Queen Anne'. Materials are red brick, red tiles, and white wood. Roofs are usually hipped, with dormer windows and the occasional gable; windows are usually sashed, with smaller panes at least in the upper half. Tile-hanging, bay windows, and verandas abound. The verandas tend to be supported on elaborately turned wooden columns, such as had already appeared on some of the porches and balconies in Bedford Park or on overmantels in 'Queen Anne' drawing-rooms. The essence of the style was to combine dormers, bays, verandas, and   176 roof into a chic and cheerful whole.[10]

Cromer was a much older seaside resort than Westgate, but it became fashionable in metro-politan terms a few years later.[11] It had been an ancient but very decayed fishing-port, which from the late eighteenth century began to be frequented by the Norfolk gentry and citizens of Norwich when on holiday. The Norwich contingent included the Quaker Gurneys and Barclays; by the mid-nineteenth century a formidable cousinhood of banking or brewing Gurneys, Barclays, Buxtons, and Hoares had established themselves in numerous holiday residences in and around the little town. But it was still a small and quiet place, and was bound to remain so until the railway came in 1877.

The development of Cromer met with considerable opposition from the Gurney cousinhood but was encouraged by the two principal ground landlords, the Bond-Cabell family, who owned the Cromer Hall estate which included most of Cromer, and Lord Suffield, who owned the manor of Cromer South and the adjacent village of Overstrand, and lived a few miles away at Gunton Hall.

In 1877 the Bond-Cabell estate prepared an elaborate scheme of villas and terraces. It proved to be as much of a flop as the 1865 Mertens scheme for Westgate. It was premature by only a few years, however, for everything was working in Cromer's favour: the railway, the climate, and the landscape. At Cromer visitors were not only braced, they were braced in a setting of woods, cornland, and gently swelling hills, a pastoral landscape such as was now coming back into fashion as the younger generation reacted against the mountains, heathland, and pine forests which had been admired by their parents.

During the 1880s a number of events occurred which were to hoist Cromer on to the peaks of late Victorian fashion. In 1883–4 the Locker-Lampsons built Newhaven Court on high ground above the Norwich road out of Cromer. Frederick Locker-Lampson ('one does not notice his

177. The Locker-Lampson children, from the dedication page of Kate Greenaway's *Little Anne*, 1883.

affected way of talking when one is used to him', a guest wrote) had a small gift for poetry and a rich wife; he knew innumerable people, many of them famous, and entertained them at Newhaven Court. In 1888 he was joined in the Cromer neighbourhood by his friend the elegantly aesthetic Cyril Flower ('artists are perpetually painting him. Bootmakers call to borrow his boots as models') who had been visiting Cromer for some years and was persuaded by Lord Suffield to buy and run together two small houses at Overstrand. He gradually enlarged them over the next few years to the designs of Lutyens, then a very young and still unknown architect. The resulting house, called at first 'The Cottage' and later 'The Pleasaunce', became a social rival to Newhaven Court, for Cyril Flower (later created Lord Battersea) and his Rothschild wife were as dedicated to entertaining as the Locker-Lampsons.[12]

Meanwhile, a popular journalist called Clement Scott, who was married to George du Maurier's sister, had been staying for several years in the Cromer neighbourhood and writing articles about it in the *Daily Telegraph*. In 1886 they were published together as a book, called *Poppyland*, which was a bestseller for many years. 'Poppyland' became a usefully picturesque tag under which travel-agents could advertise the coast. The book is little more than mildly agreeable to read today, but suggests the combination of smart simplicity on the beach with rural peace and (supposed) innocence in the surrounding countryside which is what drew late Victorian visitors to Cromer. From 1888 they found it much easier to get there, for that year saw the opening of a new railway station, conveniently near the beach instead of up above the town on the hill, with an express service from King's Cross.

So the Cromer boom was launched. Until at least 1900 it was a boom with an exclusive flavour, even if, as at Scarborough in the mid-century, the metropolitan cream lay on top of a good deal of middle-class milk. In 1885 the ten-year-old Winston Churchill was sent to Cromer with his governess and wrote to his mother 'I am not enjoying myself very much. The governess is very unkind, so strict and stiff' (a few days later he threw an ink pot at her).[13] In 1887 the infant Compton Mackenzie looked up from the sands and saw 'a beautiful lady in a beige-coloured dress' sitting next to him. This was the Empress Elizabeth of Austria, on an English holiday.[14] All around her well-born babies were being taken for trips in little goat-drawn carts, and thoroughly 'nice' Kate Greenaway children in jerseys and straw hats were paddling and making sand-castles.

177   Kate Greenaway herself was likely to be staying with the Locker-Lampsons as was Randolph Caldecott until his early death in 1886.[15] The artistic rich would meet her there when they made the customary Cromer social round: a visit to the Locker-Lampsons, a visit to the Flowers at Overstrand, and a drive inland to Blickling, to call on Constance, Lady Lothian, who was so artistic that all the animals round her had to be white—white cattle, white ponies, white pigeons, and white peacocks.[16] When not otherwise occupied they could play golf on the links, which Lord Suffield built and opened in 1887–8, with his friend the Prince of Wales as president. Here,

178. Houses of *c.* 1890 on the West Cliff at Cromer, Norfolk.

in 1892, they would have met Oscar Wilde playing golf with Lord Alfred Douglas in the intervals of composing *A Woman of No Importance* ('I find Cromer excellent for writing, and golf still better') or run into J. M. Barrie, who in that year presented a prize putter to the golf-club, to be competed for annually by his own friends.[17]

Other visitors in Cromer's heyday included Swinburne, Meredith, Walter Crane, the aged Tennyson, the Beerbohm Trees, Lady Ritchie, and Ellen Terry, besides duchesses and countesses by the dozen. All these celebrities attracted other visitors, and, inevitably, villas, terraces, and hotels sprung up to receive them. Clement Scott has a nice description in *Poppyland* of Cyril Flower and Lord Suffield, the former 'clad in white samite, as mystic as he can be, with a bath towel round his neck or a camera slung on his back' the latter 'laying out imaginary terraces and Queen Anne villa residences' with his faithful solicitor in attendance.[18] Cromer became a bigger place than Westgate, and too many interests were involved in its development for it to have the same architectural consistency; but the dominant flavour of the new buildings was 'Queen Anne'. Outbreaks of red brick, Flemish gables, cupolas, and balconies diversified the houses of the old town and spilled along the cliffs, gay and glowing above the apparently endless sands.

The architecture and the architects came from both Norfolk and London. They ranged from 'Queen Anne' strongly marked with the imprint of Norman Shaw to 'Queen Anne' in its more eccentric or commercialized varieties. Edwin Lutyens's work at the Pleasaunce was in his own highly individual version of 'Queen Anne' but was clearly out of the top drawer. The buildings put up by a mysterious 'Mr John Smith of West Kensington', a property developer who was responsible for much new building in Cromer, were equally clearly not out of the top drawer, although they varied considerably in quality.[19] In 1887 he built the mildly 'Queen Anne' Red Lion Hotel in the old town, on the cliff-top above a projected new pier which was never built. In 1890 he built a much more extraordinary pair of bungalows on the Norwich Road, in a bizarre but festive combination in which 'Queen Anne' is mixed up with cast-iron detailing that is part Japanese, part mid-nineteenth century in inspiration. Smith is also known to have been active on the West Cliff, a big westward extension of Cromer stimulated by its neighbourhood to Cromer Beach Station and by two big sales of building-land held by the Bond-Cabell family in 1890 and 1891. Was he responsible for the row of boarding-houses off the West Cliff? These   178

179. The Metropole Hotel, Cromer. By G. J. Skipper, 1893–4. (Demolished.)

are an example of Norman Shaw 'Queen Anne' put to practical purposes; the road is at right-angles to the front, and the bay windows, balconies, and dormers piled up one above the other ensure that each room gets a sideways-on view of the sea. And who was the architect or architects of the houses in the select Cliff Avenue on the other side of the town? The road was laid out in the early 1890s by Samuel Hoare, M.P., the only member of the Gurney cousinhood to get involved in property development.[20] It is lined with cheerful examples of holiday 'Queen Anne', plentifully supplied with Flemish gables, half-timbering, and elaborate wooden verandas.

The most clearly defined architectural personality in Cromer was that of G. J. Skipper, the Norwich architect. He represented the local rather than London interest in developing the town. He designed the modestly 'Queen Anne' town hall in 1889 and three far more opulent hotels along the front in the 1890s: the Grand Hotel (1889–91), the Metropole (1893–4), and the rebuilding of the Hotel de Paris (1894–5). The Grand and the Metropole, which have been demolished, were built by syndicates mostly financed by Norwich money, under the chairmanship of Sir Kenneth Kemp, a Norwich banker and businessman. The Hotel de Paris, which survives, was the personal venture of the Cromer-born Alex E. Jarvis, who was an active instigator of the development of Cromer.[21]

All four buildings were built and embellished by Norwich and Norfolk builders and craftsmen, and furnished by the Norwich firm of Trevor Page and Company, which had a financial stake in the Grand and Metropole. They were all of red brick and, in varying degrees, 'Queen Anne'. The

179   demolished Metropole was closest to Norman Shaw; the Hotel de Paris was (and is) cruder but also jollier, at once looking back to the French Empire style of the mid-century and looking forward to Edwardian Baroque. Inside, all the hotels were richly embellished with Japanese wallpapers, stained glass, and Moorish smoking-rooms; much of this has gone at the Hotel de

180   Paris, but its hall is still evocative of the period, and the upper halves of the windows in its main rooms are still rich in stained glass and leaded lights; lower down, in the usual commercial compromise with 'Queen Anne', there are sheets of plate glass through which one can look out to sea along the pier, which as a result of Alex E. Jarvis's lobbying was built immediately below his new hotel a few years after it was completed.

180. The reception hall at the Hotel de Paris, Cromer. ▷
By G. J. Skipper, 1894–5.

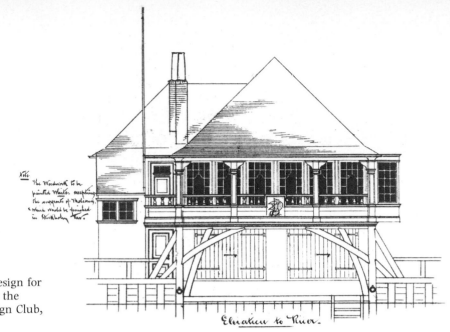

181. Anonymous design for boathouse, made for the *British Architect* Design Club, 1882.

182. Boathouse at Wallingford-on-Thames, Berkshire. By Christopher and White, 1882.

183. Unexecuted design for hotel and houses at West Bay, Dorset. By E. S. Prior, *c.* 1885.

184. Detail of a terrace house at Broadstairs, Kent.

Holiday 'Queen Anne' can be found at seaside resorts all over the country, and inland in cricket pavilions, boathouses, and riverside residences innumerable. Sometimes it is tasteful and close to Norman Shaw, as in the terraces and houses at West Bay, Dorset, a seaside development next to Bridport which never quite had the success its promoters hoped for. The architect was Shaw's pupil, E. S. Prior; his later designs for West Bay are in his own intensely idiosyncratic style, but his first terraces date from about 1885, when he was still under Shaw's influence. A delightful (unexecuted) drawing by him of a hotel and row of lodging-houses shows 'Queen Anne' at its quaintest and prettiest, firing fusillades of bay and oriel windows of every shape and size in all directions.[22]

181, 182

183

West Bay is not typical of holiday 'Queen Anne', however; it is too much a product of the inner circles of the style. Most holiday 'Queen Anne' was designed by builders or fringe architects; it was built in such large quantities that it became more or less of a vernacular at waterside resorts all over the country. It tends to be cruder than the buildings at West Bay, and also to make far more lavish use of balconies and verandas, often with a little half-timbering thrown in for variety. Much of it is humdrum, although its typical combination of red brick and white

184

185. One of the 'Seven Deadly Sins', built *c.* 1896 along the Thames at Pangbourne, Berkshire.

wood is nearly always cheerful. But there were occasions when the holiday spirit took hold of its mainly unknown designers and they broke triumphantly through the barriers of respectability.

A row of houses along the Thames just above Pangbourne is an example of how enjoyable the results could be. They were built in and around 1896, reputedly by D. H. Evans, the owner of the store of that name in Oxford Street. He was enterprising enough to buy or lease the riverside slope of the railway embankment, where most people would never think of building. He scooped away its sides and made seven holes into which he inserted seven riverside villas strung out along the roadside, with their roof tops level with the railway. He himself lived in the one nearest to Pangbourne, which carries the date 1896 and his initials.[23] The unknown architect collected together all the elements of the 'Queen Anne' style—pargeting, tile-hanging, cupolas, verandas, balconies, Flemish gables, dormers, bulging cornices, friezes decorated with swags, multiple chimney-stacks, dormer windows with little pediments, sashes, windows with multiple panes or Japanese glazing, round windows or windows with arched central lights—added a few barge-boards and a spice of half-timbering, and shovelled the whole mixture on as thick as he was able. The result is very cheerful but not calculated to appeal to Puritan tastes. Locally the houses were quickly nicknamed 'the seven deadly sins'; a contemporary guidebook described them, accurately and more tolerantly, as 'gay and variegated river residences'.[24]

'Queen Anne' Shops

In shopping streets, as in holiday resorts, 'Queen Anne' started by catering for the select few and was rapidly adapted for the less selective many. Its first appearance, as might have been expected, was in the shops which supplied artistic furnishings for artistic houses. The very first of these was for an ideally appropriate client. In 1874 Norman Shaw designed a shop-front in Oxford Street for his friend Murray Marks. Marks had been the first English dealer in blue and white china, and through him Rossetti, Whistler, and others had built up their pioneer collections in the 1860s. In the 1870s, as more and more artistic houses had more and more shelves, over-mantels, and cabinets needing to be filled, Murray Marks's business boomed. His new shop was evidence of his prosperity. Shaw designed him something based on an eighteenth-century shop-front, tastefully prettified with small panes punctuated by larger arched openings for special pieces.[25]

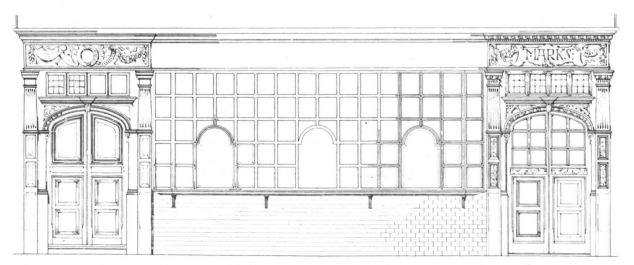

186. Shop front for Murray Marks, Oxford Street, London. By Norman Shaw, 1874. (Demolished.)

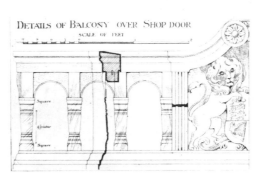

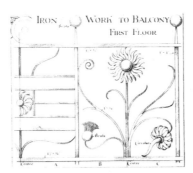

187. Thomas Goode and Co., South Audley Street, London. By Ernest George and Peto, 1876.

Murray Marks's shop was fashionable but not at all large, and in an older building. In 1876 the more formidable and equally fashionable Mayfair firm of Thomas Goode and Company, suppliers of china and glass, went over to 'Queen Anne' for their large new premises in South
187 Audley Street. Their architect was Ernest George. His design, which survives unaltered, had all the 'Queen Anne' trimmings, with one exception. It had Flemish gables; it had elegantly attenuated chimney-stacks; it had a blue and white Nankin vase in a brick alcove in the centre of the façade. But commercial caution prevented George's clients from allowing him to cut up the shop-windows with glazing bars; apart from a little 'Queen Anne' detailing, they stayed firmly within the accepted plate-glass convention.[26]

Their caution was unnecessary. Just as shop-keepers in the 1960s discovered that in a street where all the shop fronts were brightly lit the way to attract attention was to have a shop-front that was scarcely lit at all, shop-keepers of the 1870s discovered that amid acres of plate glass small panes were an excellent form of advertisement. A number of 'Queen Anne' shops, or just 'Queen Anne' shop-fronts began to appear in and around Bond Street, many of them with their shop-fronts cut up by glazing bars, and even by leaded lights.

One of the first and most elegant was Agnew's daintily fanciful new shop in Bond Street, opened in 1878 and designed by Solomons and Wornum, a partnership practising in Manchester, where Agnew's originated. Thomas Harris designed an especially pretty shop in Vigo Street,
188 which was illustrated early in 1880; and in 1877–9 at least three complete buildings with shops on the ground floor were designed by R. W. Edis in Old and New Bond Streets. That at 96 New Bond Street inspired the *Building News* to comment: 'New Bond Street will soon become one of the most interesting thoroughfares in the West of London for examples of characteristic and suitably treated modern fronts.'[27]

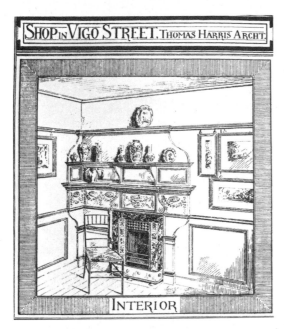

188. (*Top and bottom left*) Shop in Vigo Street, London. By Thomas Harris, 1879.

189. (*Top right*) Queen Anne Chambers, 1 Poultry, London. By J. Belcher and Son, 1875. (Demolished.)

These were all, in one way or another, select establishments, selling china, glass, pictures, or furniture to the owners of artistic houses. But meanwhile 'Queen Anne' was working its way on to a wider commercial front. Here what attracted clients was not the quaintness or old-world potentialities of 'Queen Anne' but what Norman Shaw had demonstrated in New Zealand Chambers, its ability to provide large expanses of window. The effect of New Zealand Chambers was seen as early as 1875 when J. Belcher and Son (an old-established City architect who had just taken a progressive son into partnership) designed a block aptly named Queen Anne Chambers on a prominent corner site in Poultry. The building contained a shop on the ground floor and offices above, and occupied its corner site like a lantern, with a brave array of windows of 'Sparrowe's House' and other types. In a compromise between what Shaw had done at New Zealand Chambers and what commercial clients tended to demand, the upper portions of the windows were filled with small panes and the lower with large sheets of plate glass.[28]

189

190. Shop front, originally Overfield's, in Russell Street, Leek, Staffordshire. By W. L. Sugden, *c.* 1890.

This remained the most common formula in the 'Queen Anne' commercial buildings put up in the 1880s and 1890s. In many of them the intervals between the structural members were filled, or almost filled, with glass, and this glass infill, both on ground- and upper-floor levels, often took the form of bay or oriel windows. In some designs the windows were run together to become a continuous screen of flat or shaped glazing.

190   W. L. Sugden's many 'Queen Anne' buildings in Leek include a simple but very elegant example of a glazed commercial front. It was designed about 1890 as a furniture shop for the firm of Overfield's, and still survives, although the glazing has been rather crudely altered. The roof ends in a great overriding pediment on the street-front, which is supported on a framework of single-storey columns; the space between the framework is entirely filled with windows, with bay windows in the central spaces.[29]

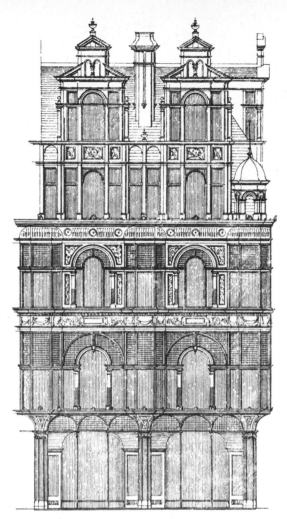

191. Design for shop and offices by
W. S. Ogden, 1885.

192. Design for shop in Albion Street, Leeds.
By Smith and Tweedale, 1886.

A block of shops and offices published by a Manchester architect, W. S. Ogden, in the second edition of his *Mercantile Architecture* (1885) is even more original. It is for a metal framed building, but the metal load-bearing columns are exposed only on the ground floor. On the first and second floors the columns are set back behind a curtain wall of glazing which projects in front of the columns in the form of half-octagonal bay windows (which rise to an octagonal turret at the corner). On the ground floor there is a similar wall of shaped glazing, but it is recessed behind the columns instead of projecting in front of them. The third and fourth floors consist of a mansard roof lit by two-storey dormer windows heavily glazed and surmounted by Flemish gables.

The design is basically imitating what Shaw had done at New Zealand Chambers, but is carried a stage further. There is no evidence that it was ever built. Ogden's book includes a number of other more or less 'Queen Anne' designs (Ogden called them 'Free Classical') detailed with a crudity that would have appalled Norman Shaw and all respectable 'Queen Anne' architects. The multi-storey glazing of a shop in Albion Street, Leeds, designed by Smith and Tweedale in 1886, is as daring and as coarse as anything by Ogden.[30] It is possible that Shaw and others failed to develop the potentialities of New Zealand Chambers because its formula was taken up by commercial architects who used it with what they would have considered an unbearably vulgar accent. It was a pity. The development was entirely in line with 'Queen Anne's' claim to be Gothic brought up to date, and if exploited by architects of the first quality might have produced exciting results.

191

192

Pubs, Improved and Otherwise

Like 'Queen Anne' shops, 'Queen Anne' pubs start by being respectable and artistic and soon become commercial and not respectable at all. The latter were often crude but also full of life and, on occasions, of originality; the potentialities of the curving glazed wall, in particular, were exploited in some pubs with results that were brilliant in all senses of the word.

The 'good' pubs were financed by philanthropic upper- or upper-middle-class patrons and were intended as rebukes and alternatives to what respectable Victorians continued to call gin-palaces—even though gin had ceased to be the principal drink sold in them many years previously. The 'bad' pubs arrived ten years or more later, and were financed mainly by publicans. They were in the gin-palace tradition but took over the 'Queen Anne' vocabulary, and adapted it to appeal to unrefined tastes. Of the two, the 'bad' pubs are rather more enjoyable.

'Good' pubs tended to be described at the time as 'improved'. They can be grouped with coffee houses or, as they were often called, coffee taverns. Victorian pubs were an obvious challenge to those among the enlightened (there were large numbers of them) who wanted to spread sweetness and light among the working classes. The pubs are the subject of so much nostalgia and admiration today that it is a little hard to appreciate the distaste, both aesthetic and moral, with which almost all educated people regarded them in the 1870s. Visually they seemed to represent commercial vulgarity at its worst; morally, they were seen as encouragers of waste and spreaders of corruption. There was widespread agreement that they needed reforming, but some disagreement about the means. The social functions of the pub were recognized; but should reform concentrate on increasing the social content and reducing the emphasis on alcohol, or should it increase the social content and get rid of the alcohol altogether?[31]

Coffee public houses were the result of the latter approach, and improved public houses of the former. Coffee public houses provided food, social facilities, and a bar at which only non-alcoholic beverages were served. At improved public houses alcoholic drink was sold but in surroundings which, it was hoped, would discourage excessive drinking, because drink would be the accompaniment to food in the restaurant or coffee-room, or social life in the club-room. At all costs their architects avoided the familiar trappings of the gin-palace of the 1870s, the lush stucco ornament and rows of large blazing gas lamps without, the mirror-lined walls and flaring lights blazing through huge plate-glass windows within.

'Queen Anne' provided builders of both coffee taverns and improved pubs with the image they wanted. Stucco was replaced by red brick and tile-hanging, plate glass by small panes, and mirrors by art tiles and panelled dados. Moreover the style had exactly the right connotations. It was 'progressive' and yet suggested a return to the good cheer and conviviality without debauch of the old English inn, an institution which was now seen through increasingly rose-coloured spectacles.

Improved pubs and coffee taverns are often architecturally indistinguishable. The pioneer 'Queen Anne' pub was Norman Shaw's Tabard in Bedford Park, designed in 1877. Its name was inspired by the Tabard from which Chaucer's Canterbury Pilgrims set out, and, according to a contemporary account, 'everywhere there is an absence of the garish glitter and the sham splendour of the modern gin palace'.[32] The pioneer 'Queen Anne' coffee tavern was the Bee Hive on Streatham Common, designed by Ernest George in 1878. Both it and the Tabard had swinging inn-signs and an abundance of small panes lighting the bars, in addition to all the normal 'Queen Anne' trimmings; over one door of the Bee Hive was the identical panel, showing Knowledge strangling Ignorance, which was originally designed for the early London Board Schools.

The best of the later 'Queen Anne' improved pubs were probably the Galleons Hotel and the Connaught Tavern, both on the edge of the Victoria and Albert Docks in the East End of London. They were designed in 1881 and 1884 by Vigers and Wagstaff for the London and St. Katherine's

193. The Galleons Hotel, off Manor Way, Royal Albert Dock, London. By Vigers and Wagstaff, 1881.

Dock Company, and imitated Norman Shaw with considerable panache.[33] The Galleons Hotel is especially lush, but it is eclipsed by Ernest George's superb and enormous Ossington Coffee Tavern of 1882 in Newark. The Bee Hive had been largely paid for by P. B. Cow, a Streatham rubber manufacturer; the Ossington Coffee Tavern was the gift of Viscountess Ossington, a leading Temperance supporter, and was built as a memorial to her husband and son. The two clients neatly suggest the social range of Victorian enlightenment, but both were equally unsuccessful. The inhabitants of Newark and Streatham proved impervious to sweetness and light, and both coffee taverns were adapted for other uses once the money to subsidize them was no longer available.

194

194. The Ossington Coffee Tavern, Newark, Nottinghamshire. By Ernest George and Peto, 1882.

The commercial pubs of the 1890s are a long way removed from the coffee taverns and improved pubs of the 1870s and 1880s. They are not in good taste and they do not suggest an old English tavern. They suggest having a good time, in uninhibited surroundings. They were, and still are, inviting and ebullient self-advertisers. But the basis of their advertisement is the 'Queen Anne' style, suitably adapted.

Their main constituents were wood and glass. Glass, in the form of engraved mirrors and windows, was elaborately framed by columns, arches, and pediments of wood; wood, in the form of immense superstructures for bottles, barrels, and glasses, or screens to conceal the more select or secretive customers from the rest of the clientele, and even from the bar staff, was lined with mirrors, or pierced with panes or hinged panels of glass. Light, from gas or electric standards of elaborate wrought metal, was reflected endlessly in the mirrors, sparkled on the facets of the glass engraving, and shone invitingly through the windows to entice the passer-by.

The decoration both of the joinery and the glass was in a commercialized version of 'Queen Anne'. The joinery made prominent use of the vocabulary of baluster-columns, broken pediments, coves and screens of turned uprights, which had been evolved by Shaw and others in the 1870s. The wall shelves and island centre-pieces (known as 'backfittings' and 'wagons' in the trade) were the publican's version of the overmantel, but used to display bottles and glasses instead of

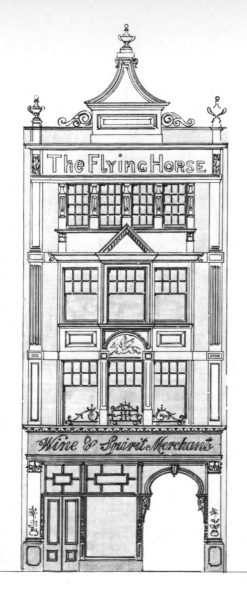

195. Design for The Flying Horse, Walworth.
By J. T. Alexander, 1888.

blue and white china and peacock-feather fans—although contemporary engravings sometimes show art-vases tastefully arranged on the upper shelves. The decoration engraved or painted on the glass was an eclectic mixture which included birds sitting on sprays of leaves, or storks perched in rushes, both motifs derived from Japan, and rococo swags and scrolls and cornucopias bursting with fruit or flowers, of Renaissance or eighteenth-century origin. The windows of the more inventive pubs projected, curved in and out, or broke up their glazing with arches and pediments in a manner which derived from New Zealand Chambers or the houses on Chelsea Embankment by way of commercial 'Queen Anne' shop-fronts. Since the bars were invariably on the ground floor this type of glazing was normally used only at that level, so that the buildings seldom, if ever, became complete lanterns of glass. But the ground-floor fronts of London pubs like the Prince Alfred in Formosa Road, Maida Vale, or the demolished Elephant and Castle, Newington Butts, with their lights glowing through a rippling wall of richly decorated glass completely divorced from the structure, were exciting and highly original creations.

197

Their 'Queen Anne' elements extended beyond windows and woodwork. Their lincrusta-lined ceilings were stamped with imitations of Jacobean plasterwork similar to those to be found in the halls and dining-rooms of 'Queen Anne' houses. The tiles which lined their walls were often decorated with designs similar to those engraved on the glass, or had borders of aesthetic sunflowers and pomegranates. The wrought-iron grilles over their entrance porches, and the immense wrought-iron tentacles supporting even more immense lanterns along their street

196. Inside the Prince Alfred, Formosa Street, Maida Vale, London. It was remodelled *c.* 1898.

fronts, were more ebullient versions of the wrought iron to be found in the balconies and railings of fashionable Chelsea or Kensington houses. And their architecture as a whole abounded with Flemish gables and cupolas, and was encrusted with terracotta or plaster panels of more or less Renaissance ornament. But these 'Queen Anne' features were often mixed up with hangovers from mid-Victorian days, such as Second Empire mansard roofs and traceried windows, or echoes of more recent fashions, varying from Art Nouveau to the neo-Flemish popularized by Ernest George.

The more respectable 'Queen Anne' architects had, of course, nothing to do with these pubs. They were designed by obscure firms sometimes specializing almost entirely in pubs, sometimes combining pub work with shops, warehouses, or speculative housing. On the other hand, some of the highest-quality firms working for 'Queen Anne' architects also did work in pubs. W. H. Lascelles and Company, who built and fitted out most of Norman Shaw's London houses in the

197. Detail of the front
of the Prince Alfred.

1870s were frequently contracting to build new pubs or refit old ones in the 1880s and 1890s.[34]
Ansell and Company, who provided woodwork and joinery of the finest quality for pubs, were
also employed by G. G. Scott, junior.[35] W. B. Simpson and Sons, art decorators and the leading
art-tile manufacturers of the 1870s, for whom Jeffreys and Company designed some of their
best aesthetic wallpapers, supplied tiles for many pubs and sometimes decorated entire pub
interiors.[36] Apart from these, at the time, extremely well-known firms, many of the innumerable
lesser 'art' manufacturers who came into existence as a result of the aesthetic movement were
doing work in pubs in the 1890s. It remains uncertain to what extent pub-architects relied on
these firms for designing fittings as well as supplying them; but the pubs of the 1890s would
certainly not have been possible without them.

IX 'Queen Anne' in America

To anyone interested in 'Queen Anne' the American Colonial Revival of the 1870s, and its development into what Vincent Scully has made familiar as the Shingle Style, presents a fascinating study. It is so obviously related to 'Queen Anne', so similar in the background social and economic factors that encouraged its birth. And yet at each stage there are increasing differences; and the style in its culmination, even though its 'Queen Anne' elements are still in evidence, is not only notably different from anything in England but also, it must be admitted, both more adventurous and more exciting.[1]

The American soil into which the seeds of 'Queen Anne' were dropped was ready to receive them. America, or at least a section of the American middle classes, was in revolt against contemporary values. This revulsion, though by no means entirely due to the scandals connected with President Grant's administration, was certainly encouraged by them. Grant and his cronies filled a role similar to that played in England by Baron Grant and the other financiers who were so bitterly satirized by Trollope in 1875 in *The Way We Live Now*.

Revulsion moved in two directions, backwards into the past and sideways into the country. A desire to escape from the wicked city into the purity of the country (at least for the holidays) was one of the motives behind the rush to the sea and the resulting boom in summer resorts along the north-east American coast. Initially, at any rate, people went to Newport (and, even more, to Maine) to lead a simple life rather than a frivolous one. And at Newport and the other old-fashioned ports along the east coast that began to attract summer trade, visitors could see modest colonial houses built in what seemed to them a simpler and better age. There are obvious parallels with England here, with the English craze for the inglenook as a symbol of old ways and values, and with the frame of mind expressed by Kate Greenaway's artless couplet:

> For oh, I love the country—the beautiful country
> Who'd live in a London street when there's the country?[2]

The 'Old English' style, which gave this frame of mind architectural expression, was correspondingly welcome in America. The first notable example of its transplantation was the Watts-Sherman house in Newport, built in 1874–5. Although nominally designed by H. H. Richardson, the house (which survives) is more likely to have been the work of his assistant Stanford White. It is a brilliantly individual version of Shaw's 'Old English' manner—chimneys, sunflowers, oriels, overhanging gables, irregularity, and all. But 'Old English' tile-hanging is replaced by a lavish use of its American equivalent, wooden shingles, and the windows, instead of being glazed with leaded lights in the Old English manner, have a close grid of wooden glazing bars. This 'Queen Anne' element probably derived from the engravings of New Zealand Chambers published in the English *Building News* and *Builder* in 1873.

By 1876 the 'Queen Anne' furore which had been raging for three years in England was having American repercussions. From May onwards *Harper's Magazine* published a series of articles by the architect Henry Hudson Holly on *Modern Dwellings; their Construction, Decoration and Furniture*. Holly had read the paper delivered by J. J. Stevenson in 1874 to the Congress of British Architects; he reproduced its arguments, and found them relevant for America. 'It has been discovered that the Gothic, however well adapted to ecclesiastical purposes, is lacking in essential points for domestic uses . . . these new reformers . . . claim that in what is loosely called the "Queen Anne" style we find the most simple mode of honest English building, worked out in an artistic and natural form'. But Holly, like other Americans at this period and later, had not appreciated the distinction between 'Old English' and 'Queen Anne'. As examples of the latter he quotes Shaw's Cragside and Grims Dyke, and Thomas Harris's English Pavilion at the 1876 Philadelphia Exhibition—all 'Old English' buildings. The confusion was understandable, in view of the common origin of the two styles, and the fact that one shaded into the other. But it meant that Holly failed to perceive the particular relevance of 'Queen Anne' for America.[3]

The relevance was pointed out in a talk by the Boston architect R. S. Peabody, given to the Boston Society of Architects and printed in the *American Architect and Building News* of 28 April 1877. This was entitled 'A Talk about "Queen Anne"', and showed a far more sophisticated appreciation of the make-up and background of the style than Holly had shown a year previously —not surprisingly, since Peabody had recently returned from a visit to London. The most important section came at the end: 'To those who do believe in revivals, "Queen Anne" is a very fit importation into our offices. There is no revival so little of an affectation on our soil, as that of the beautiful work of the Colonial days. . . . It is our legitimate field for imitation, and we have much of it to study right in our own neighbourhood. In fact, anyone who in summer drives over the ancient turnpike from Hingham to Plymouth will not only pass through a beautiful country full of old homesteads, but will find the sunflower still nodding behind the gambrel-roofed houses that line the road through Queen Anne's Corner.'[4]

Peabody was supported in a long letter from England, written by J. M. Brydon and published in the *American Architect* of 6 October 1877. Brydon took Peabody up on one point: 'Queen Anne' was not so much a revival as a development, 'an attempt to continue the work of English domestic architecture in the true spirit of English work'. But he vigorously supported Peabody's advocacy of American Colonial as the basis for an American version of 'Queen Anne'. 'If ever America is to become possessed of an historical style, it must spring from the work of the old colonists. . . . Preserve then your old colonial architecture, and it may yet bring fruit of which all the world of art may be proud.'

A revival of interest in American architecture of the seventeenth and eighteenth centuries had, in fact, begun in the late 1860s. It gathered impetus in the early 1870s. *Harper's Monthly* started to publish nostalgic articles on colonial days and buildings in 1869; in 1874 it put out a fully illustrated series on Newport, Marblehead, and Portsmouth, New Hampshire, 'An Old Town by the Sea'. Interest in colonial days was stimulated by the centenary of American Independence in 1876; one of the most popular exhibits at the Centennial International Exhibition at Philadelphia was a reconstruction of a colonial kitchen.

As early as 1872 the architect Charles F. McKim (who left Richardson's office in that year) had begun to incorporate neo-colonial details into the interiors of his houses. But the two pregnant ideas that American colonial buildings could be the starting-point for a whole new style of building, and that this should be based on free development rather than imitation, both appear to date from 1877, and were certainly inspired by English 'Queen Anne'.

Once these ideas had been put forward, American architects found them extremely exciting. Much of the freshness of English 'Queen Anne' had been the result of a sudden rediscovery of a neglected section of English architecture. But it was only a section; it provided an alternative to English Gothic or English Elizabethan. Americans, on the other hand, had long been conscious of being at the receiving end: Gothic might be truthful, but it came from Europe; the Second Empire style not only came from Europe but now seemed far from truthful; Old English might express primitive virtues, but they were English virtues. Henry Holly had found it humiliating that 'the ablest efforts of the second century of the Republic' had only resulted in 'the feeble copy of Foreign styles'.[5] Now, suddenly, he and others realized that the material for a truly American style was all around them.

At the beginning, however, the Colonial revival started off with a strong English accent, which lingered on well into the 1880s. This English element is generally recognized, but it tends to be discussed as though it were entirely the result of a study of English architectural magazines by American architects. English periodicals certainly circulated widely in America, but this was only part of the story. There were other routes by which 'Queen Anne' in particular, and the whole aesthetic movement in general, could, and in some cases certainly did, pass from England to America. Englishmen were living, or visiting, in America, and Americans living or visiting in England. Americans and Englishmen were corresponding with each other. English products were on display at American exhibitions, on sale in American shops, or on view in American houses.

Much the best known of the English writers and artists who visited America in this period was Oscar Wilde—best known, that is, in the light of subsequent events, for when Wilde toured America in 1881 he was only at the beginning of his career, and in England was still scarcely known to the general public. But Wilde's tour was successful partly because the aesthetic movement had been brought to America at least six years previously. It had become the subject of increasing discussion and interest, so that an English aesthete as lively and gifted at publicizing himself as Wilde found the ground already well prepared for him. If one is looking for a pioneer of aestheticism in America, Wilde's claims can bear no comparison to those of a much less well-known but very interesting figure, Daniel Cottier.

Cottier[6] was born in 1839, the son of a Manx sailor and a Scotswoman. He was apprenticed as a glass painter in Glasgow and around 1860 was for a time in London, where he attended Ruskin's and Ford Madox Brown's classes at the Working Men's College in Red Lion Square. Madox Brown later remarked on his great abilities as a colourist. From about 1862 to 1865 he was working in Edinburgh, and in about 1865 he started his own firm in Glasgow. The firm provided stained glass, furniture, and decoration, all of very high quality. Amongst its work was the stencilled polychromatic decoration of Alexander Thomson's wood-lined Queen's Park church in Glasgow. Madox Brown was later to describe the result of Thomson's and Cottier's collaboration as 'above everything I have seen in modern Europe' and to exclaim 'Why didn't Thomson come to London? And why did Cottier leave it for New York?'[7]

In Glasgow Cottier almost certainly knew J. J. Stevenson and Bruce Talbert, and seems to have been especially friendly with J. M. Brydon. Like them he moved to London. In 1867, or perhaps a year or two later, he opened an office at 2 Langham Place, and subsequently moved it to 8 Pall Mall (in about 1875) and then to 32 Argyll Street.[8] For a time he was in partnership with J. M. Brydon and another Glasgow friend, William Wallace. In 1873 he opened further branches in New York and Sydney, the latter in association with J. L. Lyon, who had been an apprentice with him in early Glasgow days and had emigrated to Australia. In spite of Madox Brown's remark Cottier seems never to have been permanently resident in America, but to have moved around between his various branches. He died in Florida in 1891.

W. E. Henley, who wrote a memorial essay on him, said that he 'could throw off enough designs in an hour to keep a factory going for weeks'.[9] His shop in New York (which was managed by James W. Inglis) rapidly became one of the main centres from which the aesthetic movement was introduced to America. The first important American articles on the movement were written under Cottier's influence. These were 'Beds and Tables, Stools and Candlesticks', a series of eleven illustrated articles on house furnishing by Clarence M. Cook, which appeared in *Scribner's Monthly* between June 1875 and May 1877.[10] In 1878 they were reprinted as a book *The House Beautiful*. It had a frontispiece by Walter Crane entitled 'My Lady's Chamber', showing a lady in aesthetic dress standing in her 'Queen Anne' drawing-room.

The cover of the book was designed by Cottier. The introduction acknowledges that to him, 'as friend and artist, the author has been constantly indebted for advice and practical help since he first began to write these pages'. His shop and his name figure prominently in almost every article. In the first article it is announced that 'Cottier and Co have serges in colors whose delight-

2

fulness we all recognize in the pictures that Alma Tadema and Morris, and Burne Jones and Rossetti paint. . . . the mistletoe green, the blue-green, the duck-egg, the rose-amber, the pomegranate-flower, and so forth, and so on, colors which we owe to the English poet-artists, who are oddly lumped together as the pre-Raphaelites, and who made the new rainbow to confound the scientific decorators who were so sure of what colors would go together, and what colors wouldn't.'[11]

A later article enthuses that 'next to making simplicity charming, the Cottiers have done us the greatest service, in showing us how to unite usefulness and beauty'. Goods for sale in Cottier's shops are illustrated and described, including English grates made by Morris and Co. and other firms, set in 'Queen Anne' chimney-pieces. Cottier's (along with Bumstead's of Boston) also marketed versions of the Sussex chair and Godwin's Anglo-Japanese coffee-table; according to Clarence Cook, these and other models had originally been imported from England, but since they tended to get damaged in transit, it had proved more satisfactory to manufacture similar products in America.[12]

Cottier's also sold American-designed furniture in variations of the Old English, Japanese, and 'Queen Anne' manners, designed by Cottier himself, by J. W. Inglis, and by Alexander Sandier. Some of the furniture was decorated by Francis Augustus Lathrop (1849–1909), who was also responsible for a number of the illustrations in Clarence M. Cook's book. Lathrop was recently back from three years in England (from 1870 to 1873), during which he had studied under Whistler, Ford Madox Brown, Burne-Jones, Morris, and Spencer Stanhope; as Clarence Cook put it, he had been in 'the company of the young men who are bringing back the golden days of art in England'.[13]

Architects naturally figure much less prominently in Clarence Cook's articles, which were concerned with furniture and decoration. But the sixth article, published in November 1876, contains enthusiastic praise of McKim for his restoration of an old house in Newport, in which the old was kept 'wherever it was sound enough, and suited to a new lease of life, and whatever new was added kept true to the spirit of the old time, though without any antiquarian slavishness'. McKim is described as 'one of the foremost of our young architects, who has shown an uncommon sort of skill in finding out what there is left in an old house to build upon for modern comfort and elegance'.[14]

It seems likely that Brydon's friendship and former partnership with Cottier had something to do with his appearance as the only English architect to write on the 'Queen Anne' style in the *American Architect*. Another architect who clearly influenced Cottier was E. W. Godwin. The designs of many of the goods on sale in Cottier's shop were very much in the Godwin manner. One of Clarence Cook's articles illustrated two 'Queen Anne' chimney-pieces designed by Godwin, based (with acknowledgements) on engravings published in the *British Architect* in 1874, but redrawn by Inglis, and with the figure of an aesthetic lady added by Lathrop.[15] The illustrations as re-drawn were reproduced in facsimile, without acknowledgement of either source or designers, in the English *Art at Home* series, published by Macmillan in 1876–80 and edited by the Revd. W. J. Loftie, whose wife was J. J. Stevenson's cousin. This was, on the whole, a very superficial series of little books, aimed at the popular market. It plagiarized large numbers of Clarence Cook's illustrations, all without acknowledgement. It was an early and curious example of aesthetic influence running from America to England rather than the other way round, and one that reflected little credit on either Macmillan or Loftie.[16]

198

Clarence Cook's third and fifth articles refer to the English exhibits at the Philadelphia Centennial Exhibition, with especial commendation of the embroideries executed by Mrs. Morris and her friends for the Royal School of Art Needlework, and the furniture by Collinson and Lock decorated by Morris's protégé Fairfax Murray.[17] Other English exhibits included wallpapers by Jeffrey and Co., books by Walter Crane, and Barnard, Bishop, and Barnard's amazing iron pavilion,

198. Design for a fireplace by E. W. Godwin, reproduced in *Scribner's Magazine* in 1876, with embellishments by F. A. Lathrop.

designed in the most advanced aesthetic style by Thomas Jeckyll. All this aroused much interest. English architecture, on the other hand, was badly represented; the only 'Queen Anne' work on show was a house in Park Lane by T. H. Wyatt, and unspecified designs by Maurice B. Adams.[18]

Within a few years Maurice B. Adams, Crane, and Morris and Co. had been commissioned to do work for American clients. In the early 1880s Miss Caroline Wolfe's house, Vinland, at Newport, which was designed by Peabody and Stearns, had been enriched with decorations by Morris and Co., stained glass by Burne-Jones, and a frieze by Walter Crane.[19] Meanwhile Edward S. Wilde, when on a visit to England in 1879, had commissioned Adams to design an entire neighbourhood, on the Bloomfield Estate at Chestnut Hill, New York. The houses were in an uninspired amalgamation of 'Queen Anne' and Jacobean, served by a very much prettier 'Queen Anne' railway station, also designed by Adams.[20] (Another Chestnut Hill, near Philadelphia, later acquired a group of houses very much in the Shaw manner, designed by Wilson Eyre.) All Adams's designs were sent over from England, but he may also have visited America in person in 1881 or 1882; on 28 April 1882 the *Building News* published a double spread of illustrations by him of Shingleside, a house at Swampscott, Massachusetts, designed by Arthur Little, and although these may have been made from drawings supplied by the architect a visit by Adams to America remains a possibility.[21]

During the 1870s and 1880s a lively and gifted group of Americans was living in London. The most relevant of these, as far as concerns 'Queen Anne', were J. M. Whistler, Moncure Conway, G. H. Boughton, and Edwin Abbey. Whistler first settled in England in 1859. Moncure Conway arrived in 1863, became pastor of South Place Chapel in 1864, and moved to Bedford Park in 1879. He was one of the English correspondents for *Harper's*, which published his long illustrated article on Bedford Park in March 1881. He had a wide circle of friends both English and American, and entertained freely.[22] The artist G. H. Boughton, English born but American bred, was also well known for the large but discriminating parties which he gave in the house

199. House at Chestnut Hill, Pennsylvania. By Wilson Eyre, *c.* 1881–2.

on Campden Hill which Norman Shaw designed for him in 1876.[23] Edwin Abbey arrived in London from New York in 1878, and rapidly became friendly with Whistler and Moncure Conway and close friends with G. H. Boughton and with the 'Queen Anne' set in Melbury Road—Luke Fildes, Marcus Stone, and Colin Hunter. In New York he had been a member—as had G. H. Boughton—of the Tile Club, a dining-club of artists and their friends to which the architect Stanford White belonged. He had also had a studio next door to that of F. A. Lathrop; Lathrop probably encouraged him to go to England, for Abbey later described how he used to read Browning to him, told him about his experiences with the Pre-Raphaelites, and 'was altogether wonderful to me'. Abbey, like Moncure Conway, was one of *Harper's* English correspondents. He remained a social bachelor until 1890, when he married the sister of W. R. Mead, the least well-known member of the architectural partnership of McKim, Mead, and White.[24]

No American architects settled in London in the same way as American artists did, and few, if any, seem even to have studied there. American architects who came to Europe to study architecture usually went to Rome or the Beaux-Arts in Paris, rather than London, partly because there was still no full-time architectural school in London. But while in Europe they were likely to visit London and England, as did other American architects, on holiday or a sketching tour rather than attending a school.

The questions of which American architects came to England in the nineteenth century, when they came, what they saw, and who they met, seem to have been little investigated. Of architects who were to pioneer the Shingle Style, McKim was in London, on holiday from the Beaux-Arts, in the summer of 1869, when R. Phené Spiers made him a member of the Architectural Association. In the words of his biographer 'Then began that fondness for London that grew and strengthened with the years. . . . In the great houses he was called upon to design he was influenced strongly by the well-ordered, quiet, comfortable methods of English life as manifested in the houses of that country.'[25] Amongst other recorded visits (and research would surely bring

200. Shingleside, Swampscott, Massachusetts. By W. R. Emerson, 1880–1. From the illustrations in the *Building News* of 28 April 1882.

many more to light) R. S. Peabody was in London in 1871, and again in 1876.[26] Stanford White was in London in the summer of 1879, on his way back from a year on the Continent, and again in 1884.[27] W. R. Emerson visited and made friends with Walter Crane in London, probably some time in the 1880s.[28] All these architects are likely to have looked at new buildings while they were in London, and some of them must have made contact with English architects. Peabody (who was amazed at the change 'Queen Anne' had made to the English scene between 1871 and 1876) records visiting one architect who was designing a 'Queen Anne' scenario for a play, and another who was designing stained glass based on Italian Renaissance models. It is hard to believe that Stanford White, at least, when in England in 1879, did not meet either Whistler, Abbey, Boughton, or Conway, or that, since he was already an admirer of Norman Shaw, he did not see Bedford Park and some, at least, of Shaw's houses in Chelsea and Kensington. Through one of the American group he could have had access to the interiors of these, and could even have been introduced to Shaw in person.

Although a few buildings showing 'Queen Anne' influence had gone up in America in 1877 and 1878 it was not till 1879 that the style made a notable contribution to American architecture. In the relevant buildings produced in this year and the early 1880s, as well as in their furniture and fittings, English influence is much in evidence, but the best buildings are far from being copies of English work. Increasing understanding of what was happening in England and enthusiasm for doing something on the same lines in America had brought about a fusion of expertise and excitement that began to be creative.

In 1883 the American critic Montgomery Schuyler attacked both English and American 'Queen Anne' as a style which showed 'all the signs of a departure—we might say of a hurried departure—and gives no hint of an arrival or even a direction'. He had one qualification, however: 'it is only fair to say that much interesting work has been done in it, if not strictly of it, in suburban houses or sea-side cottages.'[29] As far as America is concerned one can see what he was getting at. In American towns with a tradition of building in brick there is plenty of brick 'Queen Anne'. Much of this is either incoherent or derivative; but the group contains at least a few lively and charming houses, and is in need of research, which might produce more. On the whole, however, 'Queen Anne' in America seems to have been most creative in timber-frame buildings. These can be followed west or east. Mid-West or West Coast 'Queen Anne' is equally in need of research, and is likely to be full of enjoyable surprises.[30] The timber-framed and shingle-hung buildings of East Coast suburbs and resorts have already received, and deserve, plenty of attention.

The most interesting of the buildings designed (or at least published) in 1879 are a house by W. R. Emerson at Mount Desert, Maine, and McKim, Mead, and White's Casino at Newport. The house at Mount Desert is a competent and stylish design in which obvious and prominently displayed elements derived from English 'Queen Anne' (with a little half-timbering thrown in for good measure) are neatly combined with American-style verandas and a skin of shingles. The Newport Casino was the result of a more ambitious brief which produced a more original building. The Casino, in the heart of Newport, contained shops facing the street, clubrooms, restaurant, café, and a long curving open veranda (or 'piazza' in American terminology) which enclosed a courtyard with pool and fountain on one side and looked on to tennis-courts on the other.[31] English 'Queen Anne' elements were much in evidence. The shop-fronts, delicate in scale and with their upper portions filled with small panes, were reminiscent of 'Queen Anne' shops in the Bond Street neighbourhood. The other windows were all either entirely filled with small panes or had small panes in their upper halves. The gables on the street front were elaborately pargeted. In two of the gables smaller gables of the same shape were fitted into one corner of the larger ones; this was a device which had been used several times by Norman Shaw at Bedford Park, in houses both published and unpublished, and was to become extremely popular in America. Another

201. (*Top*) Houses of *c*. 1890 on Central Avenue, San Francisco.

202. (*Bottom*) House at St. Paul's, Minnesota. By Cass Gilbert, *c*. 1890.

203. (*Top*) The Dr. H. G. Taylor house, Camden, New Jersey. By Wilson Eyre, 1885.

204. (*Bottom*) House at Mt. Desert, Maine. By W. R. Emerson, *c.* 1879.

English motif which was also to be more imitated in America than England was the cloche-shaped roof with a little spike on top, like that on a military topee, which crowned the octagonal turret on the courtyard front of the main building. Its origin must surely have been the similar features designed by Godwin for the abortive Bethell and Corder houses in Tite Street, illustrated in the *British Architect* of 3 October 1879 and 14 May 1880. More generally, the whole concept of the Newport Casino (which was immediately followed by two more casinos designed by McKim, Mead, and White at Narragansett Pier and Short Hills) with its tennis-courts, clubrooms, and facilities for both sexes, suggests an expanded version of the Bedford Park Club, conceived two years previously.

206   But there were other elements of the Casino which were not English at all. The most obvious was the concept and treatment of the piazzas. It is true that the railings and high-level screens of turned wooden columns which line portions of their open walks derive straight from similar features in Norman Shaw houses. But there is an abundance of screening on the piazzas, and the design of much of it is not 'Queen Anne' but suggests French garden trellises or the lattice screens of oriental harems.[32] Moreover, the concept of having piazzas of this type at all, screened from the sun but open on both sides to any available breeze is essentially un-English; it was designed for the American climate.

In fact at both the Mount Desert house and at the Casino one can see the beginning of the trends which were to divert the Shingle Style from 'Queen Anne'. That they did so was more or less inevitable, for the buildings were based on different methods of construction and built in a different landscape to cater for a different climate and a different social structure.

Shingle-style houses were built for very hot summers and very cold winters, and as a result were supplied with central heating, to combat the cold, and the maximum of shade and through-ventilation, to counter the heat. This meant that closed doors were unnecessary in winter and undesirable in summer. The standard method of construction was not load-bearing brick walls, as in England, but timber frames with a shingle skin, resting on a lower course of roughly-cut local stones; the shingles were genuinely functional, unlike the tile-hanging on 'Queen Anne' buildings, which tended to be purely ornamental. Frame construction, apart from anything else, made it easy to provide the free flowing of space into space and indoors into outdoors which the needs of the climate encouraged. Moreover, in America the social system which in England worked to separate men from women, grown-ups from children, and family from servants was less constrictive; spaces could open into each other without causing social embarrassment.

A typical setting for English 'Queen Anne' was a flat tree-lined street or a gentle agricultural landscape. A typical setting for the shingle style was the rocky, pine-covered, and in places mountainous North American coast—the kind of landscape in which, when faced with its English equivalent, English architects of the time tended to switch over from 'Queen Anne' to 'Old English'. Shingle-style houses were often built at the crest of rocky slopes, out of which their massive stone foundations and rusty brown shingles sprouted like an organic growth. The result was very different from the red brick and white trim seen through green leaves of English 'Queen Anne'. The patrons of both styles were reacting from contemporary cities, but in different ways. The English were thinking in terms of eighteenth-century merchants or gentleman farmers, the American in terms of eighteenth-century pioneers. Both were probably supported by comfortable dollops of urban money; they were both play-acting, but playing different roles in the same kind of play.

So the two styles went their separate ways, but continued to show their common background. Shingle-style houses of the 1880s continue to vie with 'Queen Anne' ones in picturesque irregularity and at times overpowering quaintness. This quality was beautifully caught in the
207   'Pencil Sketches' of E. Eldon Deane, published in the *American Architect*; these sketches were, in their turn, inspired by the *British Architect*'s 'Rambling Sketches', drawn by T. Raffles Davison.

205. Street front of the Casino, Newport, Rhode Island. By McKim, Mead, and White, 1879–81.

206. Detail of one of the piazzas at the Newport Casino.

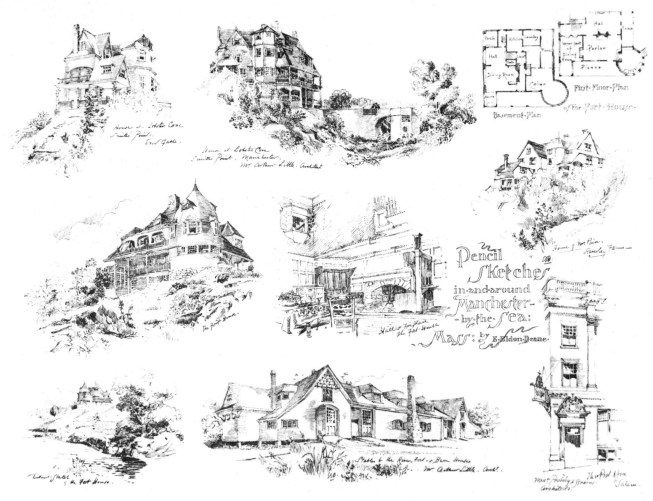

207. (*Top*) Sketches by E. Eldon Deane of houses at Manchester-by-the-Sea, Massachusetts, 1885.

208. (*Bottom*) Kragsyde, Manchester-by-the-Sea. By Peabody and Stearns, *c.* 1882.

209. House at Bar Harbor, Maine. By W. R. Emerson, *c.* 1885. From the engraving in the *Builder*, 25 December 1886.

Many of the houses continued to proliferate with small-paned sashes, oriel windows both internal and external, bay windows, domed turrets, pargeting (rather less common), inglenooks, sunflowers, and other 'Queen Anne' or aesthetic miscellanea. But their plans gradually changed; compartmented plans similar to those in England developed into open plans, with staircases that came down into living halls, halls that opened out through generous archways into living-rooms, and rooms that flowed out through French windows into verandas. From the outside, the best shingle-style houses, pierced by archways, dug into by verandas, perched on rocks, and with clusters of roofs sweeping down to the ground, were exotic and exciting creations. Sometimes, as in Peabody and Stearns's amazing 'Kragsyde' at Manchester-by-the-sea, both the name   208
and much of their detail had obvious English connotations. At other times 'Queen Anne' detail almost entirely disappeared. Huge gables, shingles rippling over smoothly swelling curves, abstract patterning of grilles, abstract curves of balconies or linked rectangles of windows joined   209
with the light and shade of solid and void to make up all the architecture.

There was, of course, another element in the Shingle Style which had nothing to do with English 'Queen Anne', namely its reminiscences of American colonial architecture. Considering the strength of feeling among Americans of the time about going back to their roots, this was less in evidence than might have been expected. Many shingle-style houses owe a great deal more to English 'Queen Anne' than to American eighteenth-century prototypes. But the colonial element was there from the start, and intensified during the 1880s. Some of the houses designed by Peabody and Stearns in the late 1870s, before English 'Queen Anne' had been fully absorbed in America, could reasonably be described as 'free colonial'. So could Arthur Little's 'Shingleside'   200
(the house drawn by Maurice B. Adams for the *Building News*), in spite of its 'Queen Anne' inglenook and oriel. A distinctively neo-colonial feature in all these houses is that the verandas are supported on classical piers or columns, rather than the wooden posts or turned balusters of 'Queen Anne' derivation. Other colonial idioms which were absorbed into the shingle-style vocabulary during the 1880s included gambrel roofs, and roofs that, in some portion of the house, swept from the ridge almost down to the ground.

210. (*Top*) The William Low House, Bristol, Rhode Island. By McKim, Mead, and White, 1887.

211. (*Bottom*) House for the Misses Appleton, Lenox, Massachusetts. By McKim, Mead, and White, 1883–4.

Roofs of this kind were typical of American farmhouses or modest homesteads of the eighteenth and even seventeenth centuries. In the mid-1880s McKim, Mead, and White began to go to grander colonial houses for inspiration. The firm produced houses of this type as an alternative to their simpler, but not necessarily smaller, shingle-style houses such as the William Low House at Bristol, Rhode Island (1887). There is a striking contrast between the latter's one immense gable and complete lack of any period detail and the house designed by the same firm for the   210
Misses Appleton at Lenox, Massachusetts (1883–4).[33] Here delicate ornamental detail abounded, but it was all of American colonial, rather than 'Queen Anne' origin. Yet the design principle   211
behind the house remained a 'Queen Anne' one. American colonial houses of any pretensions had invariably been symmetrical; the Appleton house was delicately and skilfully asymmetrical throughout.

Both McKim, Mead, and White and other firms designed many variations on this formula during the 1880s, not always with the success of the Appleton house. They developed gradually into straightforwardly imitative neo-colonialism—a counterpart to the neo-Italian palazzos and neo-Louis Seize chateaux with which McKim, Mead, and White kept up with the growing millions of their patrons. The split in the firm's own practice anticipated what was to become a split in American architecture, as it forked off in two directions, to historicism on the one side and, by way of Frank Lloyd Wright and others, to the Modern Movement on the other. It was a split from which neither wing necessarily benefited.[34]

212. Tailpiece from *At Home*, illustrated by J. G. Sowerby and Thomas Crane, 1881.

X   Epilogue

When the 'Queen Anne' architects deserted the Gothic Revival in the 1870s, the architectural press echoed with the battle-cries, groans, and recriminations of the different factions. When the same architects moved away from 'Queen Anne' a decade or two later, their abandonment of the style provoked neither fuss nor surprise. The contrast is not a surprising one. The Gothic Revival had succeeded because its claims were so ambitious; it provided a complete philosophy, and demanded total commitment from its practitioners. 'Queen Anne' succeeded because it made no demands at all. It claimed no more than that the buildings which it produced were sensible and pretty. Most 'Queen Anne' architects continued to design in other styles when the occasion suggested it. Once they had accepted 'Queen Anne' there was no reason why they should not go on to try other forms of creative eclecticism. To begin with they did so comparatively seldom, but this was not because they were committed to 'Queen Anne' but because it was so successful that there was every inducement to produce more of it. When its vogue began to subside they moved on to other things without soul-searching.

By the 1890s the architectural scene had split into at least a score of different styles. Some of these were new arrivals or revivals, some had originated in the early days of 'Queen Anne' but assumed increasing prominence as it went out of fashion. Some of them had grown out of 'Queen Anne', usually by developing one of its elements at the expense of the others. Others were the result of a reaction against both 'Queen Anne' and its offspring.

In 1874 Norman Shaw had added a strong Flemish flavour to the 'Queen Anne' cocktail when he designed 196 Queen's Gate for J. P. Heseltine. From then on Shaw and others made much use of Flemish detail, and in Shaw's Alliance Assurance Building in Pall Mall of 1882 it predominated. But the architect whose name was especially associated with the style was Ernest George; indeed, his reputation was established on the strength of it. In his houses in Collingham and Harrington Gardens, Kensington (1881–4), and Cadogan Square, Chelsea (1886), he produced (after a reasonably sober 'Queen Anne' start) a series of wildly picturesque Flemish burgher's houses, inflated to suitably Victorian size, injected with a certain amount of Jacobean and Renaissance detailing, and carried out, for the most part, in the fashionable material of the moment, yellow terracotta. The formula was soon being imitated all over London and all over the country. It had to compete, however, with a somewhat similar mixture of Elizabethan and Italian Renaissance architecture which has been christened 'Anglo-Jackson' because Thomas Graham Jackson pioneered it in 1876 with his winning design for the Examination Schools at Oxford. It remained his favourite manner, though he adventured into a number of other styles, including 'Queen Anne'. In the 1880s and 1890s he had numerous imitators; in 1892 the liveliest of them, H. T. Hare, out-trumped him on his own ground with the effervescent new Town Hall at Oxford.

In the 1870s a number of 'Queen Anne' architects attempted, without any success, to persuade the public to call their style 'Free Classic'. 'Free Classic' would, in fact, have been a more suitable name for an offshoot of 'Queen Anne' that became extremely popular in the 1880s and 1890s, especially for public buildings. In the 1880s some 'Queen Anne' architects discovered that they could treat columns, entablatures, domes, pediments, and rustication in the same enterprising and unscholarly way as they had previously treated the humbler detailing of the vernacular. The ebullient and cheerful results neatly dealt with the criticism that 'Queen Anne' was too domestic a style to be suitable for public building. Norman Shaw showed the way with New Scotland Yard in 1886, but the potentialities of this form of treatment were even more

213. 50 and 52 Cadogan Square, Chelsea. By Ernest George and Peto, 1886.

abundantly demonstrated by John Belcher, when he designed the headquarters of the Institute of Chartered Accountants in Moorgate in 1890. From then on the British Isles saw an outburst of town halls, public libraries, and art galleries where heavily rusticated colonnades appeared in unlikely places, where columns tended to bulge in the middle and pediments were invariably broken, and where classical symmetry was easily and even gleefully abandoned whenever the architect felt like adding on a cupola or pushing out an oriel.   214

This is not the place to discuss other varieties of eclecticism less closely associated with 'Queen Anne', but there was no shortage of them. Free Gothic and Free Tudor, Alma-Tadema Roman and Beresford-Pite Byzantine jostled Free Flemish, Free Elizabethan, Free Classic, and the lessening output of 'Queen Anne' along the High Streets. The buildings in these various styles were almost always designed with gusto, and sometimes with wit. But their combined effect was certainly indigestible. One can see why Goodhart-Rendel described the inevitable reaction in a chapter headed 'The Morning After'.

Reaction took the form either of attempts to reinstate discipline, scholarship, and grammar in the treatment of the styles, or of attempts to abandon them altogether. The idea that classical architecture was a language with its own grammar and inflections rather than a launching-pad for displays of personal *bravura* came as a welcome release to many architects who were bored with an excess of freedom. Shaw's Bolney House in Ennismore Gardens (1883) was closer to Queen Anne than 'Queen Anne' and its example was soon followed by his pupils. On the whole they showed more respect for authority than Shaw himself, whose own adoption of the language

214. The Institute of Chartered Accountants, Moorgate, London. By John Belcher, 1890.

of the orders retained a strong element of personal idiosyncracy. Brydon abandoned 'Queen Anne' as early as 1885, with his winning design for Chelsea Vestry Hall, and was shortly afterwards followed by Reginald Blomfield and Ernest Newton. Early in the 1900s Lutyens discovered the excitements of what he called the 'high game' of classicism.

But while one half of Shaw's office was enthusiastically rediscovering the grammar of the order, the other half was equally enthusiastically abandoning the orders altogether. During the 1890s Prior and Lethaby went back to the search for 'absence of style' which had been a feature of Webb's architecture, in particular, in the 1860s. They were joined by others, including Voysey, Maclaren, Mackmurdo, Stokes, Harrison Townshend, and Mackintosh; and Webb, whose star had been somewhat in decline in the 1880s, suddenly found himself the hero of the younger men.

Their work has been sedulously investigated, especially by those looking for possible fore-runners of the Modern Movement. In the context of their own time their buildings, however gifted, give the impression of merely adding yet more variations to the already chaotic variety of English architecture. Certainly, in contrast to the architectural scene in 1900 the architecture of the 1870s appears a relatively simple story. The contrast goes beyond architecture. The fragmentation of architectural styles echoes a related fragmentation of society. The happy hope-fulness of the 1870s, the feeling that everything could be explained and all disagreements reconciled, had largely evaporated. English society had been experiencing increasing pressure, political, moral, social, and economic. In their very different ways, the emergence of Germany and America as political and economic rivals to England, the scandal of Oscar Wilde's trial, the failure to save Gordon or to deal with Ireland, the fiascos and incompetences of the Boer War, the stepped-up campaign for women's suffrage, had begun to sap the self-confidence and amiability of late Victorian England. Society tended to polarize into different and not over-friendly groups, ranging from Imperialism at one end of the spectrum to Socialism at the other. Architecturally, Imperialism tended to affect the classicism of Blomfield and Lutyens, Socialism the anti-style of Lethaby and Voysey. The fact that these very different ways of building can both be traced back to different elements in 'Queen Anne', and that the architects who practised them included men who had once worked side by side in the same offices shows the extent to which the architectural scene had fragmented.

And so, in the early years of the 1900s, 'Queen Anne' gradually disappeared from the reper-tory even of the speculative builders among whom it had found its last home. It disappeared, at the same time, from books on architecture, until in the 1930s, when Osbert Lancaster had to think up a new name for something whose original name had long since been forgotten, the style reappeared in the comic guise of 'Pont Street Dutch'.

But 'Queen Anne' has begun to regain favour in recent years, for obvious reasons. The 1970s have certain resemblances to the 1870s. The Modern Movement, as doctrinaire and intolerant in its day as the Gothic Revival, has fallen even more heavily out of favour. Technology is suspect and escape from the city into the country is even more in vogue. Eclecticism is once more on the rampage, and once more children (and even parents) in Kate Greenaway clothes can be seen emerging from houses embellished with wallpapers by Morris and Walter Crane.

But today's eclecticism has notably failed to become creative. In the sphere of architecture, in particular, little has happened except a massive loss of confidence in and by architects. One cannot help looking back with envy at an eclecticism that worked. 'Queen Anne' can be extremely irritating. At worst it combined rather too neatly escapism with smugness. But it coalesced, not only into a recognizable style, but into one that was capable of assuming a wide variety of moods. It could be quaint at Bedford Park and dainty at Newnham, but also sensible in the Board Schools and flashy in the pubs. How did it happen? Perhaps the most relevant lesson of 'Queen Anne' for our own time is that architects should not work in isolation behind professional barriers, that Jackson was talking sense when he wrote 'Henceforth then . . . let us have artists'.

Appendix:
'Queen Anne' Architecture in Chelsea

There has been to date no adequate list of houses built on the Metropolitan Board of Works estate and the Cadogan and Hans Place Estate in Chelsea. This appendix is an interim attempt to remedy this deficiency. The list for Chelsea Embankment and the southern half of Tite Street is based on the Metropolitan Board of Works archives in the G.L.C. Record Office, and is reasonably complete. The list for Cadogan Square and the western half of Pont Street is much less comprehensive, being based on occasional architect's drawings, material in the contemporary building magazines, and analysis of the different types of ironwork used by the different contractors. It is possible that research into the records of the Cadogan Estate would fill the gaps. I have not included Lennox Gardens, where development did not start until about 1882,[1] or any of the other later Victorian terraces on the Cadogan Estate.

The Metropolitan Board of Works estate

		Date of design	Architect	Contractor	Client	
Chelsea Embankment						
1	(Shelley House)	c. 1876–8	Joseph Peacock		Sir Percy Shelley	Rebuilt
2		1876	A. W. Blomfield		J. J. Lowndes	Rebuilt
3		1876	Bodley & Garner		Hon. J. C. Dundas	
4–6		1876–8	E. W. Godwin	Gillow & Co.	Gillow & Co. (spec.)	
7		1878–9	R. Phené Spiers	Kirk & Randall	Sir Robert Collier	
8	(Clock House)	1878–80	R. Norman Shaw	J. McLachlan of Clapham	Mrs. Erskine Wemyss	
9–11		1878–80	R. Norman Shaw	W. H. Lascelles	J. W. Temple (spec.)	Altered
12		1877	Hungerford Pollen		Lord Wentworth	Altered
13		c. 1878–80	E. I'Anson			
15		1877–9	R. Norman Shaw		W. J. Armitage	Altered
16		1877–8	A. Croft	Gillow & Co.	W. J. Alt	
17	(Old Swan House)	1875–7	R. Norman Shaw	Chas. Jarrett of Croydon	Wickham Flower	
18	(Cheyne House)	1875–7	R. Norman Shaw	Chas. Jarrett of Croydon	G. Matthey	
Tite Street						
East side						
29		1879	E. W. Godwin		A. Stuart-Wortley	Demolished
31		1879	R. W. Edis		Frank Dicey	
33		1880	R. W. Edis	Jackson & Graham	Jackson & Graham (spec.)	
35		1877–8	E. W. Godwin	Nightingale	J. M. Whistler	Rebuilt
West side						
28–42		1879–80	Francis Butler & Frederick Beeston		Butler & Beeston (spec.)	
44		1878	E. W. Godwin	Sharpe & Everard	Frank Miles	
46	(Tower House)	c. 1884	E. W. Godwin		E. W. Godwin? (spec.)	Altered

	Date of design	Architect	Contractor	Client	
48	1894	Charles J. C. Pawley			
50	1881	F. S. Waller & Sons		Anna Leigh Merritt	
52	1881	F. S. Waller & Sons		John Collier	
56 (site of)	1878	Joseph Peacock		Sir Percy Shelley (private theatre)	Rebuilt as Shelley Mansions
58 (Chelsea Lodge)	1878	E. W. Godwin	Nightingale	A. Stuart-Wortley & C. Pellegrini	Rebuilt

The Cadogan and Hans Place Estate

	Date of design	Architect	Contractor	Client (if other than contractor)
Cadogan Square				
East side (odd numbers)				
1–13	1876– *c.* 1879	G. T. Robinson[2]	Trollope & Sons	
15–57	*c.* 1879–86	G. T. Robinson?	Trollope & Sons?	
North side (even numbers)				
4	1879	G. E. Street		The Misses Monk
6–18	*c.* 1885–7	G. T. Robinson?	Trollope & Sons?	No. 16 for Lady Ashburton
West side (even numbers)				
22–6	*c.* 1888	E. T. Hall	Foster & Dicksee of Rugby	
28–36	*c.* 1885	George Devey	Trollope & Sons	
38–48	late 1880s		Trollope & Sons?	
50	1886	Ernest George & Peto	R. A. J. Simpson & Sons	Col. Thynne
52	1886	Ernest George & Peto	R. A. J. Simpson & Sons	T. A. De la Rue
54–8	1877	William Young[3]		
62	1881–3	R. Norman Shaw	William Brass	E. H. Palmer
64–6	*c.* 1877	A. J. Adams	Thomas Pink & Son	
68	1877–8	R. Norman Shaw	Thomas Pink & Son	Laurence Harrison
70, 74	*c.* 1877	A. J. Adams	Thomas Pink & Son	
72	1877–9	R. Norman Shaw	Thomas Pink & Son	
76–82	*c.* 1885		Thomas Pink & Son?	
84 (Stuart House)	1884	Hunt & Steward with F. G. Knight	Titmas	O. L. Stephen
South side (odd numbers)				
63–73	*c.* 1884	J. J. Stevenson	Holland & Hannen	
75–9	1879–81	J. J. Stevenson	Thomas Pink & Son?	
Pont Street				
South side (odd numbers)				
23–9	1876	G. T. Robinson	Trollope & Sons	
31–9	*c.* 1883	G. T. Robinson?	Trollope & Sons	
45–7	*c.* 1886	E. T. Hall?	Foster & Dicksee?	
49–53	*c.* 1886	E. T. Hall	Foster & Dicksee	
67	1885	C. W. Stephens		Sir Herbert Stewart
North side (even numbers)				
18–24	*c.* 1888	H. B. Measures	William Willett	
42–58	1876–7	J. J. Stevenson	Thomas Pink & Son	
60–6	*c.* 1877	W. Niven[4]	Thomas Pink & Son	

Notes

The relevant page-number is given in italics before each note

Chapter I. Sweetness and Light

1 (*4*). e.g. Julian Sturgis, *Stephen Calinari* (London, 1901), p. 68, describing the opening of the Grosvenor Gallery in 1877: 'Indeed, in England at large a great deal of emotion which had been absorbed by religion was in need of a new object. . . . Others . . . sought a substitute for the unknown God by spelling humanity with a capital letter. But Art—art also with a capital letter—had at the moment the strongest attraction, the most alluring charm . . . Art for Art was the phrase, and to live for Art seemed the best substitute available at the moment for a life of self sacrifice.'

2 (*5*). Walter Pater, *Studies in the History of the Renaissance* (1873), Preface.

3 (*5*). Mary Eliza Haweis, *Beautiful Houses* (London, 1882), p. iv.

4 (*5*). *Robert Elsmere* (1888), Book II, Chapter XII.

5 (*7*). Thomas Wright, *The Life of Walter Pater* (London, 1907), ii. 30–1, 34–47.

6 (*7*). Walter Pater, op. cit., Conclusion.

7 (*7*). Thomas Wright, op. cit., p. 260.

8 (*7*). Ibid.

9 (*8*). Walter Crane, *An Artist's Reminiscences* (London, 1907), p. 164.

10 (*8*). 'Art at Home', *Saturday Review*, 20 Dec. 1873, pp. 777–8.

11 (*9*). *Robert Elsmere*, Book III, Chapter XXI.

Chapter II. The Origins of 'Queen Anne'

1 (*10*). (1855), Part III, Chapters III and XVII.

2 (*10*). Elizabeth Coxhead, 'Miss Nightingale's Country Hospital', *Country Life*, 23 Nov. 1972, pp. 1362–4.

3 (*11*). For Thackeray's house (now No. 2 Palace Green) see the *Survey of London*, ed. F. H. W. Sheppard, vol. xxxvii: *Northern Kensington* (London, 1973), pp. 187–9.

4 (*12*). *Culture and Anarchy*, Chapter V ('Porro unum est necessarium.').

5 (*12*). *Studies in the History of the Renaissance*, Preface.

6 (*13*). *Building News*, 26 June 1874, p. 689, reporting Stevenson's address to the 3rd General Conference of Architects.

7 (*14*). For Taylor see W. R. Lethaby, *Philip Webb and his Work* (London, 1935), pp. 47–62, and Georgiana Burne-Jones, *Memorials of Edward Burne-Jones* (London, 1904), pp. 290–1. For Taylor's friendship with Robson, and other biographical details, see a letter from Robson to Georgiana Burne-Jones of 17 Nov. 1905, filed with the Robson–Taylor Correspondence in the Fitzwilliam

Museum, Cambridge. Taylor's correspondence with Webb is in the Victoria and Albert Museum; it throws much light on the early days of the Morris firm, but comparatively little on the origins of 'Queen Anne'. Very few of Taylor's letters to Robson are dated, but many can be assigned dates with reasonable accuracy owing to their frequent references to new books and articles, and to contemporary events.

8 (*14*). For Robson see the memoir by his son Philip A. Robson in *R.I.B.A. Journal* (3rd Series), xxiv (1917), 93–6. The memoir does not mention his activities as a furniture designer, but they are implicit in Taylor's letters to him, and a notebook of biographical details concerning J. J. Stevenson, apparently compiled by his wife and now belonging to Mrs. Amy Maddox, records that in October 1862 Stevenson had an oak wardrobe made for £24. 10s. 0d. by R. Robson and Son of Claypoth, Durham. It is possible that the 'son' was Robson's brother, and that his own contribution to the firm was limited to the provision of designs.

9 (*14*). Robson to Georgiana Burne-Jones, Robson–Taylor Correspondence.

10 (*15*). William Allingham, *Diary*, ed. H. Allingham and D. Radford (London, 1907; facsimile 1967).

11 (*15*). Taylor–Robson Correspondence, fos. 5, 7.

12 (*15*). Ibid., fos. 22b, 25a.

13 (*15*). Ibid., fo. 22b.

14 (*15*). Ibid., fos. 5, 28.

15 (*15*). Ibid., fos. 3, 23a, 18.

16 (*16*). Ibid., fo. 5.

17 (*16*). Ibid., fos. 24a, 25a.

18 (*16*). For post-Gothic elements in Butterfield's work see Paul Thompson, *William Butterfield* (London, 1971), pp. 89–90, 154–5, and the numerous illustrations of his domestic work.

19 (*17*). The best account of the Sussex chair and its origins is by Simon Jervis, 'Sussex Chairs in 1820', *Furniture History*, 1974, p. 99.

20 (*18*). Taylor–Robson Correspondence, fos. 12, 13.

21 (*18*). In an article, 'The Revival of Architecture', in the *Fortnightly Review*, May 1888, reprinted in *Works* (London, 1910–15), xxii. 329.

22 (*18*). Taylor–Webb Correspondence, Victoria and Albert Museum RC/JJ/35, fo. 17(34). Taylor sent Webb a photograph of the school.

23 (*20*). For the Prinsep House see *Survey of London*, ed. F. H. W. Sheppard, vol. xxxvii: *Northern Kensington* (London, 1973), pp. 141–2. Webb's designs for the house and subsequent additions are in the Victoria and Albert Museum.

24 (*20*). Washington Hall is now re-named the Dame Margaret Training Centre and is occupied by the Coal Board. Designs survive at the R.I.B.A., those for a small rear addition dated 1865 and those (with almost identical detailing) for the new entrance front undated. Webb's Account Books, in the possession of John Brandon-Jones, record payments by Bell of £100 in 1865 and £247. 12s. in 1867.

25 (*24*). For the George Howard house (now slightly altered externally and largely remodelled internally) see *Survey of London*, ed. F. H. W. Sheppard, vol. xxxvii: *Northern Kensington*, pp. 185–7.

26 (*25*). Webb's designs for the Boyce house are in the Victoria and Albert Museum. A wing was added, designed by Webb, in 1876.

27 (*25*). For Shaw's friendship with Aldam Heaton at this period see Andrew Saint, *Richard Norman Shaw* (London and New Haven, 1976), pp. 54–5, and *passim*.

28 (*25*). L. M. Lamont, *Thomas Armstrong C.B.: A Memoir* (London, 1912), p. 194.

29 (*25*). R.I.B.A. Drawings Collection: Nesfield Sketch-Book, ii, fos. 33–6.

30 (*25*). *The Swinburne Letters* (ed. Cecil Y. Lang, Yale, 1959–62), ii. 32.

31 (*25*). J. M. Brydon, 'William Eden Nesfield, 1835–88', *Architectural Review*, i (1897), 286.

32 (*27*). Designs for both the warehouse and cottages are in the Royal Academy library, Shaw Collection, Box I. The cottage designs are undated, but designs for other cottages at Bromley are dated 1863–6. See Nos. 5A, 5B, in the invaluable catalogue of Shaw's works in Saint, op. cit.

33 (*27*). Designs in Royal Academy library, Box I. The house has been demolished.

34 (*28*). Designs for the Kew Gardens lodge are in the Victoria and Albert Museum.

35 (*29*). e.g. *The Blessed Damozel* (1857), *The King's Daughters* (1858), *Ladies and Death* (1860), *Childe Roland* (1861), *Wine of Circe* (1863–9), and stained-glass windows of Adam and Eve at Bradfield College (1857) and St. Martin's, Scarborough (1862).

36 (*29*). Virginia Surtees, *The Paintings and Drawings of Dante Gabriel Rossetti* (Oxford, 1971), i. 62–5 and ii, Pl. 156. A number of different versions were in circulation.

37 (*29*). *Survey of London*, ed. F. H. W. Sheppard, vol. xxxviii: *The Museums Area of Kensington and Westminster* (London, 1976), p. 11 and Pl. 15.

38 (*32*). Reproduced in G. P. Bankar, *Art of the Plasterer* (London, 1908), fig. 82. Two-handled pots of rather different form appear in Rossetti's *The Girlhood of Mary* (1849, containing a lily) and various paintings by Albert Moore (who, however, kept clear of sunflowers).

39 (*32*). Designs in R. A. Shaw Collection, Box I. The house, on the main street of West Wickham, survives, but has been considerably altered.

40 (*33*). For Bodley and Robson see P. A. Robson's memoir of E. R. Robson. For Watts and Company see the historical note by Anthony Symondson, in the brochure put out by the firm, which is still in business, in Tufton St., Westminster.

41 (*33*). For Bodley's 'Queen Anne' vicarages see F. M. Simpson's Memoir of Bodley, *R.I.B.A. Journal* (3rd Series), xv (1908), 150–2, and Edward Warren, 'The Life and Work of G. F. Bodley', ibid., xvii (1910), 308–9.

42 (*33*). For Father Herbert and the Community of the Holy Name see Una C. Hannam, *Portrait of a Community* (Malvern, 1972). Further information about the Malvern houses was kindly supplied to me by members of the Community.

43 (*33*). For Robson's friendship with G. G. Scott see P. A. Robson, op. cit., where it is also stated that 'I have letters from him to my father of an interesting and intimate character'.

44 (*33*). H. Luxmoore, of Eton College, recalls in a letter to Sydney Cockerell of 1 Aug. 1915 that he used to meet Warrington Taylor in 'early days in Queen Square or Red Lion Square . . . with the gifted and ill fated George Gilbert Scott then my contemporary, with whom I used to visit and exchange admiration of the shop' (Letter bound with Taylor–Webb Correspondence). Another example of the constant visiting between members of the group is recorded in G. P. Boyce's diary entry for 23 Feb. 1870: 'Gilbert Scott called. Showed him over my new house' (*Old Water Colour Society Club*, xix (1941), 58).

45 (*35*). The best source of information on G. G. Scott is the section (compiled by Gavin Stamp) devoted to him in *The Scott Family*, a separate volume of the catalogue of the R.I.B.A. Drawings Collection (forthcoming, 1977). Drawings and payments for Garboldisham show that work on the house was well advanced by 1870, in which year earlier material in Scott's office was destroyed by fire. As no drawings survive for the stables, it seems probable that they had been completed before 1870.

46 (*37*). *Building News*, 26 May, 1865, p. 373.

47 (*37*). *Architect*, 13 Mar. 1875, p. 161.

48 (*37*). *Building News*, 18 Mar. 1870, p. 210.

Chapter III. 'Queen Anne' Goes Public

1 (*38*). For J. J. Stevenson and the Stevenson family see Mark Girouard, 'The Architecture of John James Stevenson', *Connoisseur*, Nov. 1973, pp. 166–74, and Feb. 1974, pp. 106–12, with accompanying references.

2 (*39*). Brydon worked for both Nesfield and Shaw from 1867 to 1869 according to Saint, *Richard Norman Shaw* (London and New Haven, 1976), p. 438. Another former assistant to Campbell Douglas and Stevenson was the furniture designer Bruce Talbert, whose Introduction to *Gothic forms applied to Furniture Decoration*, dated Jan. 1868, acknowledges Brydon's assistance.

3 (*39*). The Red House has been demolished. The designs are in the Victoria and Albert Museum; the exterior was illustrated and briefly described in *Building News*, 18 Sept. 1874, and illustrated (with accompanying plans) and more fully described, inside and out, by Henry Cowell

Boyes in the *Portfolio* of 1879, pp. 51–5. Photographs in the National Monuments Record show the house inside and out shortly before demolition.

4 (*41*). Stevenson thought that 'a man really cannot always be sitting and looking at his own work', according to his obituary in the *R.I.B.A. Journal* (3rd Series), xv (1908), 482.

5 (*42*). For the Makins house see *Survey of London*, ed. F. H. W. Sheppard, vol. xxxviii: *The Museums Area of Kensington and Westminster* (London, 1976), pp. 46–8, with plans and sections. Designs by Stevenson are in the Victoria and Albert Museum. When a drawing of the house was exhibited at the Royal Academy in 1875 the *Builder* (8 May 1875) described it as 'a typical Queen Anne House' which 'completely succeeds in imposing itself upon the spectator as a house of the period'.

6 (*42*). Designs by Shaw are in the R.I.B.A. and Royal Academy. The building was illustrated and briefly described in the *Building News*, 5 Sept. 1873, and the *Builder*, 2 Aug. 1873. The top floor as executed was different from the original design.

7 (*45*). For Shaw's tussles with the District Surveyor see Saint, *Richard Norman Shaw*, pp. 136–7.

8 (*45*). For Kinmel see Mark Girouard, *The Victorian Country House* (Oxford, 1971), pp. 137–40, and *Country Life*, 4 and 11 Sept. 1969. The numerous surviving designs in the Victoria and Albert Museum unfortunately include nothing before 1871. The house has recently been severely damaged by fire, and at the time of writing its future is uncertain.

9 (*46*). For Bodrhyddan see Mark Girouard, *The Victorian Country House*, pp. 55 and 176, and Pls. 58 and 382. There are designs in the Victoria and Albert Museum and at the house, and photographs in the National Monuments Record.

10 (*48*). For Joldwynds see Webb's designs in the Victoria and Albert Museum and W. R. Lethaby, *Philip Webb and His Work* (London, 1935), p. 92. For Rounton see Lethaby, op. cit., pp. 93–5 and *Country Life*, xxxvii (1915, 1), pp. 906–12.

11 (*49*). Champneys died in 1935, when interest in Victorian architecture was at its nadir. As a result there were no adequate obituaries of him, and no adequate biographical account of him has been written apart from the brief and unsatisfactory one in the *Dictionary of National Biography*. His friendship with Sidney Colvin is documented in E. V. Lucas, *The Colvins and Their Friends* (London, 1928). His moves to Queen Square and Great Marlborough Street can be traced in the Post Office directories. Champneys's interests were literary as well as architectural: through Colvin he got to know Robert Louis Stevenson, Rossetti, and other writers and artists; he also became friends with Walter Pater, and with Coventry Patmore, whose biography he published in 1900. Like Sidgwick he was one of the first members of the Savile Club, the leading literary club of the 1870s and 1880s. According to John Betjeman, who visited him in the 1930s, he was then much prouder of his literary connections than his architecture.

12 (*49*). For Holiday see Henry Holiday, *Reminiscences of my Life* (London, 1914).

13 (*49*). Oak Tree House is illustrated and described in Holiday, op. cit., pp. 236–7, 240–1, and Maurice B. Adams, *Artists' Homes* (London, 1883), pp. 2–3, based on the *Building News*, 4 June 1880. Tenders for building it (from £3640 to £3230) were published in the *Architect*, 25 Jan. 1873.

14 (*50*). For Lowther Lodge see Saint, *Richard Norman Shaw*, pp. 137–42, and *Survey of London*, ed. F. H. W. Sheppard, vol. xxxviii: *The Museums Area of Kensington and Westminster* (London, 1976), pp. 327–31. The contract drawings, July 1873, are in the possession of the Royal Geographical Society, who now occupy the house; other drawings are at R.I.B.A. and the Royal Academy. Shaw's bird's-eye view, exhibited at the Royal Academy in 1874, was engraved in the *Building News* of 25 June 1875, with an enthusiastic description of the house.

15 (*52*). But it was originally planned with no bathroom at all. J. J. Stevenson, in answer to a letter from Scott, advised in favour of a bathroom, and of deal instead of mahogany for window frames, as at the Red House (Letter of 15 Apr. (1873?) in Scott Collection, R.I.B.A., kindly communicated by Gavin Stamp).

16 (*52*). For Leamington House see Scott's designs in the R.I.B.A. Drawings Collection, and accompanying entry in the Catalogue.

17 (*53*). The houses were illustrated and briefly described in the *Architect*, 1 May 1875. In the illustration the rainwater head of No. 2 is dated 1873. See also J. J. Stevenson, *What are the Best Methods of Securing the Improvement of Street Architecture, especially as regards its connection with Public Building?* (a paper read at the Social Science Congress at Liverpool, Oct. 1876, published in pamphlet form, London, 1877), p. 8.

18 (*54*). Jo Manton, *Elizabeth Garrett Anderson* (London, 1965), p. 239. For the Garretts' training under Brydon (after a brief preliminary period with Daniel Cottier) see Moncure D. Conway, *Travels in South Kensington* (London, 1882), pp. 168–70.

19 (*54*). Edis, like Champneys, lived on well into the twentieth century, and apart from giving the year when he joined the Volunteers, his obituary in the *Builder*, 1 July 1927, has little to say about his background, training, or early career.

20 (*54*). John Summerson, *The Architectural Association 1847–1947* (London, 1947), p. 17. Edis was president of the A.A., 1865–7.

21 (*55*). For Johnson see the obituary in the *Builder*, 1892 (1), p. 353, and *Archaeologia Aeliana* (Journal of the Newcastle on Tyne Society of Antiquaries), 3rd Series, vol. x (1913). The *Builder* described him as 'one of the very few men standing in the front rank of the profession who continued to practise in the country instead of being absorbed in the great vortex of London'.

22 (*55*). *Shields Gazette*, 3 June 1873; information in notebook of J. C. Stevenson, now belonging to Hew Shannan Stevenson. Johnson later collaborated with Stevenson on the offices of the Tyne Improvement Commission in Newcastle (1882).

23 (*55*). *Shields Gazette*, 3 June 1873.

24 (*55*). Johnson's Municipal College of Commerce, College Street (originally Dame Allan's Schools), Newcastle on Tyne (1882), is described by Pevsner (*Buildings of England: Northumberland*, London, 1957, p. 241) as 'in the Norman Shaw style, both his Chelsea and his Queen's Gate variety'. Johnson restored Vanbrugh's Morpeth Town Hall for the Earl of Carlisle in 1869–70 (ibid., p. 215), and supervised the redecoration of the chapel at Castle Howard in 1875–8. The commissions suggest a link with George Howard, not unexpected as both men moved in 'Queen Anne' circles.

25 (*56*). *Architect*, 10 May 1873, pp. 248–9, along with illustration of the exterior and a copy of Bodley's report. The building as executed was slightly different from the *Architect* engraving; for a photograph see Saint, *Richard Norman Shaw*, Pl. 176.

26 (*57*). Reginald Blomfield, *Richard Norman Shaw, R.A.* (London, 1940), p. 9.

27 (*57*). *Building News*, 31 May 1872, p. 430; 9 July 1872, p. 35.

28 (*57*). *Architect*, 8 June 1872, p. 305.

29 (*57*). According to a letter from E. W. H. Piper, a former member of the staff (*Architect and Building News*, 1 Sept. 1933, p. 238), Adams was the 'artist-editor' by 1875. For Passmore Edwards (1823–1911) see the *D.N.B.*

30 (*57*). *Building News*, 9 May 1873, p. 524.

31 (*58*). Loc. cit.; *Architect*, 17 May 1873, p. 258.

32 (*58*). *Builder*, 10 May 1873, p. 358.

33 (*58*). *Building News*, 23 May 1873, p. 584; *Architect*, 24 May 1873, p. 271.

34 (*58*). *Builder*, 9 Aug. 1873, p. 632.

35 (*59*). *Architect*, 31 Jan. 1874, pp. 63–6.

36 (*59*). Ibid., 3 Jan. 1874, pp. 1–2; *Building News*, 26 June 1874, pp. 689–92; *Builder*, 27 June 1874, pp. 537–8. In the discussion after his paper Stevenson cited as examples of 'Queen Anne' Bodley's London School Board Offices, T. H. Wyatt's Upper Berkeley Street houses, buildings by Webb, Nesfield, and Champneys, especially the latter's work for the London School Board, Shaw's New Zealand Chambers, and (according to the *Builder* but not the *Building News*) M. D. Wyatt's Alford House on Kensington Gore.

37 (*59*). *Architect*, 27 Feb. 1875, pp. 125–6.

38 (*59*). Ibid., 13 Mar. 1875, p. 159.

39 (*59*). *Saturday Review*, 31 July 1875, pp. 142–3.

40 (*59*). *R.I.B.A. Transactions*, 1881–2, p. 24 (reporting a remark made in 1876).

41 (*60*). Thomas Graham Jackson, *Recollections*, ed. Basil H. Jackson (London, 1950), pp. 122–3.

42 (*60*). Thomas Graham Jackson, *Modern Gothic Architecture* (London, 1873), pp. 34, 109, 113.

43 (*61*). Ibid., p. 111.

44 (*61*). The arguments and quotations in this and the following paragraph derive from Stevenson's articles in the *Building News*, 26 June 1874, pp. 689–92, and *Architect*, 27 Feb. 1875, pp. 125–6. Similar arguments occur in his *House Architecture* (London, 1880) and in E. R. Robson, *School Architecture* (London, 1874), pp. 321–3.

45 (*61*). Jackson, *Modern Gothic Architecture*, p. 117.

46 (*61*). *Portfolio*, vol. 3 (1873), p. 8.

47 (*61*). *Building News*, 26 Feb. 1875, p. 248.

48 (*62*). *Portfolio*, vol. 4 (1874), p. 9.

49 (*62*). *Building News*, 26 Feb. 1875, p. 247.

50 (*62*). Ibid., p. 248.

51 (*62*). *Building News*, 26 June, 1874, p. 690.

52 (*62*). Jackson, *Modern Gothic Architecture*, p. 189.

53 (*62*). 'Our Dwelling-Houses', *Good Words*, Oct. 1873.

54 (*62*). For Champneys's acquaintance with Walter Pater see A. C. Benson, *Walter Pater* (London, 1906), p. 192, and Thomas Wright, *The Life of Walter Pater* (London, 1907), p. 260.

55 (*62*). *Portfolio*, vol. 4 (1874), p. 10.

56 (*63*). Moncure Daniel Conway, *Autobiography* (London, 1905), ii. 339.

Chapter IV. The Architecture of Light

1 (*64*). Arthur Conan Doyle, *The Complete Sherlock Holmes Short Stories* (London, 1928), p. 515.

2 (*64*). Charles Booth (ed.), *Life and Labours of the People in London*, vol. iii (London, 1892), p. 204.

3 (*64*). The Hon. William Francis Cowper (1811–88), from 1869 Cowper-Temple, created Lord Mount Temple, 1880.

4 (*65*). Currie's obituary in *The Times*, 14 May 1913, p. 9. He was later one of the founders of the People's Palace in Mile End Road and brought Robson in as architect. For Chatfield Clarke see 'Contemporary British Architects', *Building News*, 5 Sept. 1890, p. 342.

5 (*65*). G.L.C. archives, School Board of London Minutes, 31 May, 28 June, and 5 July 1871.

6 (*65*). For Charles Reed's partnership with Plint see Reed's entry in the *D.N.B.*

7 (*65*). G.L.C. archives: SBL/927A/253 (5 Feb. 1872); SBL Minutes, 26 June and 31 July 1872. Schools designed by outside architects are dealt with in the minutes of the Works Committee, SBL/927, etc. For some reason two schools (Shakespeare Walk and Brewhouse Lane) were put out to E. C. Robins in 1873.

8 (*65*). SBL/927, *passim*.

9 (*65*). SBL/927/144.

10 (*66*). SBL Minutes, 18 Sept. 1872 and 15 Jan. 1873.

11 (*66*). *Old Water Colour Society Club*, xix (1941), 61–2. The copious extracts from Boyce's diary published in this volume are all that survive its unfortunate destruction in the war.

12 (*66*). T. G. Jackson, *Recollections*, ed. B. H. Jackson (London, 1950), p. 60.

13 (*66*). P. A. Robson, Memoir of E. R. Robson, *R.I.B.A. Journal* (3rd Series), xxiv. 9.

14 (*66*). SBL Minutes, 5 June and 31 July 1872. Tenders were published in the *Architect*, 14 Dec. 1872.

15 (*67*). Design and progress of individual schools can be followed in detail in the minutes of the Works Committee (SBL 927–1025) and those of the subcommittee on designs, working drawings, and specifications (SBL 1034), and its successor, the subcommittee on buildings (SBL 1033). The designs for many of the schools are preserved in the G.L.C. archives (for demolished or disused schools) or Architect's Department (for schools still in use). An album in the G.L.C. Photographic Department (635/49) contains contemporary photographs of the exterior of twenty-four schools. *The Work of the London School Board* and the *Final Report of the London School Board 1870–1904* (both printed in L.C.C. Official Publications, vol. 64) contain a useful account of the Board's history and maps showing the location of all the schools.

16 (*68*). E. R. Robson, *School Architecture* (London, 1874; facsimile, with introduction by Malcolm Seaborne, London, 1972), p. xi; Stevenson, *House Architecture* (London, 1880), i. 348.

17 (*69*). SBL Minutes, 6 Jan. 1875; 19 Jan. 1876.

18 (*69*). E. R. Robson, op. cit., p. 314.

19 (*70*). For the general history of Newnham and the background of women's schools and colleges in general see Alice Gardner, *A Short History of Newnham College* (Cambridge, 1921).

20 (*70*). List of shareholders, Newnham Hall Company, 1874, in Newnham College Muniments.

21 (*70*). A. and E. M. Sidgwick, *Henry Sidgwick: A Memoir* (London, 1906), p. 247.

22 (*71*). Alice Gardner, op. cit., p. 23: Victoria Glendinning, *A Suppressed Cry* (London, 1969), p. 51.

23 (*71*). Hester Burton, *Barbara Bodichon 1827–1891* (London, 1949), p. 164.

24 (*71*). In a letter of condolence to Mrs. Sidgwick in 1900 Champneys says it was 'all but forty years' since he made his acquaintance (Trinity College Add. MS. c.101/19). Sidney Colvin met Sidgwick at dinner with Champneys in 1863 when he and Champneys were undergraduates at Trinity. E. V. Lucas, *The Colvins and Their Friends* (London, 1928), p. 9.

25 (*71*). Newnham College Muniments, including letters from Champneys to Miss Ewart in Building Papers, Box 1.

26 (*71*). Newnham Hall Company Minutes (Newnham Muniments). A perspective view was published in the *Building News*, 4 Sept. 1874.

27 (*71*). Alice Gardner, op. cit., *passim*; Box file of 'Building 1874–1910', Newnham Muniments.

28 (*71*). Alice Gardner, op. cit., p. 21.

29 (*73*). Building Papers, Box 1.

30 (*75*). B. A. Clough, *Memoir of Anne J. Clough* (1897), p. 205.

31 (*75*). Mary Paley Marshall, *What I Remember* (Cambridge, 1947), p. 20.

32 (*76*). *Newnham Letter*, 1929, p. 63, quoted in Jessie Stewart, *Jane Ellen Harrison: A Portrait from Letters* (London, 1959); Jane Ellen Harrison, *Reminiscences of a Student's Life* (London, 1925), p. 54.

33 (*76*). J. E. Harrison, op. cit., pp. 44–6. While at Newnham she visited Oxford in 1877, to play Alcestis for the Oxford University Dramatic Society, and was entertained by Walter Pater whom she found 'a soft, kind cat' (p. 46).

34 (*76*). Victoria Glendinning, op. cit., p. 71.

35 (*76*). Gwen Raverat, *Period Piece: A Cambridge Childhood* (London, 1952), p. 26.

36 (*76*). Ibid., p. 45.

37 (*76*). For the first Leicester competition see *Architect*, 22 July 1871, pp. 37–8.

38 (*77*). *Building News*, 6 June 1873; *Builder*, 21 June 1875.

39 (*77*). *Building News*, 18 and 25 July 1873. Hames's design illustrated in *Building News*, 19 Sept. 1873.

40 (*77*). For F. J. Hames's Leicester connections see *Builder*, 15 Aug. 1874, p. 694. Neither here nor in the other building periodicals is he identified with Nesfield's assistant, but they were almost certainly the same person. Francis Hames was still working for Nesfield in July 1872, when he witnessed Nesfield's designs for the Rose and Crown Hotel, Saffron Walden (now in the V. and A.), a modest but pleasing 'Queen Anne' building destroyed by fire a few years ago. His sketchbook contains a number of drawings of Leicester buildings.

41 (*78*). J. W. Walker, *Wakefield, its History and People* (Wakefield, 1939), pp. 552–4; *Building News*, 13 Apr. 1877; *Wakefield Express*, Supplement, 19 Oct. 1877.

42 (*78*). Ibid., 28 Apr. and 5 and 12 May 1877. Collcutt's winning design illustrated in *Building News*, 4 May 1877.

43 (*78*). *Wakefield Express*, 20 Oct. 1877, 13 Mar. and 24 Apr. 1880.

44 (*81*). The design was illustrated in *Building News*, 29 June 1877.

45 (*81*). Street's report published in *Building News*, 11 May 1877, p. 463.

46 (*81*). Second and third premium designs illustrated in *Building News*, 1 and 8 June 1877.

47 (*81*). *Wakefield Express*, 12 May 1877.

48 (*81*). See Chapter III, n. 26.

49 (*81*). *Wakefield Express*, 20 Oct. 1877.

50 (*81*). *Building News*, 4 May 1877.

51 (*82*). *Wakefield Express*, 23 Oct. 1880, has a detailed description of the completed building, with names of the craftsmen and firms involved. Sketches of the interior by Raffles Davison are in *British Architect*, 31 Mar., 7 and 14 Apr. 1882.

52 (*82*). *Building News*, 16 Mar. 1877, p. 278; 20 Apr. 1877, p. 381.

53 (*82*). *Building News*, 27 Apr. 1877, pp. 407–9. *Builder*, 28 Apr. 1877, p. 415.

54 (*83*). Stevenson and Adams's entry was illustrated in *Building News*, 10 May 1878; Brydon's in *Building News*, 28 Sept. 1877; J. O. Scott's in *Building News*, 26 Oct. 1877, with Scott's own description. A sketch for 'Xmas', captioned by Godwin, is in the R.I.B.A. Drawings Collection (Ran 7/M/27/5), and an uncaptioned sketch in similar style by him in the Victoria and Albert Museum is certainly for Kensington.

55 (*83*). *Building News*, 27 July 1877, p. 89; 3 Aug. 1877, p. 99.

56 (*84*). Illustrated in *Building News*, 20 Dec. 1878.

57 (*84*). *Builder*, 29 Sept. 1877, p. 990; *Building News*, 19 Oct. 1877.

58 (*84*). Illustrated in *British Architect*, 15 Apr. 1881 (Pontefract); 13 July, 3 Aug. 1883 (Yarmouth).

59 (*84*). Somerville was illustrated in *Building News*, 5 Jan. 1883.

60 (*84*). For North London Collegiate School see *Builder*, 10 Apr. 1880, and *Building News*, 21 June 1881. For Blackheath High School for Girls, *Builder*, 3 Apr. 1880, p. 417. There is a good selection of illustrations of late nineteenth-century schools in Felix Clay, *Modern School Building* (London, 1902).

61 (*84*). Both illustrated in *British Architect*, 14 May 1886.

62 (*84*). Illustrated in *Building News*, 27 July 1877.

63 (*86*). *Building News*, 24 June 1881.

64 (*86*). Jo Manton, *Elizabeth Garrett Anderson* (London, 1865), p. 286 and Pl. 11a.

65 (*86*). Illustrated in *British Architect*, 10 Dec. 1880, 21 Jan. 1881 (Newmarket); *Building News*, 13 May 1887, 12 Aug. 1881; *Architect*, 1 Sept. 1883 (St. Leonard's).

66 (*86*). T. G. Jackson, *Recollections*, p. 163, Pl. XIII.

67 (*87*). 'Down Memory Lane', *Leek Post and Times*, 10 May 1973.

68 (*87*). Paul Thompson, *William Morris* (London, 1967), p. 110. *Leek Times*, 19 Nov. 1881. The Royal School of Art Needlework was later renamed Royal School of Needlework.

69 (*87*). Thompson, op. cit., pp. 96–9.

70 (*88*). For Sugden see G. A. Lovenbury, 'The House of Sugden', *Leek Post and Times*, 29 Mar., 19 Apr., and 10 May, 1973, including a list of his buildings on 10 May, and 'Sugden: The Final Chapter', *Leek Post and Times*, 23 Aug. 1973. Obituaries were published in *Leek Times*, 22 and 29 June 1901, and *Clarion*, 29 June 1901. Keir Hardie's funeral address is in *Labour Leader*, 29 June 1901, p. 203 (communicated to me by Robert Thorne). Another list of his works is in *Leek and District Illustrated* (1896, copy in Leek Public Library).

71 (*88*). Saint, *Richard Norman Shaw*, Cat. no. 42.

72 (*88*). *Leek Times*, 19 Nov. 1881.

73 (*88*). *Leek Times*, 18 Oct. 1884; illustrated and described in *Builder*, 18 Oct. 1884, and *British Architect*, 27 Mar. and 3 Apr. 1885. The old house in front of the institute was lived in by Arthur Nicholson, one of the founders of the Leek coffee tavern, and probably Joshua Nicholson's son.

Chapter V. Sweetness at Home

1 (*90*). *The Burlington*, July 1882, pp. 235–8.

2 (*92*). For the development of Hampstead see F. M. L. Thompson, *Hampstead: Building a Borough 1650–1964* (London, 1974). An excellent example of Batterbury and Huxley housing is Hampstead Hill Gardens, designed in 1877 (Thompson, pp. 266–7).

3 (*92*). For the development of the Holland estate at this period see *Survey of London*, ed. F. H. W. Sheppard, vol. xxxvii: *Northern Kensington* (London, 1973), pp. 126–9, 136–50.

4 (*92*). The development of the Metropolitan Board of Works' property along Chelsea Embankment can be traced in detail in the M.B.W. papers, in the Greater London Record Office, especially the Minutes of the Works and General Purposes Committee (M.B.W. 1129–1244) and the Valuer's Department plans and drawings, listed in the L.C.C. Register of Approved Drawings (which includes M.B.W.). For a catalogue of houses and architects in Chelsea Embankment and Tite Street see the Appendix.

5 (*92*). The surviving papers of the Cadogan and Hans Place Estate Ltd. (registered 1875) are in the Public Record Office BT/31/2131/9767. Much of the capital was subscribed from Birmingham, especially by Joseph Chamberlain and members of his family. The biggest shareholder was Robert Heath, the hatter. Colonel Makins, who was made a baronet in 1903, was also Governor of the Gas, Light and Coke Company.

6 (*92*). For the architectural development of the estate see *Builder*, 6 May 1876, p. 425; *Building News*, 28 Apr. 1876, p. 413 (houses by Stevenson and Robinson); *Building News*, 16 June 1876, 19 Jan. and 12 Oct. 1877 (illustrations of houses by Young Nesbitt and Niven); *Building News*, 17 Jan. 1879, pp. 57–8 ('New Buildings at Chelsea', a detailed account of progress on the estate); *Building News*, 27 June 1879, 16 July 1880, 11 May 1883 (illustrations of houses by Shaw and A. J. Adams); *Building News*, 25 June 1886 (illustration of later Stevenson houses); *Builder*, 2 June, 27 Nov. 1888; *Architect*, 16 Aug. 1884, 21 Sept. 1888 (houses by other architects). The only Gothic house in Cadogan Square was No. 4, by G. E. Street (illustrated in *Building News*, 7 Apr. 1882). Sketch designs by Devey are in the R.I.B.A. I have not worked on the records of the Cadogan or Smith's Charity estates.

For a catalogue of houses and architects in Cadogan Square and Pont Street see the Appendix.

7 (*94*). *Building News*, 12 Oct. 1877.

8 (*97*). *Survey of London*, ed. F. H. W. Sheppard, vol. xxxvii: *Northern Kensington* (London, 1973), p. 144.

9 (*99*). For an account of Show Sunday as seen by a Victorian artist and his family see L. V. Fildes, *Luke Fildes, R.A.; A Victorian Painter* (London, 1968), pp. 46, 86.

10 (*99*). Ibid., pp. 17, 19.

11 (*99*). For the Tite Street studios see Chapter VII. A good surviving example of a group of studios of the 1880s is Pembroke Studios, built to either side of a pedestrian court off Pembroke Road, Kensington.

12 (*99*). For Albert Hall Mansions see *Survey of London*, ed. F. H. W. Sheppard, vol. xxxviii: *The Museums Area of Kensington and Westminster* (London, 1976), pp. 342–5.

13 (*99*). William Morris, *Works* (London, 1909–14), xxii. 329, from 'The Revival of Architecture', first published in *Fortnightly Review*, May 1888.

14 (*99*). Shaw's London houses are discussed at length in Chapter 6 of Saint, *Richard Norman Shaw* (London and New Haven, 1976).

15 (*100*). W. H. Mallock, *Memoirs of Life and Literature* (London, 1920), p. 88.

16 (*103*). The contract drawings are in the Victoria and Albert Museum; elevation, section, and plans were reproduced in John Physick and Michael Darby, *Marble Halls: Drawings and Models for Victorian Secular Buildings* (London, 1973) (catalogue of an exhibition held at the Victoria and Albert Museum), pp. 86–7.

17 (*105*). They are dealt with in some detail in *Survey of London*, ed. F. H. W. Sheppard, vol. xxxvii: *Northern Kensington* (London, 1973), pp. 143–4, 148–9.

18 (*109*). Drawing for the house in the R.A. and R.I.B.A. Illustrations and photographs of interior in *British Architect*, 1876 and 1880, and W. Shaw Sparrow (ed.), *The British Home of Today* (1904).

19 (*111*). J. J. Stevenson, *House Architecture* (London, 1880), i. 349.

20 (*111*). Maurice B. Adams, *Artists' Homes* (London, 1883), p. 2.

21 (*112*). *Building News*, 20 Sept. 1878 (Lowther Gardens, with illustration and plan); *Building News*, 17 Jan. 1879 (Pont Street and Cadogan Square). Designs for some of the Pont Street and Cadogan Square houses in the Victoria and Albert Museum.

22 (*116*). For Verrall and Ward see the *D.N.B.* The date of the houses can be approximately fixed by their first appearance in the Cambridge Directories.

23 (*116*). For Southgarth see Amy C. Flagg, 'Westoe Village' (typescript in South Shields Public Library); the plans are reproduced in Stevenson's *House Architecture*, ii. 134–5 and the house is illustrated in the *Connoisseur* of Nov. 1973 (see Chapter III, n. 1). Designs for the Banbury Road houses are in the Victoria and Albert Museum.

24 (*116*). The house is illustrated and described in Maurice B. Adams, *Artists' Houses*. Contract drawings, dated August 1876, in Victoria and Albert Museum. See also *Survey of London*, ed. F. H. W. Sheppard, vol. xxxvii: *Northern Kensington* (London, 1973), p. 144.

25 (*116*). For Balliol Croft see Mary Paley Marshall, *What I Remember* (Cambridge, 1947), p. 43 and Pl. 10. For the Old Granary see Gwen Raverat, *Period Piece* (London, 1952), pp. 39–40. The architect is there not named, but described as having written 'a book on house design' in which he said: 'The coal store should be placed as far as possible from the kitchen, in order to induce economy in the use of fuel', a quotation clearly derived from Stevenson's *House Architecture*, ii. 108.

26 (*118*). For T. H. Green see R. L. Nettleship, *Memoir of Thomas Hill Green* (London, 1906), and Melvin Richter, *The Politics of Conscience: T. H. Green and his Age* (London, 1964).

27 (*118*). Mary Paley Marshall, op. cit., p. 10. A. C. Pigou (ed.), *Memorials of Alfred Marshall* (London, 1925).

28 (*118*). For Ken Hill see Mark Girouard, *The Victorian Country House* (Oxford, 1971), pp. 161–4, and *Country Life*, 21 and 28 Dec. 1967. The hall (or saloon) was illustrated in *Building News*, 25 June 1880.

29 (*119*). *Building News*, 2 May 1879.

30 (*120*). W. R. Lethaby, *Philip Webb and his Work* (Oxford, 1935), p. 136.

31 (*120*). Ibid., p. 121.

32 (*120*). For Smeaton Manor see John Brandon-Jones, 'Notes on the Building of Smeaton Manor', *Architectural History*, vol. i (1958), pp. 31–58, which reproduces the original designs and many letters from Webb to the client.

33 (*121*). Designs for Westcombe Park and Loughton are in the Victoria and Albert Museum; elevations and plans of the latter reproduced in *Marble Halls*, op. cit., pp. 74–5.

34 (*121*). Designs in the Greater London Record Office, among Metropolitan Board of Works' Valuers' Plans, listed in L.C.C. Register of Approved Drawings.

35 (*121*). Miss Peddie's house (now 26 Bolingbroke Grove) was illustrated in *Building News*, 23 June 1876. *Building News*, 5 Sept. 1890, p. 342, lists 'houses on Bolingbroke Grove Estate' as by Robson, and Nos. 23–5 Bolingbroke Grove are clearly his work. The Westcombe Park houses are mentioned in P. A. Robson, Memoir of E. R. Robson, *R.I.B.A. Journal* (3rd Series), xxiv. 96, and can perhaps be identified as the houses on Westcombe Park Road between Foyle and Coleraine Roads, dated 1883–5.

36 (*123*). For the Pevensey and Middlesbrough houses see the designs in the R.I.B.A. Drawings Collection and accompanying entries in the catalogue.

37 (*123*). See R.I.B.A. Drawings Collection and Gavin Stamp, 'Scott in Hull', *Architectural Review*, Oct. 1974, p. 251.

38 (*125*). Illustrated in *Building News*, 3 May 1878.

39 (*125*). Described and illustrated in Maurice B. Adams, *Artists' Houses* (London, 1883), based on *Building News*, 9 July 1880, and *British Architect*, 9 Jan. 1885, with numerous drawings of exterior and interior by T. Raffles Davison.

40 (*125*). For the Ascot and Sunningdale Estate Ltd. see *British Architect*, 23 Jan. 1885 and 26 Mar. and 16 July 1886, with illustrations, and Public Record Office BT/31/3270/19244. The company was registered on 27 Dec. 1883, and wound up in Mar. 1887, it being considered 'expedient to reconstruct the Company on an extended basis'. Only about 450 of the 2,500 £10 shares on offer had been taken up, 50 of them by Champneys.

41 (*125*). For Burn and St. Chad's see the *D.N.B.* and the Cambridge Directories. The house is now occupied by St. Catharine's College.

42 (*126*). For Grove Park see illustrations in *Building News*, 26 Dec. 1879, 17 Feb. 1882, 30 Mar. and 9 Nov. 1883. Designs for Prior's houses on Byron Hill and an early photograph of the Red House are in the R.I.B.A. Drawings Collection.

43 (*126*). Illustrated in *Building News*, 13 June 1879.

44 (*128*). Illustrated in *Architect*, 4 Aug. 1883, and see Amy C. Flagg, op. cit.

45 (*129*). Fremington illustrated in *Building News*, 18 Aug. 1882; Dunley House in *Building News*, 13 May 1887. As built Fremington is a much simplified version of the original design.

Chapter VI. Fitting Out the House Beautiful

1 (*130*). Mrs. Haweis, *Beautiful Houses* (London, 1882), p. 47.

2 (*132*). *Art Furniture designed by Edward W. Godwin, FSA, and manufactured by William Watt* (London, 1877); *Building News*, 26 May 1881, 10 Nov. 1882, 23 Feb., 20 Apr., and 23 Nov. 1883 (furniture by M. B. Adams). The Shoolbred catalogue is in the Handley–Read Collection in the R.I.B.A. library, which contains probably the best surviving collection of books related to furniture of this date.

3 (*136*). e.g. the model bedroom exhibited by Jackson and Graham, illustrated in *British Architect*, 20 June 1884.

4 (*136*). An increasingly common side-product of the 'Queen Anne' movement was straightforward reproduction 'Chippendale', 'Sheraton', or 'Hepplewhite' furniture. One of the firms specializing in this was Wright and Mansfield, who exhibited a selection at the Philadelphia Centennial Exhibition in 1876. See Clive Wainwright, 'The Age before Enlightenment', *The Times* (Saturday Review section, 7 Feb. 1976). Morris and Company were making reproduction eighteenth-century furniture from about 1880.

5 (*137*). The Ken Hill grate is illustrated in M. Girouard, *Victorian Country House* (Oxford, 1971), Pl. 346, and Elsley's design in R. W. Edis, *Decoration and Furniture of Town Houses* (London, 1881), p. 270.

6 (*138*). For Orchardson see *Sir William Quiller Orchardson, R.A.* (Catalogue of Scottish Arts Council exhibition, 1972) with accompanying bibliography, and for his friendship with Stevenson see the latter's obituary in *R.I.B.A. Journal* (3rd Series), vol. xv (1903), and Hilda Orchardson Gray, *Life of Sir William Quiller Orchardson* (London, 1930), pp. 207, 244. For Marcus Stone see Alfred L. Baldry, 'Marcus Stone R.A.', *Art Annual*, 1904 (complete volume). Stone designed the sets for *Olivia*, a dramatization of the *Vicar of Wakefield* by W. G. Wills, which was put on at the Court Theatre in 1878, with Ellen Terry in the leading role. I owe this reference to David Cheshire.

7 (*139*). *Ellen Terry's Memoirs*, ed. E. Craig and C. St. John (London, 1933), p. 67.

8 (*139*). Walter Crane, *An Artist's Reminiscences* (London, 1907), pp. 80, 94–5, 102.

9 (*139*). Ibid., p. 107.

10 (*139*). Ibid., pp. 103–4.

11 (*140*). Crane's 6*d.* and 1*s.* toy books are all undated and their bibliography is extremely complicated. The dates given in G. C. E. Massé, *Bibliography of First Editions of Books Illustrated by Walter Crane* (1923), are, on the whole, wildly inaccurate. Mine are based on date stamps in the British Museum copies, and references in *An Artist's Reminiscences*.

12 (*142*). *Cinderella*, c. 1872–3. Jack Sprat from *Alphabet of Old Friends*, c. 1873–4. *Three Bears*, c. 1872–3. *Princess Belle Étoile*, c. 1874–5. *Frog Prince* and *Beauty and the Beast*, 1873–4. Drawings were often made the year before publication. Crane's taste for neo-classicism may date from a winter spent in Rome, 1872–3. It became part of the eclectic stock-in-trade of 'Queen Anne'. See Mrs. Haweis, *Beautiful Houses* (London, 1882), p. 106 n.: 'The slang term "Queen Anne" means almost anything just now, but is oftenest applied to the pseudo-classic fashions of the First Empire'.

13 (*144*). Walter Crane, op. cit., p. 156.

14 (*146*). For Kate Greenaway see *Reminiscences of Edmund Evans*, ed. Ruari Maclean (Oxford, 1967), pp. 59–61, and M. H. Spielmann and G. S. Layard, *Kate Greenaway* (London, 1905).

15 (*146*). Spielmann and Layard, op. cit., pp. 63–4.

16 (*148*). Henry Blackburn, *Randolph Caldecott, A Personal Memoir of his Early Art Career* (London, 1886).

17 (*149*). Ibid., pp. 87–8, 196. Some of the panels are illustrated in colour in Mark Girouard, 'Pattern and Colour in Design: Victorian decoration in houses', *Country Life Annual*, 1970, pp. 29–36.

18 (*150*). See Mark Girouard, 'Entertaining Victorian Royalty', *Country Life*, 4 Dec. 1969, pp. 1446–50.

19 (*152*). John D. Sedding, *Gardencraft Old and New* (London, 1891), based on a talk given to the Art Worker's Guild in 1889. Reginald Blomfield and F. Inigo Thomas, *The Formal Garden in England* (London, 1892), incorporating portions of an article on 'Gardens', from the *Portfolio*, Dec. 1889. William Robinson, *Garden Design and English Gardens* (London, 1892).

20 (*153*). Both pictures are in the Tate Gallery.

21 (*153*). William Morris, *Works* (1910–14), i. 151 (first published in the *Oxford and Cambridge Magazine*, 1856).

22 (*153*). See Lethaby, *Philip Webb and his Work* (London, 1935), p. 28.

23 (*153*). O. Doughty and J. R. Wahl (eds.), *Letters of Dante Gabriel Rossetti* (Oxford, 1965), pp. 609, 611. Laura Hain Friswell, *In the Sixties and Seventies* (London, 1905), p. 270.

24 (*153*). Taylor–Robson correspondence, Fitzwilliam Museum, fo. 29.

25 (*153*). John George Marks, *Life and Letters of Frederick Walker* (London, 1896), pp. 145, 154–5, 186, and reproductions, pp. 159, 192.

26 (*154*). William Bell Scott, *Poems* (London, 1875), p. 102.

27 (*155*). *Saturday Review*, 20 Feb. 1875, pp. 245–6. The article was published anonymously, but reprinted in Mrs. Loftie, *Social Twitters* (London, 1879).

28 (*156*). *Art Journal*, 1890, quoted in A. M. W. Stirling, *The Richmond Papers* (London, 1926), pp. 249–50. For Burne-Jones's garden see, e.g., Mary Gladstone, *Diaries and Letters* (London, 1930), p. 97: 'June 25, 1875. With Frances at 4 o'clock to Mr. Burne Jones's . . . Had tea in his big studio, and then strolled about the pretty, old-fashioned garden and picked roses.'

29 (*156*). *Bedford Park Gazette*, Sept. 1883.

30 (*157*). Blomfield and Inigo Thomas, op. cit., pp. 217–18.

31 (*157*). Louisa Egerton's responsibility for the garden, and her pleasure when visitors mistook it for the original layout, is described in her manuscript notes on the 6th Duke of Devonshire's *Guide to Chatsworth and Hardwick*, in the possession of the National Trust. For her friendship with the George Howards (he was also a cousin) see Dorothy Henley, *Rosalind Howard Countess of Carlisle* (London, 1958), p. 112.

32 (*158*). Augustus Hare, *The Story of my Life* (London, 1896–1900), v. 452. For the garden at Blickling as it was in the 1890s see *Country Life*, 29 Jan. and 5 Feb. 1898. Plans for the terraces are among the Blickling papers at the Norfolk County Record Office.

33 (*158*). Illustrated in *Country Life*, 6 Dec. 1902 (vol. xii), pp. 732–41.

34 (*158*). For Mrs. Boyle see her obituary in *The Times*, 18 Aug. 1916, and William Bell Scott, *Autobiography* (London, 1892), i. 325. For supporters of the old-fashioned garden see also Mrs. Kegan Paul, 'Old Fashioned Gardening', *Nineteenth Century*, Jan. 1880, and Mrs. J. Francis Foster, *On the Art of Gardening* (London, 1881). The Huntercombe gardens are illustrated in *Country Life*, 6 May 1899 (vol. v), pp. 560–5.

Chapter VII. Two 'Queen Anne' Communities

1 (*160*). Moncure D. Conway, *Travels in South Kensington* (London, 1882), p. 218, from an illustrated article on Bedford Park reprinted from *Harper's Monthly*, lxii (Mar. 1881), pp. 481–90.

2 (*160*). Reginald Blomfield, *Richard Norman Shaw, R.A.* (London, 1940), p. 37.

3 (*160*). The main source for Carr's life is his obituary in *Chiswick Times*, 5 Feb. 1915, p. 6. There is a certain amount about his family and their background in his brother, J. Comyns Carr's book, *Some Eminent Victorians: Personal Recollections in the World of Art and Letters* (London, 1908), and Mrs. J. Comyns Carr, *Reminiscences* (London, 1926), p. 278, neither of which, curiously, mentions Jonathan Carr or Bedford Park.

4 (*160*). For Bedford Park see especially Ian Fletcher, 'Bedford Park: Aesthetes' Elysium', *Romantic Mythologies* (London, 1967), pp. 169–207, a study of Bedford Park, its inhabitants, and contemporary reactions to it and them; T. Affleck Greeves, 'London's First Garden Suburb' and 'The Making of a Community', *Country Life*, 7 and 14 Dec. 1967, and *Bedford Park: the First Garden Suburb* (London, 1975), the latter predominantly a picture-book, but with a useful introduction and architectural analysis of house types. The large Bedford Park Collection in the Chiswick Public Library includes sets of the lithographs and a run of the *Bedford Park Gazette* (1883–4), which contains much material on the estate and its origins.

5 (*161*). T. Affleck Greeves, *Country Life*, 7 Dec. 1967, p. 1526. The 'parsonage house in Northamptonshire' of the story must refer to the Moor Green parsonage in Nottinghamshire, which was the only Godwin parsonage to be published. For Comyns Carr see n. 3.

6 (*161*). Benjamin Ward Richardson, *Hygeia: A City of Health* (London, 1876).

7 (*161*). M. Ward, *Return to Chesterton* (London, 1952), p. 25, retelling a story told to Chesterton by Lucien Oldenshaw. In the 1890s Chesterton courted his future wife in Bedford Park, which features as 'Saffron Park' in *The Man Who was Thursday*.

8 (*162*). For Bedford Park Ltd. see Public Records Office BT 31/2849/15674, with lists of shareholders. The company went into liquidation in Aug. 1886, but was not finally wound up until Dec. 1892. In 1884, according to the *Stock Exchange Yearbook*, 'the whole of the completed property' was resold by the company to Carr, in return for his paying off the mortgage (by then reduced to £160,000) and taking out a mortgage for £40,000 in favour of the company. From then on the Company was presumably only concerned with developing (or failing to develop) the remainder of the property. For Whitehall Court Ltd. see *Stock Exchange Yearbook* for 1884. For Kensington Court Ltd. see Public Records Office BT 31/3168/18375. The company was registered in May 1883; its purpose was to buy the Kensington Court estate from Carr and develop it. Carr was the principle shareholder, and J. Comyns Carr was one of the directors. The company was dissolved in June 1894.

Carr's last financial enterprise seems to have been an abortive attempt to develop a new town to be called Burlingwick on 330 acres of undeveloped land belonging to the Duke of Devonshire along the Thames at Chiswick (*Chiswick Times*, 18 and 25 Apr. 1902).

9 (*162*). For Comyns Carr's silence about his brother see n. 3, and for the Fulton family's possible embarrassment see *Bedford Park 1875–1975* (the catalogue of a centenary exhibition held by the Victorian Society, with bibliographical notes on some thirty-five residents of Bedford Park), p. 13.

10 (*162*). Godwin's houses illustrated in *Building News*, 22 Dec. 1876, 12 Jan. 1877, Coe & Robinson's, 23 Feb. 1877.

11 (*164*). *Building News*, 9, 16, 23 Nov. and 21 Dec. 1877, 11 Jan. and 19 Apr. 1878 (housing); 31 Oct. 1879 (Tower House); 2 Jan. 1880 (Tabard).

12 (*164*). See T. A. Greeves (works cited in n. 4) and illustrations in *Building News*, 3 May 1878 (club); 21 Jan. and 25 Nov. 1881 (School of Art); 13 Aug. 1880 (Dollman house); 17 June 1881, 3 Nov. 1882, 16 Mar. 1883 (houses by May).

13 (*168*). *Builder*, 13 Jan. 1880, p. 139, and 7 Feb. 1880, p. 169. Shaw's friend Aldam Heaton was the consultant decorator for the estate.

14 (*171*). A good example of a 'Queen Anne' chapel is the Islington Congregational Church, Upper Street, Islington (Bonella and Paull, 1888). Elaborate unexecuted designs by G. G. Scott, jun., for rebuilding Moncure Conway's chapel in South Place in 'Queen Anne' style are in the R.I.B.A. Drawings Collection.

15 (*171*). Letter in R.I.B.A. Drawings Collection, quoted in T. A. Greeves, *Country Life*, 14 Dec. 1967, p. 1601.

16 (*171*). *Building News*, 9 Mar. 1877, p. 253.

17 (*171*). M. D. Conway, op. cit., p. 232.

18 (*172*). For the early residents see especially Fletcher, op. cit., and *Bedford Park 1875–1975*.

19 (*172*). *Building News*, 23 Nov. 1882. Hogg's obituary is in *Chiswick Times*, 12 Nov. 1915.

20 (*172*). For O'Leary see Oliver Elton, *Frederick York Powell* (Oxford, 1906), i. 64, 221, 375; he seems to have been an habitué of the Yeatses rather than a resident.

21 (*172*). Ibid. i. 64.

22 (*174*). For the two schools see *Bedford Park Gazette*, Nov. 1883–June 1884.

23 (*175*). *British Architect*, 3 Dec. 1880.

24 (*176*). Estate advertisement in *Builder*, 6 Nov. 1880, p. xxvii, and subsequent issues (Streatham Park); *Building News*, 9 Apr. 1880 (Telford Park).

25 (*176*). For Bush Hill Park see *British Architect*, 3 and 17 Aug., 5 Oct., 2 Nov., and 28 Dec. 1883, 21 Mar. 1884, and Public Records Office BT 31/3985/25340.

26 (*177*). A private theatre seating 250 people was erected by Sir Percy Shelley (son of the poet) to the designs of Joseph Peacock on the site of what is now Shelley Mansions in 1878–9.

27 (*177*). Daphne du Maurier, *The Young George du Maurier* (London, 1961), p. 235.

28 (*177*). E. R. and J. Pennell, *The Life of James McNeill Whistler* (revised edn. London, 1911), pp. 161–80, etc., gives the main outlines of Whistler's Tite Street connections and the White House story. Its architectural progress, and that of all the houses in Tite Street and on Chelsea Embankment, can be followed in detail at the G.L.C. Records Office, in the Minutes of the Works and General Purposes Committee, and the Valuers' Approved Drawings (listed in L.C.C. Register of Approved Drawings). There are designs for all the houses in the R.I.B.A. and V. & A., including a number of variants. Godwin's houses were illustrated in *British Architect*, 15 and 22 Feb., 13 Mar., and 2 Apr. 1878 (Chelsea Embankment houses); 29 Nov. 1878 (Wortley–Pellegrini house); 6 Dec. 1878, 24 Oct., and 7 Nov. 1879 (White House); 6 Dec. 1878, 11 June 1880 (Miles house); 3 Oct. 1879 (Corder House); 4 July 1884 (2nd Stuart-Wortley house); 14 May 1880 (group of Tite Street studios and houses).

29 (*177*). For Pellegrini see Eileen Harris, 'Carlo Pellegrini: Man and "Ape"', *Apollo*, Jan. 1976, pp. 53–7.

According to Frank Harris (ibid., p. 57) Pellegrini was homosexual, which suggests that Stuart-Wortley, like others in Tite Street, may have had a foot in both camps. For Stuart-Wortley and Nelly Bromley see *Burke's Peerage* under Wharncliffe, and Lady Augusta Fane, *Chit-Chat* (London, 1926), pp. 74, 104.

30 (*178*). There is a short entry on Frank (George Francis) Miles (1852–91) in the *D.N.B.* His movements and those of Oscar Wilde in this period can be plotted with reasonable accuracy in *The Letters of Oscar Wilde* (ed. Rupert Hart-Davis, London, 1962), pp. xxii, 67–80, 166. See also Rupert Croft-Cooke, *The Unrecorded Life of Oscar Wilde* (London, 1972), pp. 40–6.

31 (*178*). For the Edis buildings (both of which survive) see the *Architect*, 12 June 1880, p. 407 and illustration. What is probably Godwin's first project for a studio tower, in the Gothic style and designed to be built in a row of unidentified eighteenth-century houses, is in the R.I.B.A. Drawings Collection, RAN 7/L/19.

32 (*178*). E. R. and J. Pennell, *The Whistler Journal* (Philadelphia, 1921), p. 119.

33 (*178*). The designs are in the Victoria and Albert Museum. Elevations of the studio and adjacent stables are illustrated in John Physick and Michael Darby, *Marble Halls* (London, 1973), p. 89. See also *Building News*, 2 May 1879, p. 468, and 27 June 1879, p. 720 (illustration).

34 (*178*). Valuers' Approved Drawings, 68/C1.

35 (*179*). Other later occupants of the studios included Wilson Steer and Charles Furse.

36 (*180*). G.L.C. Records M.B.W./1194 (26 Nov. 1877).

37 (*181*). The letters are filed in M.B.W./1291/47 (papers presented for committees of 20 and 23 May).

38 (*181*). The house was demolished between the wars. In addition to the *British Architect* engraving, there are designs in the Victoria and Albert Museum and a good photograph in E. V. Lucas, *Edwin Austin Abbey* (London, 1921), ii. 341. Abbey lived in the house, then known as Chelsea Lodge, from 1899 until his death in 1911.

39 (*181*). Godwin told the story of the Frank Miles designs in an article on studios in *Building News*, 7 Mar. 1879, p. 261.

40 (*184*). For the Tower House site see especially G.L.C. Records, M.B.W./1199 (9 Aug. 1878), M.B.W./1216 (13 Dec. 1880), M.B.W./1221 (16 Jan. 1882), M.B.W./1228 (4 June 1883), M.B.W./1230 (17 Dec. 1883). Mrs. Bagot's site included the area now occupied by 48 Tite Street, which was not built on until 1894, to the designs of Charles J. C. Pawley (Valuers' Drawings 419/135). The Tower House was described as 'rapidly approaching completion' in *British Architect*, 22 May 1885, p. 252. The L.C.C. Register of Approved Drawings lists 'specification only' as on the file for the Tower House (this has disappeared) and gives E. W. Godwin, not Mrs. Bagot, as the lessee. A specification probably had to be submitted to the M.B.W. even after the site had been sold because (according to a note on the Pawley design) they retained the right to check that it complied with the Metropolitan Building Acts, etc.

Chapter VIII. The Architecture of Enjoyment

1 (*186*). e.g. 'There can be no doubt that a northerly outlook over the sea is an important element among the conditions which render a local climate bracing and exhilarating.' *A Pictorial and Descriptive Guide to Cromer* (Ward Lock and Co., 5th edn., 1906).

2 (*186*). *Seaside Watering Places* (published L. Upcott Gill, 1896–7 edn.).

3 (*186*). *Keble's Gazette*, 9, 16, and 23 Oct. 1880.

4 (*187*). *Keble's Gazette*, 25 Sept. 1880.

5 (*187*). I have been able to find out little about Beazley, except that he was a member of the Arts Club from 1863 to 1871—along with Whistler, Godwin, Swinburne, Fred Walker, and many others. He was presumably related to Samuel Beazley (1786–1851), architect and playwright.

6 (*187*). Margate Public Library, Local History Section.

7 (*187*). *Keble's Gazette*, 1880 *passim*.

8 (*187*). Illustrated in *Building News*, 2 July 1880, where it was described as 'in one of the healthiest positions of this healthiest of seaside places'.

9 (*189*). G.L.C. Records, M.B.W./1194 (15 Oct. 1877).

10 (*189*). A design for a house for Robert Whyte at Westgate by George Sherrin was published in *British Architect*, 11 Sept. 1885.

11 (*189*). For Cromer see articles by Mark Girouard, *Country Life*, 19 and 26 Aug. 1971, based mainly on material from the *Norfolk Chronicle* and on photographs, cuttings, old guidebooks, etc., in the possession of C. Crawford Holden of Cromer.

12 (*190*). For the Locker-Lampsons and Flowers at Cromer and Overstrand see Emily Lutyens, *The Blessed Girl* (London, 1953), pp. 151–7; Victoria Glendinning, *A Suppressed Cry* (London, 1969), pp. 21–5, 31–42, 58–60; Lucy Cohen, *Lady de Rothschild and her Daughters* (London, 1935), pp. 217–27; Lady Battersea, *Reminiscences* (London, 1922), pp. 324–408. The description of Cyril Flower comes from Lucy Cohen, op. cit., p. 170. The tender for Newhaven Court is in the *Builder*, 18 Aug. 1883, p. 237.

13 (*190*). Randolph S. Churchill, *Winston S. Churchill* (London, 1966), i. 67.

14 (*190*). Compton Mackenzie, *My Life and Times: Octave 1* (London, 1963), p. 144.

15 (*190*). Glendinning, op. cit., pp. 24, 60; M. H. Spielmann and G. S. Layard, *Kate Greenaway* (London, 1905), pp. 69, 86; Walter Crane, *An Artist's Reminiscences* (London, 1907), pp. 210–12.

16 (*190*). Crane, op. cit., p. 215.

17 (*191*). Oscar Wilde, *Letters* (ed. Rupert Hart-Davis, London, 1962), p. 320; *Norfolk Chronicle*, 31 May 1890.

18 (*191*). Clement Scott, *Poppyland*, quoted in Lady Battersea, *Reminiscences* (1922), p. 379. The passage is not in the book as published in 1886 and was presumably cut when the original *Telegraph* articles were edited.

19 (*191*). His building and other activities can be traced in the *Eastern Daily Press*, 22 Sept. 1888; *Norfolk Chronicle*, 22 Feb. and 3 Sept. 1890, 6 June 1891, 11 May 1895, etc.

20 (*192*). *Norfolk Chronicle*, 8 Nov. 1890, 26 May 1894.

21 (*192*). *Norfolk Chronicle*, 24 Aug. 1889, 1 Jan. 1890 (Town Hall); 5 Oct. 1889, 18 July 1891 (Grand Hotel); 2 Sept. 1893, 28 July 1894 (Hotel Metropole); 10 Aug. 1895 (Hotel de Paris). Other seaside buildings by Skipper were the Sheringham Hotel, Sheringham; the Cliff Hotel, Gorleston; the Centre Cliff Hotel, Southwold; and Victoria Mansions, Lowestoft (*Who's Who in Architecture*, Technical Journals Ltd., London, 1914).

22 (*195*). Designs in the R.I.B.A. (RAN 5/9/5/1), illustrated in John Physick and Michael Darby, *Marble Halls* (London, 1973), p. 188.

23 (*197*). The D. H. Evans story was told me by a resident; the initials are certainly there but I have not been able to corroborate it.

24 (*197*). *New Pictorial and Descriptive Guide to the Thames* (London, Ward Lock and Co., 1909–10).

25 (*197*). See G. C. Williamson, *Murray Marks and his friends* (London, 1919), pp. 12–14 and endpapers. A grangerized edition in the V. & A. contains letters from Shaw to Marks showing that Nesfield and Shaw had known him since at least 1868. Shaw's original design is at the Royal Academy.

26 (*198*). Illustrated in *Building News*, 12 May 1876. Extensions to the south by George and Peto in similar style were illustrated in *Architect*, 16 May 1890.

27 (*198*). *Building News*, 19 Oct. 1877 (Agnew's); 26 Jan. 1877, 20 Dec. 1878, 23 May 1879 (Edis); *Architect*, 25 Jan. 1879 (Harris). Another Bond Street example of 'Queen Anne' was Watson and Collins's Clifford Chambers, illustrated in *Building News*, 14 Sept. 1877.

28 (*199*). Illustrated in *Building News*, 17 Dec. 1875.

29 (*200*). 'Down Memory Lane', *Leek Post and Times*, 14 June 1973; 'The House of Sugden part Three', ibid., 10 May 1973.

30 (*201*). Illustrated in *British Architect*, 23 Apr. 1886.

31 (*202*). Pubs, improved and otherwise, and coffee-houses are discussed at much greater length in Mark Girouard, *Victorian Pubs* (London, 1975).

32 (*202*). Walter Hamilton, *The Aesthetic Movement in England* (3rd edn., London, 1882), p. 127.

33 (*203*). Illustrated and described in *Building News*, 22 July 1881 and 1 Aug. 1884. In about 1880–2 Vigers and Wagstaff had in their office the young Herbert P. Horne, later to be A. H. Mackmurdo's partner and editor of the *Hobby Horse*. His family lived in Bedford Park (*Bedford Park 1875–1975*, p. 25).

34 (*207*). Mark Girouard, *Victorian Pubs*, pp. 98, 162.

35 (*207*). They are in his address book, now in the R.I.B.A. Drawings Collection.

36 (*207*). Mark Girouard, *Victorian Pubs*, pp. 98, 132–5. The most notable example of their work is the Princess Louise at Holborn, with joinery probably by Lascelles.

Chapter IX. 'Queen Anne' in America

1 (*208*). This chapter is heavily indebted to Vincent J. Scully's classic work on the subject, *The Shingle Style and the Stick Style* (New Haven, 1955, revised edn., 1971). My own researches have been almost entirely limited to trying to work out in more detail the links between England and America in this period.

2 (*208*). Kate Greenaway, *Marigold Garden* (London, 1885), p. 27.

3 (*209*). *Harper's Magazine*, liii (June–Nov. 1876), 49–64. Holly's 'City Mansion, Queen Anne style' (p. 58) is convincingly 'Queen Anne', his 'Queen Anne' country mansion (p. 54) if anything Old English.

4 (*209*). Peabody enlarged on his views in a second article, 'Georgian Homes of New England' (signed 'Georgian'), in *American Architect*, 2 (1877), 338–9.

5 (*209*). Letter entitled 'The American Style', *American Architect*, 18 Aug. 1877, p. 267.

6 (*210*). For Cottier see Brian Gould, *Two Van Gogh Contacts: E. J. Wisselingh, Art Dealer; Daniel Cottier, Glass Painter and Decorator* (London, 1969).

7 (*210*). On a visit to Glasgow in Dec. 1883, as reported in the Glasgow *Evening Times*, 9 Oct. 1893. I owe this reference to an unpublished thesis by G. C. Law, 'Alexander ("Greek") Thomson, I.A.', Cambridge, 1950.

8 (*210*). For his movements see Gould, op. cit., and the Post Office Directories. In the latter he is first listed in Langham Place (and London) in 1871.

9 (*210*). *Collection Cottier* (Edinburgh and Paris, 1892), a catalogue with a biographical introduction signed 'W.E.H.', almost certainly W. E. Henley.

10 (*210*). *Scribner's Monthly*, June 1875, Jan., Feb., Apr., June, Oct., Nov. 1876, May 1877.

11 (*211*). Ibid., June 1875, p. 179.

12 (*211*). Ibid., Jan. 1876, pp. 346, 354.

13 (*211*). Ibid., June 1875, p. 182. For Lathrop in England see also his entry in *Dictionary of American Biography*.

14 (*211*). *Scribner's*, Nov. 1876, pp. 88, 90.

15 (*211*). Ibid., Jan. 1876, pp. 342–3; *British Architect*, 3 July 1874.

16 (*211*). But since Agnes and Rhoda Garrett, who contributed to the series and were connected by marriage to W. J. Loftie, had studied under Cottier in London, the plagiarism may have been by agreement.

17 (*211*). *Scribner's*, Oct. 1876, pp. 802–3.

18 (*212*). *Architect*, 14 Oct. 1876, p. 233; *Building News*, 13 Oct. 1876, p. 363.

19 (*212*). Walter Crane, *An Artist's Reminiscences* (London, 1907), pp. 239, 374.

20 (*212*). Illustrated in *Building News*, 15 Aug. 1879 and 23 July 1880.

21 (*212*). According to *Building News*, 3 Jan. 1890, p. 51, R. W. Edis 'went to America some years ago to lay out a city there'.

22 (*212*). For Conway see Moncure D. Conway, *Autobiography* (London, 1905).

23 (*213*). For G. H. Boughton see A. L. Baldry, 'George Henry Boughton R.A.', *Art Annual*, 1904 (separate volume). His house was described by Mrs. Haweis in *Beautiful Houses* (London, 1882), pp. 45–52.

24 (*213*). E. V. Lucas, *Edwin Austin Abbey* (London, 1921), *passim*. McKim is referred to as 'Abbey's old friend' in 1890 (ii. 227).

25 (*213*). Charles Moore, *Charles Follen McKim* (1929), p. 34.

26 (*215*). R. S. Peabody, 'A Talk about Queen Anne', *American Architect*, 28 Apr. 1877, pp. 133–4.

27 (*215*). Charles C. Baldwin, *Stanford White* (New York, 1931), p. 170.

28 (*215*). Walter Crane, op. cit., pp. 370, 403. Crane was in America in 1891–2, when he re-met Emerson and visited his Loring house at Manchester-by-the-sea.

29 (*215*). 'Recent Building in New York', first published in *Harper's*, Sept. 1883, reprinted as 'Concerning Queen Anne' in Montgomery Schuyler, *American Architecture and other writings*, ed. W. H. Jordy and Ralph Coe (Cambridge, Mass., 1961), pp. 453, 468.

30 (*215*). For urban 'Queen Anne' in Boston see Bainbridge Bunting, *Houses of Boston's Back Bay* (Cambridge, Mass., 1967), pp. 167–287. Professor Jordy, to whom I am grateful for the Schuyler and Bunting references, tells me that an English architect, Ernest Coxhead, settled in San Francisco and designed shingle houses there in a version of 'Queen Anne'. 'Queen Anne' can be seen at work in many of the buildings illustrated by Curt Bruce and Thomas Aidala in *The Great Houses of San Francisco* (London, 1974). Other West Coast houses, even so bizarre an example as the famous Carson Mansion in Eureka, Northern California, show an element of 'Queen Anne' influence.

31 (*215*). For the Casino see Scully, op. cit., pp. 131–3, figs. 111–13.

32 (*218*). But oriental-type lattice work was to be found in England, e.g., in Moorish rooms of the type of the Arab Hall at Leighton House, which Stanford White could have seen when in London in 1879.

33 (*223*). Scully, op. cit., figs. 142–3, 153.

34 (*223*). American buildings, including Shingle Style houses, were increasingly illustrated in the English architectural periodicals during the 1880s. A 'portable shingle house' by Stent and Co. of New York was at the American exhibition in West Kensington in 1887. The *Building News* illustrated it on 15 July and commented: 'We believe that company have already secured important orders for these houses. . . . We shall welcome the erection of many such houses at the seaside for instance.' It seems possible that Westgate-type seaside houses were influenced by America.

Appendix: 'Queen Anne' Architecture in Chelsea

1 (*228*). For Lennox Gardens see Dorothy Stroud, *The South Kensington Estate of Henry Smith's Charity* (published by the Trustees, 1975), pp. 46–9.

2 (*229*). George Thomas Robinson (1828/9–97) first practised in Manchester, where he was in partnership with H. J. Paull. He was in Paris during the siege of 1870, as correspondent to the *Manchester Guardian*, and was the first person to send messages out by balloon. He later moved to London, and from about 1877 was the Art Director of Trollope and Sons' 'Museum of Decorative Art' which supplied interior decor of almost every description from premises in West Halkin Street. In the 1880s he contributed articles on furniture and decoration, etc., to the *Art Journal*. He had literary tastes (and a literary daughter), and held a salon which Walter Pater, among others, attended. (*Art Journal*, July 1897, p. 222; Alistair Horne, *The Fall of Paris* (London, 1965); advertisements for Museum of Decorative Art in building periodicals.)

3 (*229*). The designs were published in William Young's *Town and Country Mansions and Suburban Houses* (London, 1879), Pls. I–III. The elevation shows four houses, one of them dated 1877, but in fact No. 60 was built to a different design, and probably by a different architect, and the houses seem not to have been finished until well into the 1880s. Other designs by Young for the estate, published in the *Building News* on 16 June 1876, were never executed.

4 (*229*). Niven later wrote *The Churches of the City of London* (London, 1887). Designs by him for houses on the west side of Cadogan Square, published in the *Building News* of 12 Oct. 1877, were never executed; the accompanying description in the text refers to the Pont Street houses as already being built.

215. Title-page illustration by Walter Crane, from *The Cuckoo Clock* by Mrs. Molesworth, 1877.

Index